Administering Windows Vista™ Security

Mark Minasi
Windows® Administrator
Library

Administering Windows Vista™ Security
The Big Surprises

Mark Minasi

Byron Hynes

1807
WILEY
2007

Wiley Publishing, Inc.

Mark Minasi
Windows® Administrator
Library

Acquisitions and Development Editor: Tom Cirtin
Technical Editors: John Paul Mueller and Russ Mullen
Production Editor: Rachel Gunn
Copy Editor: Cheryl Hauser
Production Manager: Tim Tate
Vice President and Executive Group Publisher: Richard Swadley
Vice President and Executive Publisher: Joseph B. Wikert
Vice President and Publisher: Neil Edde
Book Designer: Maureen Forys and Judy Fung
Compositor: Craig Woods, Happenstance Type-O-Rama
Proofreader: Nancy Riddiough
Indexer: Nancy Guenther
Anniversary Logo Design: Richard Pacifico
Cover Designer: Ryan Sneed
Copyright © 2007 by Wiley Publishing, Inc., Indianapolis, Indiana
Published simultaneously in Canada
ISBN: 978-0-470-10832-1

For general information on our other products and services or to obtain technical support, please contact our Customer Care Department within the U.S. at (800) 762-2974, outside the U.S. at (317) 572-3993 or fax (317) 572-4002.

Wiley also publishes its books in a variety of electronic formats. Some content that appears in print may not be available in electronic books.

Library of Congress Cataloging-in-Publication Data is available from the publisher.

10 9 8 7 6 5 4 3 2 1

This is to my mother, Virginia Marie Minasi, nee Hartley. While she is no longer with us, my brothers and I carry much of what she was inside of us and always will. Mom, we miss you, and we hope that where you've gone you've found some rest, and who knows, maybe a few wonderful "big surprises" of your own.

Acknowledgments

As the Introduction will describe, I got the idea for this book in late June 2006 and knew almost instantly that if it were to be written, it had to be written fast. You see, once an author's finished with his work, there's lots more to do, months more ahead of editing, revisions, layout, galleys, printing, binding, boxing, and trucking off to your nearby bookstore. But I also knew that this book needed to be out by the end of 2006, as it deals with the things that I felt all Vista administrators needed to know, preferably before they even start deploying Vista.

(Don't misunderstand — that absolutely doesn't mean that if you're looking at this in August 2007 you're wasting your time. XP's a pretty good desktop OS, and I think it'll be quite some time before most folks even look at Vista. No matter what time you start learning how to administer Vista, I believe this will be a useful book. I just wanted to be sure to get it into the hands of the early adopters.)

But before anything happens in the publishing industry, there is much to be done in terms of getting the wheels turning, and that, too, takes time. So I talked to my development editor, Tom Cirtin, and begged him to grease the gears of the Great Machine that is book publishing. Tom agreed to, and as I write this, it looks as if this book will indeed appear in your bookstore before the coming of 2007. That happened with the help of many people.

First, my co-authors, Byron Hynes and Jennifer Allen, took up the task of writing a chapter each to fill out the book, and in very short time. I greatly appreciate their doing that in such good time, particularly inasmuch as they've already got day jobs! My editors—Tom Cirtin, Rachel Gunn, and Cheryl Hauser—sanded my rough drafts into smooth shape in record time, and tech editors John Mueller and Russ Mullen caught me when I slipped up while still providing moral support. (We're all still figuring Vista out. And I suspect that we will be for quite a while, given that it's a near-complete rewrite of XP.) Craig Woods laid out the pages and made the book look good.

One thing that greatly sped up this process was the amount of information I got from the folks inside Microsoft. In following the development process of some earlier versions of Windows, I have sadly come to expect fairly unresponsive, terse answers to my questions, but most of that changed quite significantly during the Vista beta process. I found not only a much more open attitude but a real interest in what people would need from Vista as well. It was sometimes strange to find the roles of interviewer and interviewee switched, as someone responsible for some small but important part of Vista would answer a question with "Well, how do you think we should solve such-and-such problem?" I hope that openness works to Microsoft's benefit and helps lead Vista to real success.

But I can't forget one of the other essential sources of support: my assistant, Jean Snead. Without her, the press of constant things-in-need-of-fixing would keep me from doing anything. Finally, thanks to all of you for buying my books; if you folks weren't so good about that, I don't think this book would have seen the light of day. My thanks to all!

Contents at a Glance

Table of Contents

Introduction

How to Keep Vista Security from Giving You a Stroke

In June 2006, I was sitting in a session on Windows Vista security at Microsoft's TechEd, and heard some things that made my head explode. (But in a *good* way. Kind of. I'll explain more in a minute.) What I learned impelled me to write this book, because on the one hand I believe that these new technologies will ultimately make your job as an administrator easier, and that's good, but on the other hand, some of them are *so* new that it may cause some techies to shy away from rolling out Vista, and that'd be a shame, as Vista seems to me to be a significantly more secure operating system than its forebears. It's my hope that by making Vista's new security concepts easy to understand, you'll choose to use it earlier, and end up with a more secure network sooner. In laying this book out, my goal was to create a book that was short, readable, hands-on where possible, and focused on the stuff that doesn't get much coverage—but should. More specifically:

- First, while this book covers security-related issues, it's aimed not just at security experts, but instead at the broader audience of admins and the IT professional population in general. Security experts already know what `SeChangeNotifyPrivilege` is and why anyone cares, but I think most admins will have perhaps seen something like it without having the time to find out more about it. Similarly, I think that many admins have heard of DACEs versus SACEs, but don't understand them well enough to understand the true import of tools like the new Windows integrity mechanism. In cases like that, you'll get some quick background and review on the pre-Vista security situation in Windows. The security experts in the crowd can, of course, just skip past those sections, as they're brief.

- Second, the book explains in some detail the eight things that bring significant structural changes to Windows that will make life much more difficult for the dirtbags who are trying to attack our privacy or our wallets, but that aren't nearly as well-known as the new Explorer, or the new Windows image file format.

- Third, this book covers those topics in a readable, practical sense; we'll start out with the big concepts and, where possible, end up with practical examples—things you can try out right on your system. I find high-level presentations about integral, this-could-break-something security technologies frustrating because if I can't see it, I have trouble understanding it. This book offers step-by-step demonstrations of the new security technologies where possible and, in case they *do* break something, I'll show you how to turn them off or partially disable them. I don't *recommend* doing that, but if you have to, you have to, and I want you to be able to do that as quickly as possible!

- Finally, we wanted to keep the book small so that we could get it out the door and into your hands around the time that Microsoft releases Vista or, if we're lucky, a bit earlier. To that end, this isn't about every single Vista security technology—that'd be a *big* book!—it's just a closely focused explanation of the big "paradigm shifters," the cranial-infarction-causing new technologies.

But I couldn't get it all done by myself because, as I just mentioned, I wanted to get this book out fairly early and keep it relatively short so that overworked admins (yeah, I know, "overworked admins" is a horribly redundant phrase) could get through it quickly while trying to figure out their Vista deployment plans. The short time frame meant that I wouldn't have time to write the whole thing, so I enlisted the aid of some folks who are extremely smart about both security *and* Vista.

In the rest of this introduction, I'll explain more about why I think these new security features are so important, what we'll cover in the book, and introduce the other authors.

Vista Turns Out to Be More Than Just a Pretty Face. Who Knew?

What did I mean when I said that my "head exploded?" It all started like this....

I've played with the various Vista betas since the early pre-beta ("technology preview") Microsoft released in 2003, and to be honest I'd not been impressed. It seemed to me that Vista mostly offered neat new stuff for programmers. The new "Aero Glass" desktop seemed like pretty eye candy, but my inclination with GUIs is turn off all of the visual effects immediately anyway—I've got *plans* for those CPU cycles that fading menu would suck up!—and so a look at one of my Vista desktops might lead the casual observer to guess that I was running Server 2003 rather than Vista. Yes, there was great stuff coming in Windows, I'd heard...but the version of Windows delivering that great stuff was Windows Server 2007, "the operating system formerly known as Longhorn," rather than Vista.

In the first half of 2006, however, that all changed. The Vista betas started strutting their stuff, and I was surprised to discover that a lot of that "stuff" turned out to be many of the features that I'd originally told would not appear until Server 2007. From that point on, I started spending a lot more time with the Vista betas and customer technology previews. But playing with a beta only reveals the things that the OS designer exposes through the GUI and the built-in applications; it usually doesn't reveal all that much about any changes to the OS's internals. That's why it was possible to surprise me so significantly at the June 2006 show.

I'd already sat in several sessions about new security technologies in the Vista. Some of what I was hearing was, to be honest, sort of disquieting. A new laptop protection technology named "BitLocker" would protect your laptop *so* well that you if you weren't careful, losing your password might mean losing your *data*. When installed, Vista appeared not to have a built-in Administrator account anymore, just a kind of "junior administrator" who seemed unable to do many basic administrative chores. Bunches of security tweaks in the file system and the Registry might render tons of XP-compatible applications useless. Every time you wanted to do something vaguely administrative, Vista annoyed you with an "are you sure?" sort of dialog box.

All of this new security stuff was starting to sound like it'd be a source of new chores for us admin types, and I can't say that made me eager for Vista's arrival. Then, to make matters worse, the speaker said something about "mandatory integrity control" or MIC— later renamed "Windows integrity control" and for all I know, they'll change it again before it ships—a new layer of security in Vista that I'd already heard about but hadn't really considered. My attention was drifting until I heard the speaker say "and a side effect of this is that there could be files on Vista that no one, not even an administrator, could delete." At that moment, I realized why MIC had seemed kind of familiar; you see, it's based on a method of securing files that's been incorporated into operating systems for decades...but only on *military* computers.

That was what triggered the brain combustion.

Why on earth, I asked myself, would we *want* an operating system like this? Good lord, I'm not running a blasted missile silo or storing national secrets on my own confounded computer!

But, after Krazy Glue-ing my head back together, I remembered some things. Things like the fact that in the past couple of years, I have removed truly scary spyware, keystroke loggers, and even a rootkit from virtually *every single computer* that I've been asked to look at by friends and family. And if you're a fellow admin type, then I'll bet your reaction to that wasn't shock or amazement. No, I'd guess that you were nodding your head in recognition as you read that; I'd imagine that every XP techie out there has had experiences like mine. Nor are those friends and family dummies; they're mostly smart people who aren't computer experts, and every one of them had picked up something potentially lethal, because there are so many new ways to pick up something bad.

That led me to also remember all of the fake security alerts that I've gotten from financial institutions that I'm not even a member of, the "phishing" attacks that use social engineering to trick people into giving random servers their names, passwords, and account numbers. I've never been taken in by one, but I wouldn't ascribe that to any genius on my part; no, it's probably because I don't use a PayPal account, and they seem to be the biggest phishing target. Additionally, as a writer I have something of a secret weapon: I'm a bit more likely to notice the spelling and grammatical mistakes endemic to 99 percent of the phishing messages out there than the average bear. There's the constant assault on my privacy from websites that want me to click some graphic and hit a monkey or claim my free iPod, all with the same desire: to put the links in place necessary to track my every move on the Internet and sell it to people who can then plague me with spam. (Why do you think Google gives away e-mail accounts?)

And then it dawned on me: I guess it's true that my computer can't launch ICBMs and doesn't contain any national secrets…but it *does* hold *personal* secrets like my passwords, personal business affairs, and financial information, and if the bad guys were to get that, then I could be in some serious trouble money-wise.

The world of malware—viruses, worms, bots, Trojans, rootkits, phishing, you name it—has changed drastically in just the past few years, and not everyone understands that. Yes, jerks have been writing malware for years, but the *motivation* to write the malware has changed. Not that long ago, viruses and the like were written by pathetic wannabes who mostly just sought bragging rights about how many systems they'd infected. Nowadays, the dweebs are gone, and the goal of the new malware authors isn't bragging rights: it's your bank account. There are truly bad people out there, thousands and thousands of them, they want to hurt you, and, worst of all, they live in your neighborhood. (The Internet, that is.) We're at war with a much tougher enemy than we faced just a few years ago when viruses were the worst thing we ran into, and we're under siege…so adding a few Cold War notions into our OS is, unfortunately, probably not such a bad idea.

Think of it this way. In the late 1990s, our foes were essentially nothing more than annoying kids who liked to break into houses when people were away just to do it. Putting locks on doors that had never had them, remembering to actually *lock* those locks when leaving the house, and perhaps installing a simple burglar alarm were sufficient for most people's needs. Nowadays, in contrast, we're up against an intelligent, highly motivated army of thieves with automatic lock picks and vacuum cleaners that can leave an account as empty as a politician's promise, and do it in seconds. That sort of enemy calls for more powerful defenses, like bulletproof walls, guards, fences, and smart cards as well as better keys. That means more work and new things to learn…but the alternative is losing the fight. Vista provides a lot of those new weapons, and you need to understand them.

With that said, here's a more specific explanation of why I felt that this book needed to be written, and written as soon as possible. Vista changes a lot of things, and that makes sense because Vista is the first completely new OS that Microsoft has created since they "got religion" about security. And yes, I know that Server 2003 shipped after Bill Gates had his big security epiphany in early 2002, but I'm not counting 2003 as the first "post-religion" OS. I think Microsoft still had a few lessons to learn after 2003 appeared in April 2003. They understood that security was a big deal, but they weren't yet ready to sacrifice much of anything in the way of backward compatibility to achieve it. But it seemed to me that the Blaster worm in August 2003 was the final nail in the "security's important, but only so long as we can still run 1992 programs" way of thinking.

But don't misunderstand me when I say that. I surely hate running up against compatibility issues with old software, and I realize that a significant number of Windows users will find not being to run some old apps on Vista to be a real problem. But consider two things. First, even if we're talking, say, one in five users being adversely affected by not being able to run some subset of applications, compare that to *five in five* Windows users facing ever-more-destructive malware. But with a little work, Vista may not even cause that much trouble for old applications, as it's got some impressive tools for offering backward compatibility without sacrificing security. We'll examine one of them, file and Registry virtualization, in Chapter 3.

Blaster was incredibly embarrassing to Microsoft, and from what I've heard it was the seminal event that led Microsoft to basically throw away all of the Vista work that they'd done to that point and start from scratch. I don't have access to either XP or Vista's source code, but I'm told that a very high percentage of Vista's programs are all-new code, and I can believe it from the multitude of things that run *just* a little differently under Vista.

Anyway, the fact that so much of Vista is new and security-centric means that I *could* point to dozens or perhaps hundreds of things in Vista and say, "these are very different, you should know about them," and in fact our wider-focus books *Mastering Windows Vista Professional* and, in 2007, *Mastering Windows Server 2003* will cover all of those topics. But there are a few things that I felt that every Windows admin needs to know about, but that there's little available about, or little accurate information on.

Meet the Coauthors

I couldn't have gotten this book out quickly enough without the hard work of my coauthors Byron Hynes and Jennifer Allen.

I met Byron Hynes at TechEd through a mutual friend, Steve Riley, at Microsoft. Byron is a guy who's spent many years teaching technical seminars and writing documentation. He just joined Microsoft a year ago and is hard at work doing the security-related documentation about Server 2007. He also may be the single human being on the planet who best understands the new BitLocker encryption system that arrives with Vista—so I was pretty happy to hear that he'd do the BitLocker chapter for this book. But don't worry that you'll just get a sales pitch from him— Byron's a straight shooter when it comes to talking about Windows strengths, as well as weaknesses. Jennifer Allen is a technical writer and editor in the Microsoft Security Technology group, where she manages and creates documentation for security technologies. Jennifer resides in Seattle, Washington, and is a native of Washington state.

I greatly appreciate each coauthor's hard work, and I think you'll enjoy their contributions.

What's Inside This Book

Here's a quick look at the things that you'll learn in this book.

As I've said, we'll see some real paradigm-busters in this book, but I wanted to start you off gently with Chapter 1. In that chapter, I tell you how to solve a few annoying problems (like restoring the Administrator account, which is disabled by default) and then, I explain a dozen or so subtle changes to security defaults. These are things that you might well not notice...until you trip over one of them. (For example, did you know that in Vista, Power Users go away?) But not all of the surprises are bad ones, as I'll walk you through an unexpected bright star in the Vista constellation—the Event Viewer. Covering *that* will also let me do some drill-down on Windows Remote Management, a new piece of Windows infrastructure that we're all going to have to get facile with.

In Chapter 2, we dive right into Vista security with the first of those eight biggies that I've mentioned. And, unlike most of the new Vista security technologies that we'll cover, this is one that you probably *have* heard of or come across: User Account Control or UAC, also known as "the Vista feature that everyone loves to hate." It's Microsoft's significant shift in Windows functionality intended to help the Windows community, who are all used to running as full-power administrators, make the painful shift to running as a user. UAC is definitely a good thing in the long run, but it can be frustrating for the veteran administrator, if not understood. That veteran admin could choose to simply tweak a couple of group policies to shut UAC off—and this chapter shows how—but that admin just might choose differently if she understood exactly what UAC does. This chapter goes beyond the UI and explains the new concept of "split tokens" and what they mean for both admins and users…and how not disabling UAC may be the best thing you can do to fight rootkits, worms, Trojans, and viruses.

In Chapter 3, I explain the second of the Big Eight, file system and Registry virtualization. It's a technology built into Vista that, like UAC, helps make the transition from today's world, where 99 percent of us spend our days logged in as an administrator, to a safer world of tomorrow, where we spend most of our time logged on as standard users. We need that because a lot of malware can't possibly infect our systems if we're logged on as standard users rather than administrators. *But* one of the biggest obstacles that well-informed techies see to moving to a world where most of us run as a user is the objection that "hey, I'd *love* to run as a user, but my stupid apps won't run unless I'm an admin because they try to write to places on the disk and in the Registry where user types can't go. What am I gonna do, find the developer and hit him in the head until he rewrites his code?" It's a very valid objection, or *was*, anyway…until Vista. Vista does a bit of sleight of hand letting folks with normal user levels of privilege to run what once were just badly written applications…automatically. Called "virtualization," it's got nothing to do with VMWare or Virtual Server, and everything to do with making things easier to run in lower power. With virtualization, you really *can* run apps that write to HKEY_LOCAL_MACHINE or System32, even if you're not an admin, just like magic. But as with all magic, there are some gotchas. This chapter explains how virtualization works, where it doesn't work, and how to know when it can and can't help you.

Chapter 4 introduces the technology that caused my cranial pop: the Windows integrity control, formerly known as Mandatory Integrity Control or MIC. In an effort to stem the tide of malware, Microsoft has, believe it or not, gone beyond the "discretionary permissions" model for NTFS and Registry permissions that we've known since its inception in 1993 and added a model that to this point has not appeared in any operating systems on the planet, except for ones used in some special-purpose OSes designed for military and national security applications. This new layer of security is called the "Windows Integrity control" and, well, it's no exaggeration to say that if you're a long-time Windows admin, you've never seen anything like this. In this chapter, I explain the theory behind the Windows integrity control, and then dive into your system's insides to show you what Windows integrity is doing…and how you can get in on the act to do insert a bit more "integrity" of your own into Vista. There is one downside to this chapter, however: we must sadly warn our readers that this chapter cannot not be read by persons without the proper security clearances.

Okay, just joking on the last item. But as I was writing this on the eve of Vista's release in late October 2006, its name was *still* in flux so for all I know it'll have another name.

In Chapter 5, Byron joins us to explain the fourth in my list of big new security technologies, the one piece of "Palladium," Microsoft's vision of security way back in 2002, that has actually seen the light of day: BitLocker Full Volume Encryption. Every year, American companies lose 600,000 laptops that are sometimes stolen but often just left in cabs and airports. But no matter how they're lost, they sometimes contain data that can make or break organizations. For example, you may recall the recent story about a Veteran's Administration employee who brought home a laptop whose hard disk contained the records of all veterans, including all of the information needed for a bad guy to commit identity theft against them... and the laptop was stolen from his home. Yikes! The answer? (Besides shooting the dummy who did that, that is.) Encrypt the entire hard disk, and hide the key where it can't be found. That's in Vista in a new tool called BitLocker.

When Microsoft first talked about BitLocker, it seemed like an interesting but impractical technology because it required that any system using BitLocker have a cryptographic chip called a Trusted Platform Module (TPM) chip on its motherboard. The Vista implementation of BitLocker, however, lets you encrypt any system so long as it's got either a TPM chip or a USB slot. If you've got a laptop, or if you're in charge of a fleet of laptops, then this may be the single most gotta-have-it feature of Vista!

In Chapter 6, Jennifer Allen joins us to explain three more of my list of significant Vista security technologies: code integrity, new driver signing rules, and PatchGuard. By this point in the book, you will have seen that Vista may be the first version of Windows with "Paranoia Inside," to borrow from Intel's well-known logo. In a change from all previous versions of Windows, Vista randomly reassigns the locations of basic Windows services, making the job of worm writers all the more difficult. One more set of anti-malware provisions includes code integrity, a boot-time check of digital signatures on files, and a new set of rules for 64-bit Windows only. Under these rules, all drivers must be signed. This chapter explains both of those protections in detail. But that's not all for 64-bit systems: the 64-bit kernel contains a feature called PatchGuard that attempts to intelligently detect and stop malware.

Chapter 7 I discuss that old security bugbear, Windows services. Although much maligned in security literature, services are helpful processes that get a lot of the job of keeping Windows running done. But because they run all of the time, services with bugs quickly become some of the lowest of low-hanging fruit for attackers. Over the years, Microsoft has sought to make services harder to attack with simple adjustments and those changes have been valuable, but Vista takes things a step further and rewrites the rules of how services are built. In this chapter, I explain how Vista services have changed, and how that affects administering Windows systems.

At that point, we'll be done with our quick look at Vista security's big surprises. I suspect that by then, you'll agree that at least security-wise, Vista is as different from previous versions of Windows as a Rolls-Royce is from a roller skate.

Stay Up to Date with My Free Newsletter

Keeping track of Windows administration and security is a job in itself, as it changes so fast. We did our best in this book to get you information that's as up to date as is possible, but remember that we wrote this from the betas, and things can and will change. (Heck, as I write this, no one seems to have any really strong feel for when Vista will ship. But the technologies that we're discussing here will appear in Vista *and* Server 2007 whether they ship late or early, so the sooner you're acquainted with them, the better.) I don't know if we'll get around to writing a second edition of this, but whether we do or not, why wait for another edition to stay up to date?

So I'm extending the following offer to my readers. Visit my website at http://www .minasi.com and register to receive my free Windows Networking newsletter. It covers everything from NT 4 to 2000 to XP to 2003, Vista and even a little Linux. Every month that I can, I send you a short update on tips and things that I've learned, as well as any significant errata that appear in the book (which I'm praying don't appear). It won't be spam—as the saying goes, "Spammers must die!"—just a short heads-up on whatever I've come across that's new (to me) and interesting about NT, 2000, XP, 2003, or Vista. I've been doing this newsletter since 1999, so you can also peruse the newsletter archives. Past newsletters have also included lengthy articles on running and securing Microsoft's free database servers MSDE and SQL Server Express, DNS troubleshooting, configuring the Indexing Service, and IPSec, so I think you'll find it a worthwhile newsletter for the price.

Contacting Us

If you've got a question, comment, or think you've caught us in some egregious error, then we want to hear from you! You can e-mail me at help@minasi.com, although before you do, please take a look at http://www.minasi.com/gethelp for my FAQ information.

I assembled this book not because we want every reader to agree with us with our assessments of these new paradigm-busters, although I think that many will; instead, I put this book together because there are some seriously big (and often quiet) changes in how Windows works under the hood from a security point of view, and I wanted to save you the time of having *your* head explode with realization that you'd have to figure all of this new stuff out. Thanks for picking it up, and we hope you enjoy it!

Administering Vista Security: The Little Surprises

Much of this book shows you how Vista's new big security technologies work, how they'll affect you, and where you can control them. This chapter, however, doesn't hit the big stuff; instead, in this chapter I want to introduce you to a bunch of changes in Vista that are fairly significant, but not obvious...until you run up against the kind of strange, unexpected, or puzzling behavior that I've come to think of as "Vysteries." Now, you might think "hey, if this is a potpourri of small Vista administration and security surprises, why not put it at the *end* of the book?" I thought about that but realized that if you *did* want to fire up a copy of Vista and work through some of the things we cover in the rest of the book, then you might find yourself more aggravated from tripping over the small brambles at your feet than from trying to scale the high towers of User Account Control internals and the like—so the first chapter seemed a practical place to put these items.

But let me stress that these aren't all *bad* surprises. All I'm trying to do in this chapter is give you a quick heads-up about things that I feel have changed most significantly administration-wise, particularly from a security point of view, with a view to highlighting the not-so-well-publicized changes. That way, you can decide best where to spend your time in Windows new doodads. (In addition, I'm hoping to show you these things before some client mentions it in a meeting. Don't you just hate *those* kinds of surprises?) These aren't in any particular order; it is, again, a potpourri.

Because, as I mentioned in the Introduction, I'm trying to keep this short and because I'm working from pre-release versions of Vista, I'll assume that you've already figured out how to get Vista up and running in at least a minimal manner on a test system or two. That way, we can move right along to the surprises.

Restoring the Administrator

You go to log onto Vista for the first time, and want to log on as the Administrator, just as you always have. But there's this hitch because, well, there doesn't seem to *be* an Administrator account anymore. Arrgh.

Actually, the Administrator account's still there and can be logged onto. It's just disabled. So here's how to get it back.

First, log onto the Vista system as a local administrator. If you're on a domain, that means that you'll probably need to log on with a domain administrator account, or, if you're not in charge of your domain, then ask your domain administrator to put your domain account in the Administrators group of your Vista machine. If you're using a computer that's a member of a domain, but you *can't* do either of those things then you're probably stuck, unless you reinstall the Vista box as a member of a workgroup rather than a domain.

Making Your Own Administrator

If, on the other hand, you're running a Vista box that is *not* a member of a domain, then Vista will prompt you to create a user account when it first starts up. Vista then automatically puts that account in the Administrators group, just as XP did. It won't *force* you to give that account a password, but it's a good idea to do it anyway because Vista, like XP and 2003, treats accounts with blank passwords as sort of second-class citizens in that they can't be used over a network.

Because that first account is a local administrator, you may not actually need to revivify the Administrator account.

Activating the Administrator Account

Do you, then, need to activate the Administrator account? Probably not. I figured out how to activate the Administrator account in the early days of Vista, but soon realized that I could accomplish anything with that account that Vista prompted me to create that I could do with the Administrator account. In fact, when testing Vista builds 5472, 5536, and RC1 I never even bothered with activating the Administrator account.

I have heard of people needing the Administrator for application compatibility; as some folks have apps coded to run using the Administrator account (not a good idea, but, again, I've been told that some need it). In any case, if you need the Administrator back, then here's the sequence. First, the Administrator account needs a password, as it's currently blank and, as we all know, having an account on a system named "Administrator" with a blank password and that is a member of the Administrators group is a terribly bad idea.

Also, if your system is a member of a domain that has minimum password requirements installed, then you won't be able to activate an Administrator account with a blank password. (Not that the error message that you get from Windows is crystal clear in explaining why it errors out when you try to activate an Administrator account with a lame password; you tell it to activate the Administrator account and it replies something to the effect that "the password does not meet the minimum requirements of this system." You then scratch your head and say, "I wasn't *trying* to do anything with a password!")

We'll give the Administrator a good password and activate it at the same time. Here's how.

Note that in my instructions, I'm using the "Classic Start menu." You'll see that I also run using the Windows Classic theme, which leads to my Vista desktops looking sort of like Windows 2000. I do that mainly for the sake of better speed and quicker response time.

1. Log onto your Vista system with whatever local administrator account you've wangled.

2. Start up a command prompt: click the Start button (it doesn't say "Start" anymore, but it's in the same place as the old Start button, the lower left-hand corner by default and is a circular representation of the Windows flag). Then click All Programs, and then Accessories.

3. I know, I've lulled you into a false sense of "I know what I'm doing now," and you're about to click the Command Prompt icon. *Don't*. Instead, right-click the Command Prompt icon and choose "Run as administrator." You will see your desktop go gray and you'll see a dialog box warning you that you're about to do something administrator-like, and did you really mean to do that? You then click either a Continue or Cancel button.

4. This is called the "Consent user interface" because the program that kicks it off is called `consent.exe`. It's part of User Account Control (UAC), which we'll discuss in Chapter 2. You'll see this dialog box every time you do something that requires even mildly "administrator-ness" to work right. It stays up for two minutes, and if you don't respond in those two minutes, you get a dialog box announcing that Windows won't run the program because "The operation returned because the timeout period expired." In any case, click Continue to get Vista to open a command prompt.

5. Now that you've got the command prompt, set the Administrator's password to something other than blank. (And, if necessary, something that makes your domain's group policies happy.) That command looks like net user administrator *newpassword*. In my case, I'll type **net user administrator swordfish** to give it the password "swordfish." As with virtually all Windows command-line commands, case does not matter except in the password itself, and you've got to press the Enter key once done. You should get "The command completed successfully."

But what if you didn't? If you get "System error 5 has occurred. Access is denied," then you didn't start up the command prompt by right-clicking and choosing "Run as administrator." Yes, I know, you're logged on as an administrator, you should be able to do administrator things...but it's a longer story having to do with UAC, and we'll cover it later. For now, just please remember to always start your command prompts with "Run as administrator" if you want to do anything administrative.

6. Now we've got an administrator with a good password; finish the job and activate the account. From the command prompt, type **net user administrator /active:yes** and press Enter.

I did that as two commands for clarity's sake, but you *can* do it in one: **net user administrator swordfish /active:yes** will work as well.

And no matter which path you took, be sure to clear your screen or prying eyes might see that new password. In fact, closing the command prompt window at that point might be a good idea so that no one can press the Up arrow to see what you typed.

Power Users Are Essentially Gone

The Power Users group has always been an attempt by Microsoft to provide a group that wasn't quite as powerful as the Administrators group, but more powerful than the Users group. That need, as you probably know, grew out of the fact that the permissions and rights that you get from being a member of the Users group just aren't sufficient to allow you to run many applications. Many of us administrators know that we need to wean users away from having local administration accounts, but need to give them more power so that they can run applications. For some folks, the Power Users group was the answer.

Unfortunately, it wasn't a very good answer. Because Power Users have the ability to write to `ntoskrnl.exe`, the basic Windows program, then an evil (and, of necessity, very smart) Power User could modify that file, giving themselves more powers and escalating their privileges. They also have the ability to modify at least one system service that runs as the LocalSystem account, which would let a crafty Power User log onto the system as the LocalSystem account. (See Mark Russinovich's blog entry at `http://www.sysinternals.com/blog/2006/05/power-in-power-users.html` for a more detailed write-up of how these attacks would be launched.)

Power Users was created as a Band-Aid to help solve the overall problem of application compatibility because many applications won't work when run from a so-called standard user account.

Jargon alert: "standard user" is a relatively new Microsoft phrase that you'll hear more and more as you start using Vista. It means "a user who's basically just a member of the local Users group on a machine," with no special administrative powers at all. You'll see this appear in phrases like "once you have all of your users running as standard users...."

The idea with Power Users was to create a group that had just enough administrative powers to allow users to run those troublesome "gotta be an admin to run me" applications. In other words, Microsoft created Power Users to work around the fact that many Windows developers did a lousy job of testing their applications. (And, unfortunately, some of those developers work for Microsoft.) That has led to a world where millions of users are logged into their systems all day as administrators or power users, with the result that the millions of machines that they're working on are prone to security problems.

The alternative solution to the problem of applications that require administrator-level power—chivvying developers into writing software that works properly when run by a standard user—seemed too highly priced before we all starting facing the worms and spyware du jour, but Microsoft has apparently decided that the time has come to ask those developers to pitch in and help solve the security problem.

As a result, Microsoft has essentially eliminated the Power Users group. It's still present in case you've got some resource that has a permission that refers to the Power Users group, but it's "Power" Users in name only, as it basically has the same power as the Users group. To see this change, try creating a member of the Power Users group on an XP system and then use the `whoami.exe` application found in various versions of Support Tools and the Resource Kit (or built into the OS, in the case of XP x64 and Vista) to find out what privileges that user has. Run `whoami /priv` and you'll get this list:

- `SeChangeNotifyPrivilege`
- `SeShutdownPrivilege`
- `SeUndockPrivilege`
- `SeSystemtimePrivilege`
- `SeProfileSingleProcessPrivilege`
- `SeCreateGlobalPrivilege`

Do the same thing with a Power User member on a Vista system, open up a command prompt and run `whoami /priv` and you'll see this:

- `SeChangeNotifyPrivilege`
- `SeShutdownPrivilege`
- `SeUndockPrivilege`
- `SeTimeZonePrivilege`
- `SeIncreaseWorkingSetPrivilege`

(If you're wondering what all of that *Sesomething* stuff means, we'll cover it the next chapter.) Let's make that a bit more understandable by looking first at the things that old and new Power Users have in common and which things they see differently. Both groups have `SeChangeNotifyPrivilege`, which you may know better as "bypass traverse checking." It means that if a user has NTFS permissions to access a particular folder, but the folder is nested inside folders that the user is denied access, then the user can get to the folder that they *do* have permission to. (Users have had this permission since NT 3.1.) The other two rights that both XP and Vista Power Users have are `SeShutdownPrivilege` and `SeUndockPrivilege`, which mean pretty much what they sound like: the power to shut a system down or to undock a laptop from a docking station.

Both XP and Vista users have the right to modify system time, but in different ways. XP Power Users could change time, date, and time zone. Vista users and Power Users have been granted an altogether new right: the ability to change just the time zone, something that Microsoft added in response to customer demand. You see, regular users don't have the right to change workstation times because Microsoft's always seen that as a security issue. (Certainly it might make Kerberos unhappy in a domain, as domain authentication breaks down if a client's clock is more than five minutes different from a domain controller's clock.) But, people argued, they had regular old users who traveled with laptops and crossed time zones. Admins wanted the itinerant laptop users to be able to change their clock's time zone, but not the time. So Vista has the new "change time zone" right, and Power Users (and Users) have it, but Power Users no longer have the right to change workstation time.

XP Power Users had two rights that Vista Power Users don't have: "profile single process" (`SeProfileSingleProcessPrivilege`) and "create global objects" (`SeCreateGlobalPrivilege`). The first was scary because it allows one user to examine a process being run by another user. The idea is this: suppose I wanted to run Performance Monitor and monitor processes that other users are running. That would require the OS to give me the right to gather statistical information about other users' processes. The power is normally used to allow someone to run a program like Performance Monitor to watch things that the system is doing but in theory could be used to spy on someone or even on the system. (There's an even more intrusive one called `SeDebugPrivilege`, but we'll meet that next chapter.)

The second is a right that controls whether or not users can create something called "file mapping objects in the global namespace." And no, that wasn't an English sentence, but I'll translate. When programs need to read or write disk files and folders, or talk to and from other programs, or control an I/O device like a printer or a serial port, there are often several ways to do that, coding-wise. But one way that's been around for a long time is to treat all of those kinds of I/O as being particular kinds of disk file reads and writes; so, for example, to let one program talk to another program, a programmer could do a lot of complicated coding, *or* she could have the two programs that she wants to communicate create a sort of imaginary file. Then, when the two programs needed to talk between themselves, they just read or write from or to that imaginary file. Where does security come in here? Well, if I'm just a regular old user and I want to run program A, which talks to program B, then those programs—which logged on as me, because I started them—will need the ability to create these imaginary files, these "file mapping objects." Clearly even the lowliest of users should be able to create one of these; no security worries there. Ah, but now let's add in Terminal Services, and we get a problem. More than one user may have a TS session running on the same system, and each user may run programs that use these file mapping objects. What if they collide, what if User 1 runs a program that creates a file mapping object named "Wally," and User 2 runs a program that tries to do the same thing? That'd be a problem, except for the fact that every user session gets its own separate area or "namespace." Each user in a Terminal Server session, then, has his own "local namespace" in which he can create file mapping objects. But Terminal Services has a way for one user's session to interact with another user's session, through a *global* namespace for file mapping objects. Being able to monkey around with the *global* namespace could enable a bad guy to affect other TS users' sessions, so Microsoft removed that ability from Power Users in Vista. Offhand I do not know of any applications that this change would break if you take this right from a user, but it's possible. In that case, just add the right to a particular group and put the user in that group because, again, Vista Power Users (and standard users) lack `SeProfileSingleProcessPrivilege` and `SeCreateGlobalPrivilege`.

The Vista Power User has one right that the XP Power User didn't—the right to bump up the amount of memory that a given application uses, the "working set" of that app. Apparently Microsoft needed to create that specific new right for some reason and needed regular users to have it.

Once you've seen the privileges and group memberships of a Vista Power User, try creating a normal user account in Vista and run `whoami /priv` on it for comparison: you'll see that members of the Users group have the exact same rights as members of Vista's Power Users group.

So Power Users are much less powerful rights-wise. How about Power Users' NTFS permissions, though? Yup, they've been circumscribed. Even my up-to-date, SP2-equipped copy of XP x64 edition that I'm writing this on gives vast powers over the System32 folder to Power Users, vast when compared to what little a member of Users can do...but there's nary a special-to-Power-User permission on *any* folder of a Vista system that I can find, much less a scary one!

"Run..." Is Off the Start Menu

I'm not sure who makes the call on the user interface stuff at Microsoft, but I get the impression that he thinks we user types are pretty dumb. It seems like every version of Windows changes the default behaviors of the Start menu in ever-increasing levels of annoyance. XP hid Administrative Tools, Server 2003 made getting to the actual Control Panel more work, and now Vista has taken away the Run... item from the Start menu. Personally, I use Run... a lot of the time, if for no other reason than to quickly get to Regedit and the local Group Policy Editor. Losing Run... on the Start menu makes me less productive on Vista.

So let's fix that, shall we?

1. Right-click the Start menu, and in the resulting context menu choose "Properties." As with earlier versions of Windows, that brings up the Taskbar and Start Menu Properties page with the "Start Menu" tab highlighted. Choose the "Customize..." button in the upper right-hand corner to bring up the Customize Start Menu dialog.

2. In the Customize Start Menu dialog, you'll see a number of radio buttons in a window with a scroll bar down its side. Scroll down almost to the bottom, and you'll see the option "Run command" with an unchecked check box next to it. Check the box.

3. Still in that window, scroll all the way down and you'll see a section called "System administrative tools." In that section, choose the radio button labeled "Display on the All Programs menu."

4. Click OK to dismiss the Customize Start Menu dialog, and again to dismiss the Taskbar and Start Menu Properties page.

The Run... command and the Administrative Tools group are now back, after a few clicks. (And they call Vista a productivity tool!)

BOOT.INI Is Gone, BCD Is Here

Now and then, I need to edit the boot.ini file in order to fix some configuration issue. Ever since NT 3.1, it's been an ASCII text file on the hard disk.

With Vista, that's all changed; it maintains a boot file called the Boot Configuration Data or BCD located on the boot volume (that is, the volume that the operating system boots from, no matter what Microsoft calls it) in a folder named BOOT. It's one of those files locked open by the operating system (like the *.EVT event log files), so you can't edit it in the normal manner, *and* because that means that it'll be tougher for the odd bit of malware to modify it.

Don't go looking to edit it from the Control Panel, either; the Startup and Recovery dialog box is still in Control Panel hidden a few layers down, but where the XP version of that dialog had a button labeled "To edit the startup options manually, press Edit," that doesn't exist in Vista anymore. Instead, there's bcdedit.exe, a command-line tool for messing with Vista boot options.

boot.ini Review

The reason why *I* needed to modify boot.ini—normally a few-minute operation that became a multi-hour process, although it'll take you much less time after reading this—is that when I'm running test machines that are not connected to the Internet, either virtual or real, I'm often using *slower* machines, and in an effort to reduce my waiting time when playing with Vista, I like to turn off Data Execution Prevention (DEP). I do *not* recommend doing this on a production machine or, for that matter, any system into which you will type any data that you wouldn't want the world to know. But for test systems that you won't be sharing your vital data with, it's a great idea. With XP and 2003 systems, I could always shut off DEP by editing the boot.ini and adding the /NoExecute=AlwaysOff option to any boot.ini entry. But how to do that (and other things) to BCD? Well, to learn that, we've got to learn BCD-ese. Here's the boot.ini on my XP workstation:

```
[boot loader]
timeout=30
default=multi(0)disk(0)rdisk(0)partition(2)\WINDOWS
```

```
[operating systems]
multi(0)disk(0)rdisk(0)partition(2)\WINDOWS="XP x64 " /fastdetect /
NoExecute=OptOut
multi(0)disk(0)rdisk(0)partition(2)\WINDOWS="XP x64 w/debug" /fastdetect /
NoExecute=OptOut /DEBUG
multi(0)disk(0)rdisk(0)partition(1)\WINDOWS="Microsoft Windows XP Professional"
/fastdetect
```

This particular `boot.ini` offers three different operating system options when booting this computer; those three options are in the section named `[operating systems]`. The three lines following it (each is long and broken on the page, but there would indeed be just three lines if we were viewing this on a wide computer screen) is called a "`boot.ini` entry." For example, consider this one:

```
multi(0)disk(0)rdisk(0)partition(2)\WINDOWS="XP x64 " /fastdetect /
NoExecute=OptOut
```

The `multi(0)disk(0)partition(2)\WINDOWS` is just an arcane way of saying "the actual operating system is on the second partition of the first hard disk, and in the Windows directory on that partition." That's followed by two "switches," `/fastdetect` (which tells Windows not to bother looking around for devices attached to parallel and serial devices, which hasn't been generally necessary since 2000 came out), and `/NoExecute=OptOut`, which is the normal setting for DEP. Because there are three operating system entries, I see a `boot.ini` menu offering those three every time I boot my workstation. Other useful switches are `/maxmem`, which tell your copy of Windows to not use your system's RAM above some level, or `/debug`, which enables system debugging, or `/numprocs`, which tells your system to ignore some number of processors.

Above the `[operating systems]` section, there is a `[boot loader]` section. It specifies two things: how long to leave the menu on the screen, and which option to make default if the `boot.ini` options time out.

Now, if you're scratching your head saying, "I never see anything like that `boot.ini` file, or a boot-time menu at all in either XP *or* in Vista," that means that you've got only one operating system entry. In that case, you don't get the menu on either XP or Vista. If you *do* have a Vista BCD with more than one entry, then you see a different boot menu from the one that you would have in the pre-Vista days, assuming that you had a multi-entry `boot.ini`. The Vista boot menu is text, but it's a bit snazzier than `boot.ini`, like the one that you see in Figure 1.1.

This menu shows two options: "Microsoft Windows Vista," the option built when Vista's installed, and "Vista without DEP," an option that I've created and that I'll show you how to create. In addition to the operating system entries, Vista's Boot Manager also offers the option of booting straight to a memory tester—a convenient touch on Microsoft's part, particularly given that Vista systems typically need quite a bit more memory than XP systems.

FIGURE 1.1   A Vista system with multiple boot options

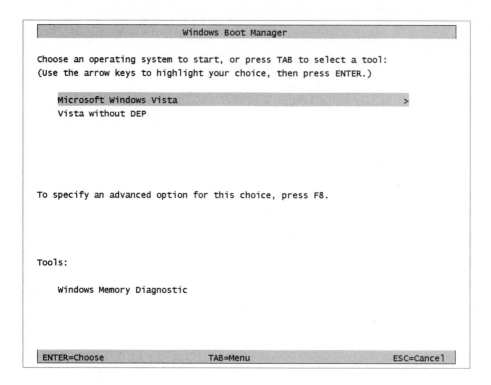

```
                        Windows Boot Manager

Choose an operating system to start, or press TAB to select a tool:
(Use the arrow keys to highlight your choice, then press ENTER.)

    Microsoft Windows Vista                                          >
    Vista without DEP




To specify an advanced option for this choice, press F8.




Tools:

    Windows Memory Diagnostic




 ENTER=Choose                    TAB=Menu                   ESC=Cancel
```

BCD Terminology

To work with BCD, we need to learn a bit of BCD-ese. What we might think of as the entire BCD "database" is called the "store" or the "system BCD store." The store contains one or more "entries," which act as boot.ini entries did; thus, were I to translate my boot.ini into a BCD, I'd have a *store* containing three *entries*. There is, in addition to the entries, a tools menu that by default contains just one entry, the memory tester. Each entry may contain what we used to call boot.ini switches, like /NoExecute=AlwaysOff, but they're not called "switches," they're called "entry options."

Let's see how to relate this to an actual BCD by telling bcdedit to dump the current configuration. Do that by opening a command prompt as an administrator (right-click the Command Prompt icon, choose Run as administrator, and confirm the choice when UAC asks), and then type just **bcdedit**. I get an output like this (I've shortened a few items for clarity):

```
C:\Users\mark>bcdedit
```

```
Windows Boot Manager
--------------------
identifier              {bootmgr}
device                  partition=D:
description             Windows Boot Manager
locale                  en-US
inherit                 {globalsettings}
default                 {current}
displayorder            {current}
                        {c0e803c8-217c-11db-8f12-0016364dab15}
toolsdisplayorder       {memdiag}
timeout                 30


Windows Boot Loader
-------------------
identifier              {current}
device                  partition=C:
path                    \Windows\system32\winload.exe
description             Microsoft Windows Vista
locale                  en-US
inherit                 {bootloadersettings}
osdevice                partition=C:
systemroot              \Windows
nx                      OptOut


Windows Boot Loader
-------------------
identifier              {c0e803c8-217c-11db-8f12-0016364dab15}
device                  partition=C:
path                    \Windows\system32\winload.exe
description             Vista without DEP
locale                  en-US
inherit                 {bootloadersettings}
osdevice                partition=C:
systemroot              \Windows
nx                      AlwaysOff
```

Notice that you see three sections in this report: a "`Windows Boot Manager`" section and two "`Windows Boot Loader`" sections. Remember the [`boot loader`] section? It has morphed into the Windows Boot Manager information. Each entry in the [`operating systems`] section gets its own Windows Boot Loader section.

Creating a Second OS Entry

Let's start putting bcdedit through its paces but…safety first! When installed, Vista creates one OS entry called "`Microsoft Windows Vista`." If you think that you'd like to play around with changing boot options then I highly recommend it, if for no other reason than to take advantage of my suggestion about speeding up test machines with that DEP configuration notion that I've already mentioned. But instead of mucking with the one boot entry that you've got, I even *more* highly recommend that you first make a second OS entry and do your experiments on *that* entry. After all, it *is* possible to make your system unable to boot with a bad OS entry, and that is guaranteed to ruin your whole day. (Unless you like watching Vista install. I mean, it *does* have that lovely "undersea view of the bottom of a kelp forest" background while installing.)

How to create a second OS entry? That's one of bcdedit's abilities. The easiest way to create a second OS entry is to just copy the existing one with the `bcdedit /copy {ID-of-entry-to-copy-from} /d description` command. I will explain *{ID-of-entry-to-copy-from}* in just a couple of paragraphs but for now we can use {`default`}, which is the identifier for the default operating system entry. Using that information, I originally created my "Vista without DEP" OS entry like this:

```
bcdedit /copy {default} /d "Vista without DEP"
```

When I did that, I got a response of

```
The entry was successfully copied to {c0e803c8-217c-11db-8f12-0016364dab15}
```

I'm going to explain that thing in the curly braces—it's called a globally unique identifier or GUID—next, but before I do, let me just summarize where we are at this point. If you try that command on a Vista system and reboot, you will get to see the Windows Boot Manager and your new "Vista without DEP" entry that, at the moment, doesn't do anything different than the "Microsoft Windows Vista" entry. *But* now you've got a safe OS boot entry to play with.

Understanding Vista Boot Manager Identifiers

What's with those {`default`} and {`c0e803c8-217c-11db-8f12-0016364dab15`} things? Windows Boot Manager needs some way to be able to identify the multiple operating system entries. Now, it *could* give them names like "default Vista OS entry," but that would be, um…okay, I don't know why they don't let you just give them arbitrary identifiers; it just seems to be something that's been in Windows since Windows 2000. The idea is, I suppose, that you might go crazy and accidentally create *two* OS entries with identifiers of "default Vista OS entry," and then your computer would implode. Anyway, when Vista creates a new OS entry, it also generates a random 128-bit number and uses that as the OS entry's "true name." Now, *inside* that OS entry is something called a "description" and you and I can fill it with text like "Vista without DEP" or the like, and you and I will use that to identify a particular OS entry, but Vista just sees that "Vista without DEP" name not as a *real* name, but instead as window dressing—{`c0e803c8-217c-11db-8f12-0016364dab15`} is the true name for our new "Vista without DEP" OS entry as far as software's concerned.

That means that when you want bcdedit to do something to a particular OS entry, then you'll usually have to identify the entry that you want to configure. Usually that'll be the GUID of the OS entry. But you will sometimes be able to save a little work, as GUIDs aren't the *only* kind of OS entry identifier that bcdedit will take. It also recognizes the {default} and {current} identifiers. Note that they're surrounded by curly braces, as are the GUIDs. {default} is an identifier that tells bcdedit, "I want you to configure that OS entry that starts up by default, but I don't want to look up its GUID." {current} does the same thing, but it identifies the OS entry that the system is currently booted into. Thus, if you're working on a Vista system that booted into the default operating system entry, then both {default} and {current} point to that OS entry.

So, back a page or two, when I offered the command bcdedit /copy {default}..., I was telling bcdedit to copy whichever operating system entry was the one I'd get by default. When bcdedit spat back the big number in the curly braces, it was telling me that GUID of the OS entry that it had just created for me.

If you ever need to *see* the GUIDs of your computer's default OS entry, just type **bcdedit /v** and you'll get the same long listing as you saw a few pages back when I typed just "bcdedit," *except* that instead of seeing {current} on the Identifier line, you'll get the GUID of that entry. Both a GUID surrounded by curly braces or the predefined {current} or {default} items are called "identifiers" by bcdedit.

Choosing Timeout and Default OS with bcdedit

Now that we're experts on identifying OS entries, let's return to some nuts and bolts. As with boot.ini, Windows Boot Manager's main jobs are to define a timeout value and a default. (Clearly there are also other things that Windows Boot Manager does, but I'm trying to cover just the essentials here.)

Changing the Boot Manager Timeout

To change the timeout value, type **bcdedit /timeout *numberofseconds*** to set the number of seconds that Windows Boot Manager waits before choosing the default operating system entry. For example, to tell Windows Boot Manager to wait 15 seconds, you'd type

```
bcdedit /timeout 15
```

The adjustment you'll want to do more often is probably choosing the default operating system instance.

Changing the Default Boot Manager Entry

You'd think the second task—telling Boot Manager which OS entry to load by default—would be a snap. It is, *almost*; you can pick any OS entry and make it the default, but, as you'd probably guess by now, you've got to refer to that OS entry by an identifier, and the chances are good that you'll have to use its GUID.

As we've already seen, the new "Vista without DEP" OS entry on my system got a GUID of {c0e803c8-217c-11db-8f12-0016364dab15}.

WARNING   Even if you type into your system exactly the same commands that I've typed, you will not get the same GUID, as they're random. So if your GUIDs look different than mine, don't panic, it's supposed to work out that way.

Using that GUID, I can then make that entry the default by typing **bcdedit /default {*guid*}**, so for example to make "Vista without DEP" the default, I'd type

```
bcdedit /default {c0e803c8-217c-11db-8f12-0016364dab15}
```

Again, you can do something similar on your system; just remember that you'll have to retrieve the particular GUID of your "Vista without DEP" OS entry; simply typing **bcdedit** by itself will, recall, show you your OS entries and their GUIDs. And don't forget to surround the GUID with curly braces; bcdedit won't work without them. Then, after typing **bcdedit** all by itself a second time, I'll see the same output, except in the "identifier" line the {c0e803c8-217c-11db-8f12-0016364dab15} will be replaced by {default}. The other OS entry, the "Microsoft Windows Vista" one, will have an identifier of {current}.

Changing an Entry Option

With our new OS entry created and set to the default, we're ready to start with playing with entry options. Recall that "entry option" is the bcdedit phrase for what we used to call "boot.ini switches." Some switches have values, like the /NoExecute=AlwaysOff example that I've already offered, and some, like /basevideo (which says to boot the system with the basic VGA driver) don't have values, and you enable them by including them in the OS entry and disable them by leaving them out. In BCD and bcdedit, however, every entry option has both a name, like NoExecute, *and* a value, like AlwaysOff. (Case seems not to matter to BCD and bcdedit, in my experience.) Boot.ini switches that didn't previously have a value, like "/basevideo," now get a value of "yes" or "no." (/basevideo is now called simply "vga," by the way.)

You can include an entry option by typing **bcdedit /set [{*entry guid*}] *entry-option-name* [*entry-option-value*]**. To set nx to AlwaysOff in the currently running operating system entry, then, we could type

```
bcdedit /set {current} nx AlwaysOff
```

If, however, we hadn't included an OS entry at all, then bcdedit would have assumed that we wanted that change done on the currently booted OS entry anyway, and so this would get the same job done:

```
bcdedit /set nx AlwaysOff
```

To set nx in the default OS entry, we'd type

```
bcdedit /set {default} nx AlwaysOff
```

To tell the OS entry with a GUID of {c0e803c8-217c-11db-8f12-0016364dab15} to boot using the standard VGA video driver, we could type

```
bcdedit /set {c0e803c8-217c-11db-8f12-0016364dab15} vga yes
```

(Just to be clear, that command would be typed as one line.)

Now that you know how to modify boot options, here are a few of the available Vista boot options in BCD and, for the boot.ini black belts out there, the corresponding boot.ini switches of each option entry:

nx, as I've mentioned, controls DEP. Its boot.ini value was just /NoExecute. nx can be can be set to AlwaysOn, which applies DEP to all user applications and operating system programs; AlwaysOff, which does not apply DEP to anything; OptOut, which applies DEP to everything except particular programs that you exclude; or OptIn, which applies DEP to all operating system programs and any applications that you add in. (You can do the excluding or including in the Control Panel's System applet.)

vga is, as I've already explained, the setting telling your system to forgo whatever video driver it's currently using and instead use the generic VGA driver. It takes values "yes" or "no." Its boot.ini counterpart was /basevideo.

numproc, which lets you limit your OS to a certain number of processors, was also /numproc in boot.ini, and takes a number; bcdedit /set numproc 1 would tell your system to only run one processor on the currently running OS entry. This can be useful because once in a while, you'll run into an application that was only tested on single-processor systems but that contains bugs that only pop up in multiprocessor computers.

removememory lets you exclude some amount of memory from Vista. Its boot.ini counterpart was called /burnmemory. It takes a value in either decimal or hex (prefix a hex number with "0x" so it recognizes it as hex) of the exact number of bytes of memory to give Vista— specifying "500000" would remove about a half a megabyte of memory from Vista, not about a half a gigabyte!

truncatememory is another command restricting the amount of RAM that you allow Vista to use. Where removememory specifies how much RAM to take away from Vista, leaving it the rest, truncatememory specifies how much RAM to *give* to Vista, denying it the rest. You wouldn't use both of these in the same OS entry, by the way. As with removememory, truncatememory takes a number as a parameter. That number is, like removememory, the exact number of bytes to give Vista. Truncatememory's name in boot.ini was /maxmem.

If that's still not clear, imagine that you've got a system with 2 GB of RAM. removememory 500000000 would remove a half gig, leaving 1.5 GB of RAM for Vista. You could do the same thing with truncatememory, but you'd feed truncatememory 1500000000.

quietboot skips the GUI's little animated rectangles that ripple left-to-right as an indicator that the OS is loading. Set it to "yes" or "no." It was /noguiboot in boot.ini.

sos, which was named /sos in boot.ini, tells the operating system to show each driver and service's name as the operating system boots. This can be useful if your system locks up on boot; just sos to "yes" and reboot (clearly you need a different way to boot to make this setting, perhaps another OS entry!), and the name of the last driver loaded may be the culprit. This takes "yes" or "no" for parameters.

bootlog tells your system to create a log of the drivers that the OS loads, in the order in which it loads them. It then saves that log in Windows directory in a file called ntbtlog.txt. This option takes "yes" or "no" and was called /bootlog in boot.ini.

Cleaning Up: Deleting OS Entries

That's about all I wanted to cover in BCD and bcdedit to help you tweak your OS's starting parameters. But if you find that you've got your OS entry just the way you like it, and don't need the one automatically built by Vista, then you might want to tidy up a bit. You can delete an OS entry with the bcdedit /delete *identifier* command. For example, on my system, I'd first type "bcdedit" to find out the GUID of the now-unused OS entry, discover that it was {24a500f3-12ea-11db-a536-b7db70c06ac2}, and type

```
bcdedit /delete {24a500f3-12ea-11db-a536-b7db70c06ac2}
```

"Documents and Settings" Is Gone, Kind Of

I liked Windows 2000's improvements over NT 4.0, but I really found one thing annoying about it: the Documents and Settings folder. I do a lot of command-line work, you see, and folder names with spaces are a pain in the neck. You've got to put quotes around them, and even if you do, some programs get a bit stupid when handed a folder name with spaces in it.

Vista, however, does make working with folders and file names with spaces in them easier. Whenever you're using a command-line tool that requires a file or folder name, you can just type as much or as little as you like of the folder or file name that you want to specify, then press the Tab key. It auto-completes the file or folder name. Thus, to change my directory to C:\Documents and Settings, I just type cd d and then press Tab, and instantly the command becomes cd 'c:\documents and settings.' If there is more than one directory starting with a "D" and it chose the wrong one, I'd just press Tab again and it'll cycle through the possibilities. It even puts the quotes around the name if there's a space in the name. (This feature existed in 2000, XP, and 2003 but was not enabled by default.)

NT originally stored user profiles in winnt\profiles, but Microsoft decided to move the profiles out of the OS's directory (which probably made sense) into a separate location. That, again, was a good idea; calling it "Documents and Settings," in contrast, was a bad one. (Not as dumb as making people learn goofy phrases like HKEY_LOCAL_MACHINE to understand the Registry, but dumb enough.) Vista changes that, creating a folder to store local profiles called \Users. You've just gotta love it: no spaces, short and sweet.

But we've been living with Documents and Settings for six and some years, so Microsoft knows that there will be *some* application out there that doesn't follow the rules, and decides to write some data to c:\documents and settings*some-users-name**some-folder-name* instead of just asking the operating system where that user's profile folder is. To combat that, Microsoft creates a Documents and Settings folder on the drive, *but hides it.* Then they take things a step further and set its NTFS permissions to—you'll love this—*deny the Everyone group read access to Documents and Settings.* The result? Any application that tries to create data in Documents and Settings, rather than just asking the OS where to put the profile information, will fail.

What should you do if you happen to find that one bad application out of thousands? Either get the developer to fix the problem, or unhide the folder and change its NTFS permissions. Or Vista's file and folder virtualization feature may fix the problem invisibly. (You'll learn more about that in Chapter 3.)

IPv6 and Network Properties

The first time I started an early copy of Vista (back when it was known as "Longhorn Desktop"), it appeared that my network connections weren't working. So I did the same thing that most network admins would do: I opened up a command prompt and typed **ipconfig**, then pressed Enter. Figure 1.2 shows something like what I saw.

FIGURE 1.2   ipconfig, with a new, scary look

First of all, this particular computer's only got two network adapters, not…umm, give me a second, let me count…*five* network adapters. Auugh. What's *going on* here, I wondered? "Why are there colons and percent signs where there are supposed to be periods, and…oh, I see. IPv6." As you may know, the version of IP that we use in TCP/IP for the Internet is actually "IPv4," IP version 4. There was an IPv5 because some folks played around with a networking tool to make transmitting multimedia stuff easier—I don't think it went anywhere—and meanwhile, while the world started worrying about running out of IP addresses, some smart folks started working on a new version of IP based on 128-bit, rather than 32-bit, addressing. Were the Internet to go IPv6, we'd *never* have to worry about running out of addresses, as a little calculation shows that we'd have 429,446,885,032,372,986,132 IP addresses for every square inch of the Earth's surface and, yes, that *does* include the part of the earth covered by water.

Now, I understand why Microsoft wanted to put IPv6 into Vista. It's the basis of a lot of interesting technologies in mobile computing; in theory, when the whole world goes IPv6 then you can get up in the morning, grab your e-mail on your notebook via the wireless network in your house, take a bus downtown and catch up on the news at your favorite websites while your laptop's connected to the municipal wireless LAN, and then finally connect to the network at work to hook up with your domain…and never change an IP address. Microsoft's committed to taking big market shares in the mobility world, so I can see that might be a reason why they installed IPv6 by default, whether I want it or not. China's working to produce a country-wide IPv6-based Internet, and China's an important sales market, so I can see why Microsoft decided to install IPv6 by default, whether I wanted it or not. Microsoft hates hearing that they're Johnny-come-latelies to any network party and most Linux distributions don't install IPv6 by default yet, so I could see that Microsoft might like using IPv6 as a chance to seem more "wave of the future" than their biggest desktop rival.

But boy, are they gonna pay for it, at least in my opinion. Microsoft hates running a tech support operation because it's not nearly as profitable as is cranking out Vista DVDs and charging a few C-notes apiece, but the need's there; turn off tech support for Windows and a lot of users will find something else.

I think, however, that Microsoft's gotten something of a free ride tech-support-wise over the years. As I've already noted, I'll bet that everyone reading this book has probably acted as a no-charge-for-services tech support person for friends, family, and neighbors. Now imagine what happens the first time one of the legions of free support folks start trying to troubleshoot a neighbor's cable modem troubles with the neighbor's brand spanking new copy of Vista. One look at *that* ipconfig output, and many of those helpful volunteers will just say "um, maybe you'd better call the cable company."

And you know how helpful the cable guys will be when they see those IPv6 numbers.

Now, let's be clear, and this is a very important point: as far as I can see, home network users can keep IPv6 running without any ill effects to their network at all. But I've run into problems with IPv6 on XP, 2003, and Vista systems in an Active Directory environment—dynamic DNS registrations run into some trouble, presumably because the IPv6 addresses were confusing, and the problem persists into RC1—and so I'd prefer to have to *add* IPv6 rather than remove it. But inasmuch as it's the default, that means that I'll have to remove it if I want my ipconfig outputs to look less cryptic. Now, you're probably thinking, "that'll be easy; just go to the Properties page of your network interface card and uncheck the boxes next to IPv6." My thoughts exactly the first time I ran Vista.

But then I went *looking* for the Properties page of my NIC. Want to find it? Well, then put on your mining helmet with the lamp on it; we're going into the bowels of Vista....

1. Click the Start button, then choose Control Panel. You'll see that on Figure 1.3, although I've added an annotation.

   This isn't a gratuitous screen shot, because I need it to illustrate a point about Control Panel. Look at the section that I outlined with a black rectangle; it's the area where you kick off network-related Control Panel pages. But here's the surprise: that's not just one section, as was the Network and Internet Connections section in XP's Control Panel. No, it's not obvious, but those are actually pointers to three separate sections: "Network and Internet," "View network status and tasks," and "Share files and folders." Each is a separate hyperlink-like thing, and each takes you to a different place. None of them, however, will take you directly to your NIC or NICs.

2. Instead, click "View network status and tasks," and, in the resulting Control Panel page, you'll see a list on the left-hand side of that page labeled "Tasks." One of those tasks is "Manage network connections;" click that to see something like Figure 1.4.

FIGURE 1.3   Vista's Control Panel

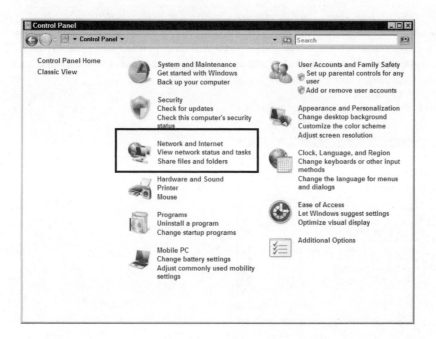

FIGURE 1.4 Network Connections, Vista style

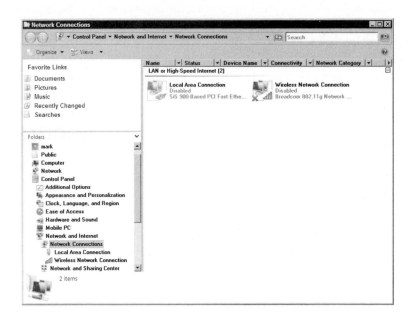

3. Now, *that* seems a bit more familiar. Ignore the fact that both NICs are designated "disabled;" that's an artifact of build 5472, the build that I took this from, and appeared fixed at RC1. Right-clicking the Ethernet NIC (yours will, of course, almost certainly be a different make or model, but the dialog will look similar) and choosing Properties shows something that looks like Figure 1.5.

FIGURE 1.5 Vista's NIC Properties page

4. Once again, a more familiar dialog box...almost. Note all of the IPv6 and IPv6-to-IPv4 compatibility tools. Uncheck any that you want, and some of the IPv6 stuff goes away; three references to "tunnel adapters" remain.

Now you've seen how to find the NIC Properties page. I should stress that I'm not instructing people in general to get rid of IPv6; I just wanted to show you how to find the NIC Properties page, and IPv6 was a good excuse.

Remote Desktop Gets a Bit More Secure

At first glance, Remote Desktop for Vista looks pretty much identical to RD on XP. But a slightly closer look shows a small but important change in security. You can see this in the Remote tab of the System property page. Get to it like so:

1. Click the Start button.

2. In the resulting menu, right-click Computer and choose Properties.

3. In the Control Panel page that appears, look at the Tasks list on the left-hand side of the page. Choose "Remote settings." You'll see a property page like Figure 1.6.

As I said, this looks similar to the corresponding page in XP, but notice that instead of two options—"enable or disable remote desktop"—there is a third offering, "Allow connections only from computers running Remote Desktop with Network Level Authentication."

FIGURE 1.6   Configuring Remote Desktop in Vista

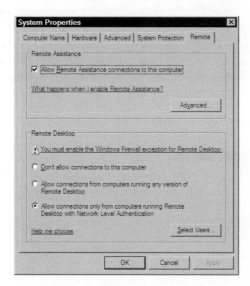

To understand this, think about what's happened every time you've tried to use Remote Desktop to remote into a system. You start up the Remote Desktop Connection (RDC) app in XP or 2003 and tell the app to connect you to some system. RDC goes out and, assuming that Remote Desktop's enabled for that system and they've got their firewall set up so that people can remote in, you get a logon screen from the remote system. Now, from the point of view of a particularly paranoid security person, this is interesting: you haven't authenticated to this system yet, but it's responded to your command for its attention nonetheless. In other words, Remote Desktop is a little bit more trusting than it could be, as the sequence of events is (1) request a Remote Desktop connection from the remote system, (2) the remote system stops what it's doing and creates a remote session to your computer, and (3) you log on.

By choosing the new third setting under Remote Desktop, you tell Remote Desktop to switch steps (2) and (3). When you try to log onto a remote system that supports this approach, which Microsoft calls "Network Level Authentication," you don't see a remote standard Windows logon dialog sitting atop a remote desktop; instead, you get a dialog box like the one in Figure 1.7.

But does this mean that a Network Level Authentication logon only works against Vista systems at the moment? Apparently yes. As I write this in September 2006, Microsoft has released a package called "Remote Desktop Connection 6.0" for XP SP2, 2003 SP1, and the x64 versions of XP and 2003. They did not release it to the general public, and it was only available from Microsoft's beta software site, but I'd be surprised if it weren't either generally available with Vista's release, or might even end up on the Vista DVD. But even with this updated RDP client, you cannot do a Network Level Authentication against a Vista system or, if you can, I've not figured out how.

What if you still want older systems to be able to remote into your system, but you'd like any Vista systems trying to log in to use Network Level Authentication? Then choose the second radio button. Vista clients will still use Network Level Authentication even if the Vista system they're remoting into doesn't require it. Is it a bad idea to enable the second radio button? Well, of course. On the one hand, enabling it means that you can RD into your Vista box from a wider variety of clients; on the other hand, the whole point of Network Level Authentication was to lessen the chance that someone could tie up your computer's CPU with bogus attempts at Remote Desktop sessions, and the second radio button leaves open that possibility. Once again, security and compatibility are sometimes tradeoffs.

FIGURE 1.7   A Network Level Authentication logon dialog

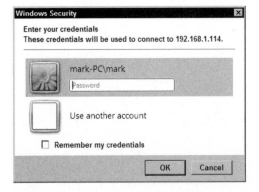

Oh, hey, I almost forgot my favorite new Remote Desktop feature. You can cut and paste files across a Remote Desktop connection. Want to deliver a folder from your desktop to the computer that you're remoting into? Just right-click it, choose Copy, and then left-click on some folder in the remote system, right-click, and choose Paste. Quite nice, although as far as I can see, the revised RDP client for XP and 2003 doesn't support this. The revised RDP client *looks* as if it'll manage that drag and drop, but when you drop, nothing happens.

NTFS and the Registry Are Transaction Based

This falls in the category of a good surprise, in fact a really nice one. Both the file system and the Registry are now transaction based in Vista. This surprised me because it was supposed to appear in Server 2007 but it's in Vista. "Transaction based" means that you can take a number of separate files, copy, move, or whatever operations you need, and essentially package them up so that they're all or nothing. If one of the operations fails, then you just "roll back" and everything done so far is undone. Here's an actual example run:

```
Microsoft Windows [Version 6.0.5456]
(C) Copyright 1985-2005 Microsoft Corp.

C:\Users\mark>transaction /start
A transaction has been successfully started.
Transaction ID: {1288b5a4-4b58-4006-88d8-6bc86f4b8ad3}

C:\Users\mark>md newfiles

C:\Users\mark>copy con newfiles\test
hi there
^Z
1 file(s) copied.

C:\Users\mark>dir newfiles
Volume in drive C has no label.
Volume Serial Number is 4834-858C

Directory of C:\Users\mark\newfiles

07/17/2006 06:48 PM <DIR> .
07/17/2006 06:48 PM <DIR> ..
07/17/2006 06:48 PM 10 test
1 File(s) 10 bytes
2 Dir(s) 15,731,507,200 bytes free
```

```
C:\Users\mark>transaction /rollback
The current transaction has been rolled back.

C:\Users\mark>dir newfiles
Volume in drive C has no label.
Volume Serial Number is 4834-858C

Directory of C:\Users\mark

File Not Found

C:\Users\mark>
```

Here, I start a transaction, then create a new folder and put a file in that folder. But then I cancel the transaction, and it's all undone; asking for a directory listing of the new folder yields "File Not Found." In contrast, typing `transaction /commit` would have said "transaction's over, make it all permanent." Where will this be useful? Well, File and Registry-based transactions will be pretty useful for applying patches. Heck, you could actually install and test a piece of software, and then uninstall it via a transaction rollback. But that'd only work if the software didn't require a reboot; any reboots act as a `transaction /rollback`. I suspect we'll find plenty of pretty valuable uses for this. (I've got to say it again: the word "patches" keeps coming to mind.)

 WARNING   Unfortunately around RC1, Microsoft took the `transaction` command out of Vista. Apparently the under-the-hood support for transaction-based NTFS and Registry is still there, but the command itself posed some theoretical problems and so Microsoft decided that letting regular users like you and me set up transactions would be a bad idea. So unless they change their minds, then transactions will be something that only programmers can set up. (Which might make sense; it's just a shame.)

Undelete Comes to Windows for Real!

If you've ever used System Restore for XP, then you know how useful it can be. System Restore takes periodic snapshots of the state of your operating system and lets you roll back to before you installed the Driver from Hell or that antivirus application that seems to work by crashing your system, which is of course one way to keep you from getting malware, although not the optimal one. Now, with Vista, System Restore does the same thing for your *files*. Right-click any file or folder and choose Properties, and you'll see a dialog box like Figure 1.8.

Note the tab named Previous Versions. That's right, version*s* with an "s." Decided that your version of the Great American Novel was better two days ago and you didn't back up? No worries; check out Previous Versions and just grab the version from a couple of days ago. As before, you get a System Restore point once a day by default, or whenever you tell System Restore to create one.

FIGURE 1.8   Previous Versions tab in a file's Properties page

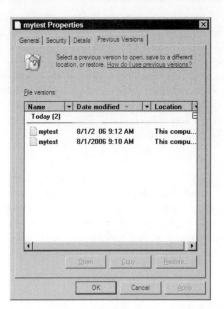

Changes in Security Options

If you've got any security-related responsibilities are all, chances are good that at some point you've opened up the Group Policy Editor either on the local group policy object or on a domain group policy object and navigated to Computer Configuration ➤ Windows Settings ➤ Security Settings ➤ Local Policies ➤ Security Options. That folder contains a grab bag of options that let you dial your security up or down. Turn 'em all off, and you're basically running a NT network, circa 1993 security-wise: loose and easily hacked, but compatible with ancient software and operating systems. Turn 'em all on and you'll need to be running only XP, 2003, and Vista systems and new applications.

But most of these security settings are just on/off ones, and they've *got* to have some default, out-of-the-box value. Microsoft's got to pick those defaults, and it's a tough job. They've been slowly tightening security not just with every version of Windows but often with every service pack, so it should be no surprise that Vista not only continues to offer the same security options as XP SP2 did, but more options, as well, *and* tighter settings on some existing options. In this section, I'll enumerate which security options settings have changed, and how that may affect your job of fitting Vista systems into your existing network.

But don't panic: yes, Vista tightens some security settings that have been left loose for a long time, but remember, these are settings in the *local* group policy object and can be easily rolled back if necessary. Furthermore, if you're connected to a domain, and that domain has a domain-based group policy object that specifies values in the Security Options folder, then those settings will override the local settings on a Vista system. The only real downside you might experience if you monkey with the security settings a lot would be a little heartburn from Vista when you try to initially join a Vista box to an existing Active Directory domain, but I'll discuss that later.

A note before we get started: when I say that something has "changed from XP" or "changed from Server 2003," I am referring to the 32-bit versions of XP and 2003. I mention this because as I look at the default settings in the local group policy object of my x64 workstation I note that some of the "new Vista settings" are actually already included in the x64 versions of XP and Server 2003.

Changes to Named Pipe Access

Named pipes are a way for programs to communicate among themselves. Years ago, most named pipes created by the OS were poorly secured or not secured at all. Many hackers successfully attacked Windows systems through poorly secured named pipes. One of the easiest avenues for these sort of attacks was by connecting as an "anonymous" user. This is a once-obscure but sadly now well-known way to connect to many Microsoft protocols and, as its name suggests, you needn't use a username and password to log in; you can, instead, remain anonymous. While allowing anonymous users *any* access to a Microsoft network resource isn't a very good idea, the fact is that for backward compatibility purposes Windows still uses some anonymous connections. Microsoft's been slowly removing the anonymous user—if I recall right, the first code to reduce the power of "anonymous" was as far back as 1998 with NT 4.0 SP3—but it's still around, and Vista takes up cudgels to reduce its power—and threat—a bit further, in these changes in how named pipes handle anonymous users.

Windows has, since XP at least, had a Security Options setting "Network access: Named Pipes that can be accessed anonymously." It lists a subset of the system's named pipes that you need the anonymous user to be able to access, and by default the group policy setting has included a bunch of stuff that doesn't really make sense:

- COMNAP and COMNODE only appear on a server running Microsoft's gateway software for talking to an IBM mainframe, their "Host Integration Server" (HIS). To the best of my knowledge, it's not possible to run HIS on any of Microsoft's desktop OSes.

- SQL\QUERY would appear on a system running Microsoft SQL Server or its equivalent. It's *possible* that a Vista system might be running SQL Server Express 2005— although not possible, I am told, to run its predecessor, Microsoft Desktop Engine (MSDE)— but not likely.

- LLSRPC appears only on servers running the Licensing Service. Why Microsoft would want anonymous people accessing the Licensing Service is a puzzle, and in no case would it appear on a desktop OS.

- BROWSER allows a system to act as either a master browser or backup browser on a subnet; this pipe is how the master and backup browsers talk. If the backup and master browser on a given subnet are not members of the same forest, then they need to be able to anonymously access the BROWSER named pipe so that the master browser can send the backup browser a copy of the segment's browse list. Microsoft has kept BROWSER in the list of named pipes that can be accessed anonymously because of that case where a workgroup might have backup and master browsers. In any case, the chances that it's a desktop OS are small, but not impossible; one could imagine a small home workgroup built entirely of Vista systems. But in that case we'd probably be talking about a single segment, where broadcasts could handle any name resolution needs.

Vista's default setting for "Network access: Named Pipes that can be accessed anonymously" removes all of those named pipes, leaving just one: SPOOLSS. That works with the print spooler, and *that's* a server role that is quite common for desktop OSes.

Why did Microsoft have so many silly named pipes in XP's default set of group policy settings? They were just saving themselves a little trouble by creating a set of defaults that they could apply both to server OSes and workstation OSes. With Vista, it looks as though that's no longer true, and the desktop has gotten its own set of settings.

Changes to Share and Registry Access

Criminals wanting to penetrate a system anonymously have avenues other than named pipes. Windows systems also feature a variety of built-in shares, and some can be accessed anonymously— or could be, before Vista. By default, XP allows two shares to be accessed anonymously. They are named in a Security Option setting named "Network access: shares that can be accessed anonymously." The two named on XP are COMCFG, which is related to the Host Integration System, and DFS$, which is necessary for a server hosting a Distributed File System root. Since Vista can't host HIS *or* a DFS root, they're both gone in Vista, and "Network access: shares that can be accessed anonymously" features an empty box.

Another avenue for bad guys is to read parts of the Registry remotely, as it reveals inner details about the system. Some Registry paths clearly must be accessible over a network for networking and remote administration to function, and those are named in the Security Option setting "Network access: remotely accessible registry paths." Where it names nine paths in XP, there are only three in Vista.

LM Deemphasized, NTLMv2 Emphasized

Vista changes two items in Security Options in a way that I personally like a lot, but I want you to understand what they might do to your network compatibility. The two settings are

- "Network security: Do not store LAN Manager hash value on next password change" is now enabled, even though it had been disabled by default until now.

- "Network security: LAN Manager authentication level" changes from "Send LM and NTLM" to "Send NTLMv2 response only."

First, a little background. It's nice that we've got machines called domain controllers (DCs) that centrally store usernames and passwords so that every machine doesn't have to carry around a complete list of all usernames and passwords. But having central logon services means that you've got to figure out how to *use* those services safely. I say that because if I'm sitting a Workstation A and offer it my domain name and password, then how's Workstation A going to ask Domain Controller B to verify it? It's not a very good idea to ask across the network "hey, Domain Controller B, I've got a guy here who says he's a guy named Mark with password 'swordfish,' does that sound right?" It'd be a bad idea because people can easily listen in on network traffic.

So, instead of making DCs and workstations reveal secrets across the wire, Microsoft and other vendors do something a bit more crafty. When the workstation says to the DC, "I want to log Mark in, can you verify that this is indeed Mark talking to me," the DC replies "okay, *I* know Mark's password, and you've got the password that the would-be Mark offers. So here's a big random number. Take it and encrypt it, using the password that this might-be-Mark guy offered. Then send the encrypted result back to me." The workstation takes the random number (which is called the *challenge*), encrypts it with offered password, and sends that encrypted number (which is called the *response*) to the DC. Meanwhile, the DC also encrypts the challenge, using the password that it has on file for Mark. If the response from the workstation matches the encrypted challenge, then the DC knows that the password typed in to the workstation is indeed the correct one, without the workstation having to transmit the proffered password.

Now, that's just the broad outline of how this kind of authentication method, called a "challenge-response mechanism," works. The devil's in the details: complex encryption's hard to crack (and that's good) but requires more CPU power, long keys are harder to crack but also require more CPU power and make logons slower (and that's bad), so the OS vendor has to weigh its choice of encryption methods and key lengths carefully. As time has gone on, Microsoft has created three different challenge-response mechanisms: the late 1980s offered "LM," short for "LAN Manager," which was replaced in the early 1990s with "NTLM," the NT version of the LAN Manager logon protocol, and in the late 1990s Microsoft created a far better challenge-response mechanism called "NTLMv2." There's also Kerberos, an authentication method used most in the time in Active Directory, and that appeared with Windows 2000 in early 2000. But even a network with the most state-of-the-art stuff will sometimes fall back from Kerberos to either LM, NTLM, or NTLMv2. That's not really a wonderful thing, as Kerberos is considerably more secure than the other three, but there is no way to banish the "LM family" altogether. But if you want to keep your network secure, then it'd be best to ensure that if

Kerberos isn't available then your systems should use NTLMv2 rather than the older, less secure challenge-response mechanisms.

If NTLMv2's been around for nearly 10 years, why aren't we all using it now? Why hasn't LM and NTLM been banished for years? It's the same story as before: compatibility. If you've got some older computers in your network (Windows 9x, for example), then it's some work getting them to talk NTLMv2; MS-DOS systems and Windows for Workgroup systems will never talk NTLMv2. Alternatively, if you've got third-party network-attached devices like some of the Network Attached Storage (NAS) boxes like, for example, an old Quantum Snap Server, then a device like that might not *understand* NTLMv2.

Every modern copy of Windows knows how to log on using either the LM, NTLM, or NTLMv2 challenge-response methods, but which of those methods does it choose? You configure that with a setting in Security Options, "Network security: LAN Manager authentication level." By default an XP box will, when offered a logon challenge, compute *two* responses: the LM and NTLM response. As both of those responses are encrypted with an encryption algorithm that has been cracked in the past and gets easier to crack with every passing year as CPUs get faster, automatically responding LM and NTLM responses becomes less and less ideal all the time. Vista's default is different, and by default it offers the NTLMv2 response.

Will this new default cause you trouble? Well, any 2000, XP, 2003, or Vista system acting as a server can understand and use an NTLMv2 response, so if your Vista clients always produce NTLMv2 responses then you'll probably be okay. But, again, check your network-attached devices, like those convenient little print server things the size of a deck of cards that will let you put a printer anywhere and make it available on the network. As with all hardening processes, testing is important.

Vista also hardens systems a bit by keeping your systems from creating something called "LM hashes." Whenever you type a password into your computer, the computer doesn't store your password anywhere. Instead, it takes you password and subjects it to a mathematical function called a "hashing function" that reduces the password, no matter what length, to a 128-bit number. *That's* what gets stored on your computer and on your domain controllers, not your password; instead, the "password hash" is stored. Why do that? Because if someone gets your hash, then reversing the hash process and figuring out your password just by looking at the hash *should* be nearly impossible, *if the system's designed right.* Microsoft first started doing this back in the LAN Manager days of the late 1980s, and the hashes created and stored by LAN Manager are known as the "LM hashes." In designing the method of storing LM hashes, Microsoft built a fairly good hashing system given the power of computers at the time, but they made one serious error. By looking at the LM hash of someone's password, anyone can instantly determine whether the password that resulted in the hash was fewer than eight characters. Being able to instantly be certain that a particular password was seven characters or fewer is a powerful tool in the hands of bad guys.

With the advent of NT 3.1 in 1993, Microsoft used a different and more secure method of hashing. But Microsoft needed to worry about backward compatibility, and so whenever you changed your password, then NT created and stored *two* hashes: the LM hash and an "NT hash." Remember, if a bad guy gets your hashes, then he doesn't need to crack them both— cracking the LM hash will give him your password without any need of help from the NT hash. Storing LM hashes is potentially security nitroglycerine, but Windows XP and 2003 still create LM hashes by default. There's been a setting in Security Options, "Network security: Do not store LAN Manager hash value on next password change" in Windows for years, but Microsoft's disabled it by default because, again, older operating systems and network-attached devices may fail if they can't get LM hashes. That changes with Vista.

Personally, I shut LM hashes off my network in 2002 and haven't missed them, and I think that if you can tell your systems to stop creating LM hashes, then you should jump on it—but, again, I would strongly suggest doing some testing first. Vista, however, takes a stronger position and is the first version of Windows to shut off LM hashes right out of the box.

No More Unsigned Driver Warnings

Just about anyone who's ever worked with 2000, XP, or 2003 for any time at all has had to load a driver for a new piece of hardware, or perhaps had to update a driver on an existing piece of hardware. A good portion of the time, trying to install that driver meets with a dialog box containing a dire-sounding message to the effect that you are trying to install a driver that has not been signed by Microsoft's Windows Hardware Quality Labs (WHQL, pronounced "whickel" so as to rhyme with "nickel."). This, the message seems to intone, is a perilously foolish idea but, hey, it's a free country and you are certainly *welcome* to destroy your operating system; *just don't say we didn't warn you*, it seems to say.

No, that's not the exact text of the dialog box, but it's the spirit. You see, Microsoft's WHQL labs offer a set of rules to follow when writing a driver or for that matter anything that contains low-level, "kernel mode" code. If you follow those rules to write the driver, and then buy a digital certificate to sign the driver, then you can submit it to Microsoft's WHQL labs to be tested for compatibility. (As of August 2006, the test costs $250 per driver per operating system; "XP" covers all varieties of XP, so submitting a driver for signing for both XP and 2003 would cost $500, according to "Global WHQL Policies Document," found at http://www.microsoft.com/whdc/whql/policies/default.mspx.) If the driver passes, then WHQL signs your driver with Microsoft's certificate. If Windows sees that signature when you try to install a driver, then you don't get the baleful-sounding warning message.

Most hardware vendors don't particularly want to have to pay Microsoft $250 every time the hardware vendor updates a driver, and so they don't bother, kicking off the warning message. I honestly don't know enough about how thorough the WHQL guys are to intelligently comment about whether or not this whole WHQL signing thing is just a revenue stream for Microsoft, or a seriously good idea. In any case, the only reason that you ever see the warning is because of a Security Options setting "Devices: Unsigned driver installation behavior." On 2000, XP, and 2003, it's got three options: "Do not allow installation," "Warn but allow installation," or "Silently succeed." The default was "Warn but allow installation." But if you look for "Devices: Unsigned driver installation behavior" in Security Options on a Vista system, you'll find that it's gone altogether. That's because Microsoft decided to take a hard line on drivers for the 64-bit version of Vista, and require that all 64-bit drivers for Vista be signed by WHQL. That's a pretty stringent requirement in my opinion, and that's not just a bystander's point of view—remember, I'm a 64-bit kinda guy, and that driver thing is in my top five reasons why I might not be able to roll out Vista as quickly as I'd like. In any case, you can read more about this 64-bit driver issue in detail in Chapter 6.

But wait a minute; the Security Options item goes away, and 64-bit Vista requires signing; what about 32-bit? Well, inasmuch as 32-bit Vista is, according to Microsoft, the last 32-bit operating system that they'll ever create, I guess they decided not to worry quite as much about security (which is the supposed reason for driver signing) and just tell 32-bit Vista to allow unsigned driver installs to silently succeed. It's a good change in my opinion, as I have never, ever seen anyone *not* load a driver because of the dialog box's message, and I *have* seen the "are you sure?" dialog get in the way of some unattended installs.

Encryption News

Security can't work without encryption, and of course Microsoft operating systems (except for MS-DOS) have all included some kind of encryption since Microsoft released OS/2 1.0 in 1987. But over the years, the sort of encryption that Microsoft builds into its OSes, and what it does with them, changes. Here are few notes on new crypto capabilities in Vista.

Vista Includes New Cryptographic Services

Every software vendor has to make the choice about whether to try creating its own encryption algorithms or to employ standard algorithms. It might seem at first glance that a software vendor would be better off building their own encryption algorithm and keeping its inner workings secret, but according to security expert Bruce Schneier, writing in his book *Secrets and Lies: Digital Security in a Networked World* (Wiley, 2000), the better route is not to build crypto algorithms that are studied and cross-checked by a handful of insiders, but instead to use a crypto algorithm that's been reviewed by hundreds of mathematical experts. In his book Schneier took Microsoft to task for this, claiming that every single time that Microsoft creates a proprietary cryptographic algorithm, it's cracked in just a few months.

I don't know if that *always* happens, but it's surely happened enough. Maybe that's why Microsoft's using more and more standard cryptographic algorithms. (Maybe they read Schneier's book?) Two that come to mind are the Secure Hashing Algorithm (SHA) and the Advanced Encryption System (AES). Both were developed under the aegis of the U.S. government's National Institute for Standards and Technology (NIST) with the intention of providing a well-thought-out set of algorithms for hashing (SHA) and encryption (AES). AES seems well thought of in the crypto community, but SHA has been attacked successfully in some specialized situations. The most recent version of SHA, "SHA-2," has not been successfully attacked as I write this.

Microsoft has had AES built into XP since SP1 and 2003 since its original release, but only in limited use; as far as I know, the only use XP had for AES was in the Encrypting File System (EFS). With Vista, Microsoft says that you will be able to use AES for encryption with IPsec. Granted, it's not earth-shaking, as previously only offered Triple DES (Data Encryption Standard), and cracking TDES probably won't be practical for some time, but it's a step ahead. Adding SHA-2 to IPsec will also be good, but I should note that as I write this, the group policy interface does not show options for either AES or SHA-2. I *can* confirm, however, that another Windows technology, BitLocker Full Volume Encryption, does indeed use AES in 128-bit and 256-bit encryption. (You can read more about BitLocker in Chapter 5.)

You Can Encrypt Your Pagefile

Here's good news for the completely paranoid: you can encrypt your pagefile. Just take my advice…don't. Not unless you want to wait, say, an hour or so every time you turn your computer on while you wait for it to decrypt a gigabyte or so of pagefile.

Offline Files Folders Are Encrypted per User

Offline Files is a great technology that allows you to cache data from oft-used file shares locally. It first appeared in Windows 2000 and while it's not for everyone, lots of people like it. But once details of how Offline Files works got out, people soon realized that it presented something of a security hole. You see, in Windows 2000, all of the cached files were stored in a directory easily viewed by any user. Thus, if I shared a computer with you and you used Offline Files, then I could poke around the folder holding the cached files—everyone on the same machine shared the same folder—and that might not be good.

When XP came around, Microsoft encrypted the folder that held the cached Offline Files data. But the process that did the encrypting was a service that ran as the LocalSystem account, which meant that the EFS encryption key for the Offline Files data was easily utilized by anyone running as LocalSystem. Unfortunately, it turned out to be really easy to log on as Local-System—just use the at.exe scheduler program to start up a command prompt; as the scheduler program runs as LocalSystem, you get a command prompt running under the Local-System account—cracking Offline Files to peek into the cached files of someone who shares your machine was still relatively easy.

Vista changes that in two ways. First of all, everyone's cached files are cached with *their* EFS key, not LocalSystem's. Second, even if Microsoft *hadn't* changed that about the operating system, it'd still be pretty tough to exploit, as logging on as LocalSystem has gotten a lot harder. All of the old tricks that I've been able to use in the past to log on as LocalSystem no longer work in Vista!

New Event Viewer

Here's a good surprise: the Event Viewer has had a complete reengineering. The new Event Viewer:

- Can collect events from many systems to one system's log, allowing you to centralize event logs.
- Lets you easily tell it what to do if particular events occur, like telling it to send you an e-mail, run a program, reboot a system, or the like.

- Allows you to create custom queries so you can essentially tweak Event Viewer to show you just the things that you want to see.
- Event Viewer Reports its data in XML.

It's beyond the scope of this book to go into Event Viewer in detail, but I'd like to show you a bit of what I think you'll like about the new Viewer, in ascending order of importance from my point of view. But before we go any further, let me show you how to start Event Viewer. As with all Windows things, there are several ways.

- If you reenabled the Start ➢ Run… command as I suggested earlier in this chapter, just click Start/Run… and then fill in **eventvwr** and click OK.
- If you restored Administrative Tools to your Start menu, then just click Start ➢ Administrative Tools ➢ Event Viewer.
- Alternatively you'll need to do a little spelunking in Control Panel: click Start ➢ Control Panel ➢ System and Maintenance and, under "Administrative Tools," click "View event logs."

As some have observed, "Vista: it's everyone's 10 favorite user interfaces."

XML Format Comes to Event Viewer

Woo, hoo, XML! Wait, wait, don't flip the page…

Yes, I know, you've heard the abbreviation "XML" far too often, but here's a case where you'll like it. Let's take an example event, a simple security event that reports that the system's time was successfully changed. The event looks graphically like Figure 1.9.

FIGURE 1.9   Typical Vista event

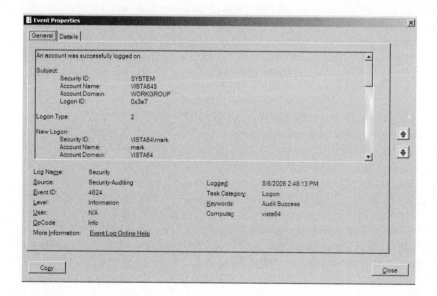

This is an event generated in the Security log because I've just logged on with a username of "Mark." You'll note at first that Event Viewer presents the event in a different format than the one that we've seen since NT 3.1. Notice that there's a button that's actually labeled "Copy" instead of hoping that you just somehow know that the button on the XP Event Viewer that looks like two pieces of paper means "click this and the relevant stuff from this event will be copied in ASCII text format to the Clipboard."

You can't see it because the text in the box is pretty big and scrolled out of the visual part of the box, but here's some of it:

```
This event is generated when a logon session is created. It is generated on the
computer that was accessed.
```

```
The subject fields indicate the account on the local system which requested the
logon. This is most commonly a service such as the Server service, or a local
process such as Winlogon.exe or Services.exe.
```

```
The logon type field indicates the kind of logon that occurred. The most common
types are 2 (interactive) and 3 (network).
```

```
The New Logon fields indicate the account for whom the new logon was created,
i.e. the account that was logged on...
```

I've looked at "logon type" in logon events in Windows for years and never bothered to look up what a "logon type" is. In contrast, Vista tells me. I didn't copy all of the information from the message, but it goes on to explain what a logon GUID, package name, and bunch of otherwise-cryptic stuff was. Very nice. In another event, one reporting that the system time changed, the explanatory text goes on to basically say "look, system time updates happen normally, so you can probably ignore it. But there are reasons why bad guys might try to change a system time."

If you click the Copy button and paste the results into Notepad, you get a lot of information. It starts off looking like event logs have always looked, telling you where the event came from, its ID and so on. Then it starts with a bunch of XML, which, shortened a bit, looks like

```
<Data Name="TargetUserSid">S-1-5-21 …-1000</Data>
<Data Name="TargetUserName">mark</Data>
<Data Name="TargetDomainName">VISTA64</Data>
<Data Name="TargetLogonId">0x20788</Data>
<Data Name="LogonType">2</Data>
<Data Name="LogonProcessName">User32 </Data>
```

What's *this* mess? It's all of the pieces of data specific to this particular event log entry. Now, event log items have always kept this kind of information, but it hasn't been very useful for two reasons. First, it's been hard to export this kind of data out of the event logs for use in scripts or other homegrown tools that might increase the value of the data in the event logs, and, second, it's hard to know what the data means. You can fairly easily write a script that grabs "data item 1," "data item 2," "data item 3," and so on from a given event, but what *is* data item 1? Well, it depends on what particular event you're looking at. But not with Vista. By storing the data in XML and making that data easy to get to from scripts or even right from the Event Viewer—you can right-click any log in Vista and choose "Save events as," and you're offered to save the files as either text files, XML files, or comma separated variable files—then not only can you get to the data, but the data identifies itself. That's the beauty of XML; the line

```
<Data Name="TargetUserName">mark</Data>
```

is XML-ese for "there's a piece of data in this event named the 'TargetUserName,' and the value of that data in this case is 'mark.'" But you needn't export the data to look at it; you can always click the Details view in any given event log entry to see something like Figure 1.10.

A moment's glance will show you, I guarantee you, that this will be a jumping-off point for a lot of neat event log management tools. But this was the least interesting of the three things that I wanted to cover about Event Viewer; let's move on to the next one.

Custom Queries Lets You Customize Event Viewer

It's always been possible to filter items in Event Viewer in a simple way by right-clicking in the Event Log, choosing New Log View, and then adjusting its filter properties. But Vista's Event Viewer takes it a bit further. To see how, take a look at the Event Viewer when started up in Figure 1.11.

FIGURE 1.10   An event log entry's details

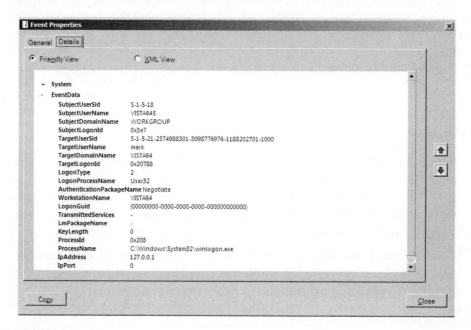

FIGURE 1.11   The Event Viewer

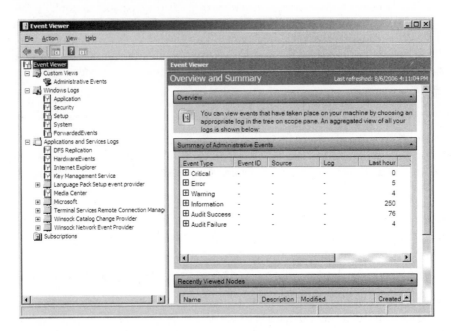

Like the old Event Viewer, you get a pane down the left-hand side listing the logs that you can peruse. But instead of the standard Application, System and Security, Vista's Event Viewer fine-tunes your events into dozens of smaller "sub-logs." You can see in its right-hand pane a summary of entries and, you'll note, there are more levels of event than Information, Warning, Error, Audit Success, and Audit Failure; now there's also Critical. But look in the upper left-hand corner and you'll notice a folder called "Custom Views" and, inside that, a folder named "Administrative Events."

I didn't create that, it was already built in Vista. It collects all of the events from all logs that are Critical, Error, or Warning. In short, it's one-stop-shopping for keeping an eye on what's broken. But what if we wanted the "auugh! log," a collection of just the Critical stuff? Simplicity itself. Just right-click the Custom Views folder and choose "Create custom view..." and you'll see a dialog like the one in Figure 1.12.

With this dialog, it's simple to see how Microsoft prebuilt the "Administrative Events" log. To create a "Criticals only" log, I'd change the dialog like so:

- Leave "Logged:" as "Any time;" this means to show any events in the log. (Remember that by default Windows only keeps as many events as it has storage to hold.)

- In "Event level:," check only "Critical."

- Choose the radio button between "Event log:" and "By log," and click the drop-down box to the right of them. Check the boxes next to "Windows Logs" and "Applications and Services Logs" to choose all logs.

- Click OK and when you get the dialog that says that this might be a bit slow and are you sure, click "Yes." You'll see a dialog like Figure 1.13.

FIGURE 1.12   Creating a custom view in Vista's Event Viewer

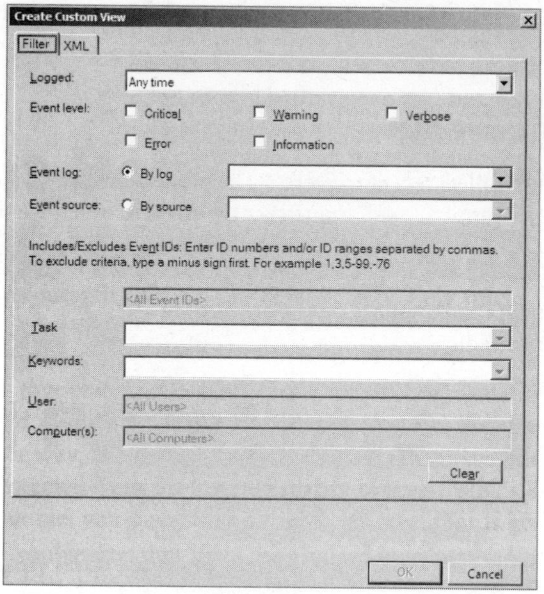

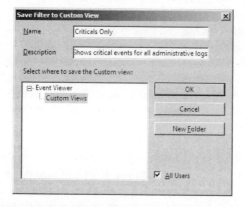

FIGURE 1.13   Name your new custom view

Here, I've filled in "Criticals Only" in the Name: field, and "Shows critical events for all administrative logs" in the Description: field. Click OK and you'll see the new view. And by the way, that's not a silly example. After running just a few days, my Vista system has generated tons of event log entries of varying levels of importance. But the "Criticals Only" log has just a dozen events in it, and they were all interesting. (My favorite was a message telling me that a particular program was "slowing down the Windows Shell," presumably meaning that shutting off this badly written program, whatever its name was, would make things faster. The program? Explorer.exe. Who says programmers lack senses of humor?)

Once you've created your ideal custom view, it's easy to back it up or spread it around. Just right-click it and export it. And guess what kind of file it creates? Yup, you got it: XML. (Perhaps they should have named Vista "Windows XML?" Then it would have sounded more like an upgrade from "XP.")

Generating Actions from Events

XP and 2003 brought a really nice feature called "event triggers." The idea was that you could use a command-line tool called "eventtriggers.exe" to instruct the Event Log service that if a particular kind of event occurred then the Event Log service would start the application of your choosing. Not many people seemed to discover it, but I wrote about it in a few magazine articles and suggested that you could build a pretty neat system for alerting you to problems in the network. There were three ingredients:

- You'd need a cell phone that could receive text messages via e-mail. For example, my cell carrier is Verizon Wireless, and you can send an SMS text message to any Verizon cell phone by sending e-mail to *cellphonenumber*@vtext.com.

- You need a program that can send simple e-mails from the command line. There's a free one called "blat" at http://www.blat.org.

- You need XP or 2003, as they support event triggers.

I put this all together by suggesting that if there were particular events that you were concerned about—say, an account lockout happened—then you could use eventtriggers.exe to tell the Event Log service, "if an account lockout happens, run such-and-such blat command line to send me an alert on my phone as a text message. It worked pretty nicely but was, admittedly, cumbersome. So the new "Attach task to event..." option is a real blessing.

To see this in action, open up the Application log and look at the events in it. If this is your first look into Vista's Event Viewer, look in the folder "Windows Logs"—it's probably already open, if not then open it—and notice that these logs bear the familiar names of Application, Security, and System, as well as two new ones named "Setup" and "ForwardedEvents." Click the Application folder in the left-hand pane and in the right-hand pane (I always close the Action pane because I think you'd need a computer with a screen that isn't just in "landscape" mode, you'd need one in "panoramic mode" in order to make use of MMC 3.0's three panes) you'll see the events in that log.

Right-click any one of them and you'll see in the resulting context menu that you've got a new option, "Attach Task To This Event...;" click that, and you'll see a wizard page like the one in Figure 1.14.

Why a wizard? Well, as it turns out, Vista's Event Viewer offers you several options on how to respond. (They even simplified setting up my suggestion about e-mailing admins when an event occurs, as you'll see.) Click Next to see a figure like Figure 1.15.

First, as with eventtriggers.exe, you can specify any given application. Or you can send an e-mail, or display a message on the server's desktop. I'll consider all three options in a moment, but for now, I'll click the radio button next to "Send an e-mail" and then Next to see something like Figure 1.16.

FIGURE 1.14   Starting the Create Basic Task Wizard

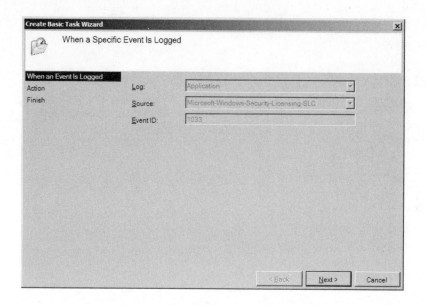

FIGURE 1.15   Event Viewer offers three kinds of responses.

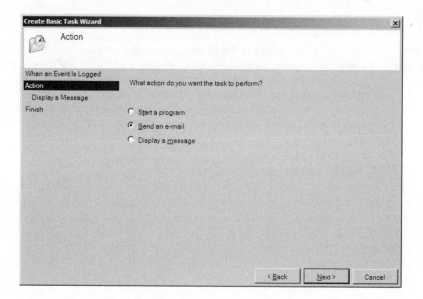

FIGURE 1.16   Setting up an e-mail notification

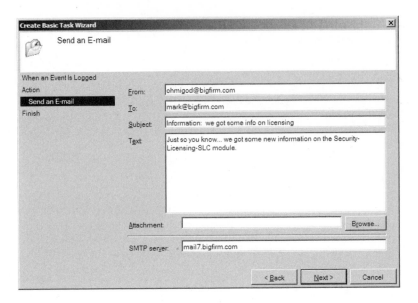

This page looks very much as you'd expect, allowing you to punch in a from address, to address, subject, and text. It even lets you add an attachment, which is a nice touch, and specify the name of the SMTP server to use to send the e-mail.

Be sure to configure the SMTP server to accept e-mails from this server, or you'll never get an alert via e-mail. All well-configured SMTP servers nowadays have strict rules restricting SMTP relaying and would probably reject the e-mail that the Event Log service tried to send to the SMTP server. And setting up random extra SMTP servers without all of those strict rules is a *really* bad idea, as it's one way that spammers send all of that junk but don't get caught.

If I click Next, I get a summary screen like the one in Figure 1.17.

This is a nice summary of what's going to happen once I click Finish, although truthfully it's not necessary. An administrator can always modify or delete an event task, as you'd expect. Ah, but *where* you modify or delete that event task, that'll surprise you. When I click Finish, I get the message box in Figure 1.18.

FIGURE 1.17   Summarizing the trigger

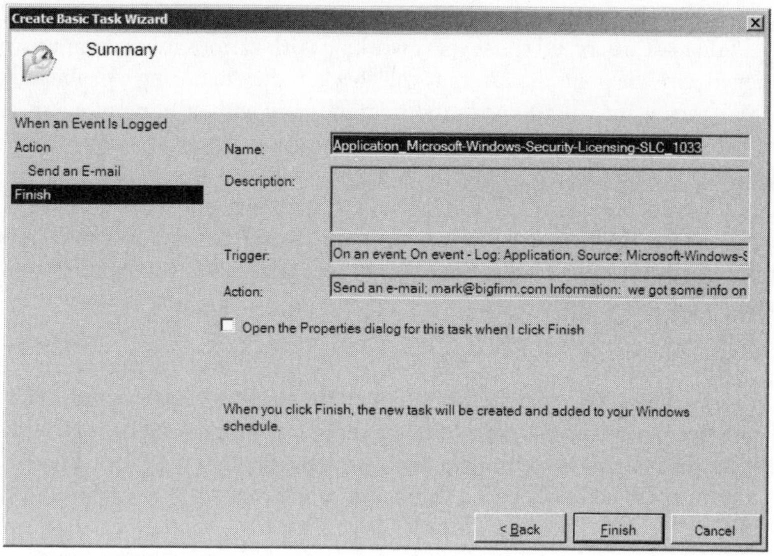

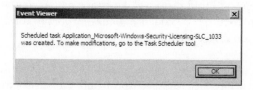

FIGURE 1.18   Changes? Off to the Task Scheduler

This seems like a bad idea to me. Vista's user interface does a fairly decent job of providing what Microsoft has come to like calling "discoverability," which is their recently coined term for "a user interface that makes figuring out what you can do with a GUI program easier." So here you've created an event task in the Event Viewer; you'd think that you could modify or delete it in the Event Viewer. But no, instead Microsoft's got you going to the Task Scheduler to do that.

Telling the Event Log Service to Display Messages

I highlighted sending a piece of mail, but Vista's Event Viewer offers a couple of other options as well, as you may recall from Figure 1.17. The "Start a program" option is pretty straightforward, so I needn't really discuss that, given that I'm not covering this in minute detail, but I wanted to talk about the last option: "Display a message." On its face, it's pretty simple; it just asks you what text to display. When the corresponding event occurs, the Event Log service just pops up a message box with whatever text you specified. But the fact that the option existed puzzled me, at first. What real good did this offer? But then it hit me.

You see, ever since I started with NT, I've always had a bit of trouble getting used to the "chatter level" that NT offers. I'd spent years working with various microcomputer operating systems designed with the point of view that well, heck, if they're having a problem, no matter how small, then they want *you* to know about it, and *now* with at minimum a message box and at maximum a "system modal dialog," one of those big annoying things that can't be resized or minimized. And, in fact, some of Windows' behavior is still like that, but in an uneven fashion. If a document doesn't print, then you get a big can't-miss-it pop-up in the system tray to that effect. Windows applications are just as bad as Windows itself, and I offer Adobe Acrobat Reader as Exhibit A. When Adobe Reader decides that you're gonna get an update, then while you're getting it, Reader puts this huge dialog box on your screen with status information, a dialog box without a "minimize" button.

But what's always puzzled me about Windows' "chatter level" is that there are things that it *doesn't* say a blessed thing about, but that might be useful. For example, I had a workstation a few years ago whose hard drive failed. I got it running long enough to get what I needed off of it and, as I waited for the files to copy, I noticed that the Event Viewer had been logging disk failures for weeks. "You'd think *that* might merit a pop-up box," I grumbled to myself. There are, similarly, a handful of Active Directory events that are downright scary, things that portend long-term unhappiness if not seen to posthaste, but does AD pop up a dire warning message? No, instead AD just quietly issues an event, sort of like an unhappy employee petulantly writing memos "to the record" to cover his backside when his company turns out to be the next Enron—"I told them so," he anticipates saying with disguised glee. (Okay, in reality I imagine that the AD coders assume—probably correctly—that, again, most domain controllers don't have people sitting and watching the DC's desktops all the day long.)

Okay, so why *is* Windows so schizophrenic about what it shouts and what it whispers? Simple: it's not like there's a central User Interface Message Approval Board at Microsoft. If Janet's working on the file sharing client and Peter's working on the shell hardware detection module (the thing that pops up a box asking you what to do every time you plug a USB device into your computer), then Janet gets to control the degree of shrillness or demureness the file sharing client displays to the user, and Peter likewise can dial up or down the hysteria level of the warnings and errors that the shell hardware detection module displays. (In my opinion Peter needs to consider more decaf, as the fireworks that start every time a USB stick drive is plugged into a system is a bit overmuch.)

The cool thing about the "Display a message" option is that it lets you increase Windows' hysteria level about any event or events that you choose. Never again will I miss a disk error that formerly would have secreted itself in the logs and, when Server 2007 comes out with the same Event Viewer, never again will I pass over a message to the effect that a particular domain controller hasn't talked to the rest of the family for a few weeks.

Forwarding Events from One Computer to Another

I imagine that I needn't explain my reasoning in saying that my number one favorite new Event Viewer feature will probably be everyone else's favorite new Event Viewer feature: event forwarding. It's always been true that NT systems have had event logs, and that those event logs are completely decentralized: if you've got 500 XP boxes that someone's been trying to hack and you want to look at all of the failed logon attempts for all of those 500 boxes...what do you do?

Well, you could walk around to 500 systems, or buy a third-party tool, or use a serviceable and nicely priced—free—but slightly rough-edged tool called eventcombmt. It's sort of amazing, but after 13 years of NT, we still don't have a built-in method of centralizing events from the event logs of scattered machines. Unless, of course, you've got Vista. It offers something called "event forwarding" that lets you collect events from other Vista systems to one single system. Just tell all of those 500 systems to report logon failure events to one of their own, and then all you need do is to sit down at that system, open up a folder called "ForwardedEvents," and it's all in one place.

So is it just Vista talking to Vista? I attended a briefing where a program manager for Vista's Event Viewer said that he thought it very likely that they'd have modules that you could add to earlier versions of Windows (I'm guessing XP and 2003) that would make it possible for a Vista system to collect events from those older OSes, so the answer seems to be "right now yes, it's just Vista, but there's a chance that earlier Windows may get event forwarders." But don't hold your breath. Back in 2002, Microsoft promised a free tool that would collect all of the Security events from 2000, XP, and 2003 systems into a centralized SQL Server. When they finally finished in late 2005, they said "oh, we changed our minds," and stuck it into Microsoft Operations Manager, which you probably know is most definitely *not* free.

Subscription Overview

Another Microsoft phrase for event forwarding is "subscription"—one computer "subscribes" to events from other computers. Here's basically how it works, in Microsoft "subscription terminology."

- In a *subscription*, you designate one Vista system to collect events from one or more other computers.
- That system is called *the collector*.
- The systems from which the collector gets events are called the *source* computers.

Once you set up a subscription, the collector then *polls* the sources every 15 minutes or so for new events. By default, those events go into a folder called "ForwardedEvents" but that can be changed. And one more thing: subscriptions work a lot easier if the collector and the sources are in the same domain. It's possible to make it work between two systems in a workgroup, but it's more trouble. How you make all of this work varies, but here's the overview of how to set up a subscription in the easiest way.

Set Up the Sources

First, go to every computer that will be a source computer and enable a service that listens for the collector's requests for events. You do that with a command-line tool named winrm. Also, adjust the permissions on the event logs of all of the sources so that when the collector asks for those logs, then the sources are willing to cough up events.

Set Up the Collector

Then, enable the software on the collector so that it can, well, collect. Every Vista box comes with it, and it's called the "Windows Event Collector" service. Just start it and tell it to start automatically henceforth, as you'd do with any service. (Actually you needn't even do that because, as you'll see, the first time that you try to create a subscription, the Event Viewer asks you if you'd like it to configure the Windows Event Collector service for you.) Then create a new subscription. In that subscription, you tell the collector exactly which events to collect, and the names of the systems to request them from. In a little while, the events will start flowing into the collector.

Creating an Example Subscription

Let's walk through setting up a simple subscription. In this example, I'll have the following settings. If you'd like to follow along, just duplicate this setup:

- Two Vista systems; one's named "Vista1" and the other will be "Vista2."
- Both Vista1 and Vista2 are members of an Active Directory domain named "bigfirm.com." I'm doing that because it makes things a bit easier than connecting two systems in a workgroup would be.
- When configuring both systems, I'll be logging on to them as an account named "mark@bigfirm.com," which is a member of the Domain Admins group.

My goal for this simple demonstration is to have the Vista1 machine act as the collector and the Vista2 machine act as its sole source. I'll have Vista1 collect all of the information-level Windows events from Vista2 machine. As I outlined before, I'll do this in two steps: first I'll visit Vista2, the source, to enable some services on it and adjust its security so that it'll let Vista1 extract events from it. Then I'll move over to Vista1, the collector, to turn on the Windows Event Collection service and create the subscription.

When we start out, I've got the two Vista systems running basically in an out-of-the-box configuration, although I've given them a very simple display theme to accommodate screen shots that are easier to read. Both have Windows Firewall up and, as is usual for Vista, WF by default has no exceptions enabled except for what it calls "core networking."

Step One: Set Up Vista2 for WinRM

First, we'll log onto Vista2, the system sending the events to the collector, and fire up the infrastructure necessary to allow it to respond to subscription requests from Vista1. In a sense, the fact that Vista2 is responding to requests from Vista1 for events makes Vista2, the source, something of a server—and so we'll have to start up a service to respond to those needs.

Microsoft built the event log stuff on top of a set of remote desktop management standards called "WS-Management," and Microsoft's name for their implementation of it is "WinRM," for "Windows Remote Management." Just fire up an elevated command prompt (right-click Command Prompt and choose Run as administrator, as always, and go ahead and respond as necessary to the UAC prompts), and type

```
winrm quickconfig
```

The Windows Remote Management Tool will respond like so:

```
WinRM is not set up to allow remote access to this machine for management.
The following changes must be made:

Set the WinRM service type to delayed auto start.
Start the WinRM service.
Create a WinRM listener on HTTP://* to accept WS-Man requests to any IP on this
machine.
Enable the WinRM firewall exception.

Make these changes [y/n]?
```

Yes, you read that right: WS-Management runs on port 80 (that's the reference to "HTTP://*") but no, you're not setting up a web server on your Vista box, at least not a full-scale one. In response, I type y and Enter to get this response:

```
WinRM has been updated for remote management.
WinRM service type changed successfully.
WinRM service started.
Created a WinRM listener on HTTP://* to accept WS-Man requests to any IP on
this machine.
WinRM firewall exception enabled.
```

Once that's done, stay at the command prompt and give the collector computer the permission to look at events on this computer. You do that by putting the collector computer's computer account into each of the source computers' "Event Log Reader" groups—and as you've probably guessed, the "Event Log Readers" group is new to Vista. We could do this with the GUI, but quite honestly I find it easier to do from the command line. There's a NET (not a .NET) command that's been around NT for over a decade that lets you put a user account into a local group that we'll find useful here. Its syntax looks like

```
net localgroup groupname accountname /add
```

The group's name is, again, "Event Log Readers." But what's the name of the Vista1 computer? Well, we want to enter the name of the Vista1 machine's domain account. Ever since Windows 2000, machines have gotten Active Directory names looking like *machinename$@DNSdomainname*. Thus, a machine named "Vista1" in a domain named "bigfirm.com" would have a domain account name of "vista1\$@bigfirm.com." (The dollar sign suffix fixed a problem that popped up back in the NT 4.0 days whenever a user had the same name as her computer.) The command I'd type at the command line, then, would be

```
net localgroup "Event Log Readers" vista1@bigfirm.com /add
```

To which Vista2 should respond The command completed successfully. Vista2's ready, let's move over to Vista1 for Act Two.

Step Two: Create the Subscription on Vista1

Now I move to Vista1 and, again, log on as mark@bigfirm.com, a domain admin. Before we get into configuring Vista1, let's take a moment and verify that we've got connectivity to Vista2, and that it's running the WS-Management software. We can do that with a command-line tool, so start up an elevated command prompt on Vista1 and type

```
winrm id -remote:vista2.bigfirm.com
```

That's the winrm command again, but this time we're using the id parameter, which is basically nothing more than a "WS-Management ping." The -remote option identifies what system to talk to. Vista2 responds in a successful fashion with output that looks something like

```
IdentifyResponse
    ProtocolVersion = http://schemas.dmtf.org/wbem/wsman/1/wsman.xsd
    ProductVendor = Microsoft Corporation
    ProductVersion = OS: 6.0.5472 SP: 0.5 Stack: 1.0
```

In contrast, bad responses would be something like "WS-Management could not connect to the specified destination." So now we know that we've got connectivity; excellent. We're ready, then, to set up Vista1 to collect.

On Vista1, we next start up the Event Viewer. Then we right-click the Subscriptions folder and choose "Create Subscription." As this is the first time that we've told Vista1 to create a subscription, we get a dialog box like the one in Figure 1.19.

FIGURE 1.19   Shall we start the Windows Event Collector service?

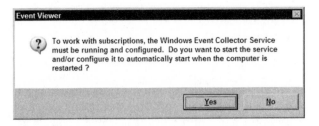

Click yes. If you'd wanted to set up the Windows Event Collector service beforehand, then you could have alternatively just opened up an elevated command prompt and typed `wecutil qc`. Had we done that, we'd not have gotten the dialog box in Figure 1.19. Anyway, after clicking Yes at the dialog box, we then get the quite formidable-looking Subscription Properties dialog box, as you see in Figure 1.20.

FIGURE 1.20   Creating a subscription, part 1

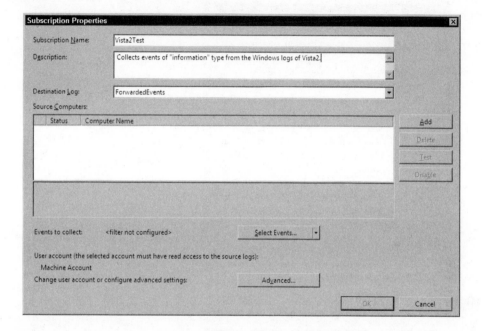

As you can see, I've started to create the subscription by filling in the "Subscription Name" and "Description" fields.

WARNING   And do yourself a favor: don't put any spaces in your subscription names. If you do, then some syntax gets ugly later.

But before this subscription will start working, we've got to tell the Event Viewer what kind of events to grab from Vista2 and oh, that's right, we need to tell it to specify that Vista2's the machine to get those events from. First, I'll specify what to look for by clicking the Select Events... button. That'll raise a dialog box like the one in Figure 1.21.

In this Query Filter dialog box, you see that you can choose the "fright level" of the events to grab (Critical, Error, etc.) with the check boxes next to "Error level:." I'll check "Information," as that's what I set out to collect. Above that, you can choose to collect every qualifying event in the source, or you can choose to only get events generated a certain number of days or hours in the past. For now, I'll leave it at "Any time."

Perhaps the biggest choice is "which logs to pull from?" A little browsing in Vista's Event Viewer will show that, as I've already mentioned, Vista has a whole lot more logs than the three or so normally found on a pre-Vista desktop operating system. If I click the drop-down box next to the "Event log:" radio button, I'll see something like Figure 1.22.

FIGURE 1.21   More creation: pick the events to track

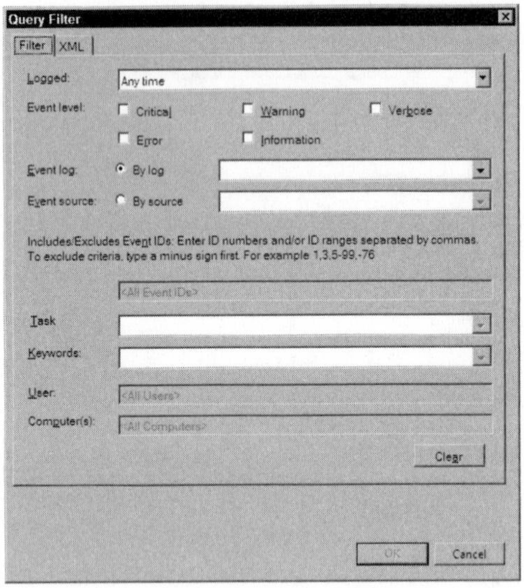

FIGURE 1.22   Just the Windows logs, please

If you're following along, then you'll just see the "Windows Logs" and "Applications and Services Logs;" I deliberately expanded the list a couple of levels to show you what's available. Nothing's checked by default—I checked all of the Windows Logs items except for "ForwardedEvents," as I had nightmare visions of accidentally setting up an infinite loop between Vista1 and Vista2 if I ever happen to set up Vista2 to grab from Vista1, instead of the vice versa situation we're setting up here. If this drop-down looks a little strange, it is—I don't recall seeing a structure like this on a Windows GUI before.

Look more closely back at Figure 1.23 and you'll see that you can *continue* to fine-tune the events that you want to grab. In sum, then, you could, if you wanted, only forward event ID 1030s but only when generated by the Group Policy service. Oh, and remember that XML centrism that we saw in Event Viewer before? You might have noticed the "XML" tab on the Query Filter page. If I click that, I see something like Figure 1.23.

That's something called "XPath," an XML-renderable way of describing a query. Basically what Microsoft's done here is to offer us a moderately easy-to-use GUI to tell the collector what to grab from the source, but, if we really want to cook up an exotic filter, then we can skip the GUI and do it in XML. Or you can spend 30 minutes fiddling around with it in the GUI, but then you'd like to be able to reproduce it on demand...so you just copy the XML to Notepad, save it somewhere, and then you can copy from the Notepad file sometime in the future and paste into the XML tab of some query that you'll create in the future. I'm not getting that fine-grained for this event forwarding tryout, however, so I'll just click OK to clear the Query Filter dialog and return to the Subscription Properties dialog.

FIGURE 1.23   XML-ese for the query

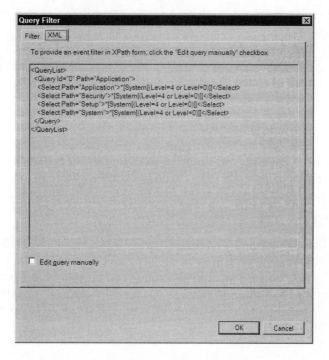

In the Subscription Properties dialog, there's just one more thing I must do before I can take this subscription out for a spin: I've got to tell the Event Viewer where to draw the events from. That's easy; I just click Add and I'll get the standard Select Computers dialog that looks exactly like the one you'd see on an XP box, so I'll skip the screen shot. I just fill in the name "Vista2," click Check Names and then OK to end up with a Subscription Properties dialog looking like Figure 1.24.

FIGURE 1.24   Subscription setup before activation

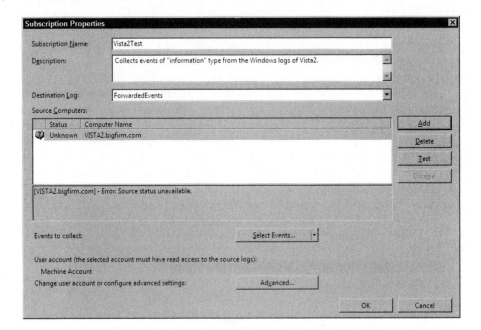

I included this screen shot because the first time you've finished crafting a subscription, then you'll look at your dialog box one last time before clicking OK…and feel your heart drop. Notice that in the "Source Computers:" field, Vista2's there, with "Unknown" next to it, and, below that, the grim report that says "[VISTA2.bigfirm.com] - Error: Source status unavailable." I mention that to let you know that you really needn't worry if you see that; it appears to be normal. Now that the subscription has been defined, I click OK.

Troubleshooting Subscription Delays

With that done, it's time to view the fruits of our labors. So we open up the ForwardedEvents log in Event Viewer, to see…nothing.

But don't panic; that's apparently normal. Just give it about 15 minutes—Microsoft's golden interval, it seems—and the events start popping up. In fact, that's an important point about subscriptions. Working with them is similar to flying somewhere on an airline in that both have the same motto: "expect delays."

Adjusting the 15 Minutes

Now, you can change some of those delays, but not all. There are two main reasons for the delays that you'll see in Event Log subscriptions. The first reason explains our current wait: "the 15 minute rule." By default, Vista systems acting as event collectors only poll their source systems every 15 minutes. Now, you'd *think* that they'd do the *first* poll the very moment that you clicked that last "OK" to create the subscription, but Vista doesn't; it seems to just wait about 15 minutes before even *starting* to grab that data.

Now, if you like, you can change that 15 minutes to something shorter. You can't do it in the GUI; you need a command-line tool called `wecutil`—Windows Event Collector utility—to do the fiddling needed on the collector. You'll need to run `wecutil` twice. First, we'll use wecutil to tell the Event Log that we don't want the standard 15-minute cycle, and instead we want to customize the subscription. That command looks like `wecutil ss` *subsname* `/cm:custom`, where *subsname* is the subscription's name. The /cm is short for "configuration mode," hence the "custom." If you wanted to return your subscription to its original standard format, you'd just replace the /cm:`custom` with /cm:`normal`. The `ss` stands for "subscription settings." To shift the Vista2Test subscription to "custom" configuration mode, then, we could type

```
wecutil ss vista2test /cm:custom
```

Press Enter, and if you get no response, that's good. Clearly `wecutil` is of the class of command-line tools who are the strong, silent types. Now that we've freed Vista2Test from the iron constraints of "normal," we can change the polling rate. We do that with the command `wecutil ss` *subsname* `/hi:`*milliseconds*, where *subsname* is, again, the subscription name, and *milliseconds* is how much time to wait between polls, in milliseconds. Try it out by setting it to 10 seconds with this command:

```
wecutil ss vista2test /hi:10000
```

If you're following along and want to try this out, then clearly you'll need a way to create an "information" event on Vista2. The easiest way I've come across is to open a command prompt of elevated privilege and type `ipconfig /renew` to renew Vista2's DHCP lease. That generates an "information" level event on Vista systems. Those events will appear on Vista1's ForwardedEvents folder nearly immediately, although you'll have to press F5 in Event Viewer on Vista1 to see them.

Understanding the "Reboot Delay"

The second reason you'll sometimes see subscriptions change slowly has to do with two services: the `winrm` service that provides the WS-Management capabilities on the side of the source computers, and `wecsvc`, the Windows Event Collector service on the side of the collector computer. Here's what you're likely to see: you boot up one of your source computers, and go over to the collector to start seeing events from that computer. So you look. And look. You check the parameters of the subscription, which you can do on the collector by typing

```
wecutil gs vista2test
```

If you do that, then you'll see, plain as day, that you've set the polling interval—wecutil calls it the "heartbeat interval"—to 10 seconds. By the time you do that, then clearly 10 seconds will have elapsed. More than a few times. And yet...no events. What's going on?

It's all due to a change that Microsoft made to the way that some services start up. Microsoft is very sensitive to the fact that their operating systems tend to, um, take a long time to boot up. So for the past few years (XP was part of this) they've been trying to find things that they could kind of *remove* from the boot process—technically, anyway—and so make their OSes (particularly the desktop OSes) seem more sprightly. Their latest plan to make Windows seem to boot more quickly involves a new class of services.

If you've been following Windows (well, the NT side of Windows) for a while, then you know that Windows services have different startup classes. But most of the run-of-the-mill services are "automatic." That means that they all start up pretty much the same time as the GUI.

Most of them? Go ahead, count the number of services in Windows. And their size. You can see what Microsoft was thinking: "holy moley! About 40 percent of the stuff that slows down Windows boots are these service things!"

So they created a new class of services: "automatic...but delayed." They get the go-ahead to start up at the same time as the "automatic" services, but they have this special note on them that says "well, yeah, they're automatic, but...take your time." Any of these so-called delayed services start up in quite low priorities. And that can mean that, well, it may take a while for those subscriptions to pop up because, as you've probably guessed by now, winrm and wecsvc are both delayed services.

The bottom line is: don't be surprised if you don't get any updates from the source systems for (in my experience) seven or eight minutes. If that's annoying, you can always bump up the winrm and wecsvc services from "automatic-delayed" to "automatic," although I'd leave them alone. (And consider joining Peter in that switch to decaf.)

Event Forwarding in Workgroups

Before I leave this introduction to event forwarding, I want to provide a more complex example of event forwarding setup because it'll give me a chance to show you some more configuration options and, even better, more troubleshooting tools. First, let's review the steps that we employed to get the two domain members Vista1 and Vista2 to talk, so that we've got a starting point in explaining how to set up forwarding in a workgroup:

- On the source computer Vista2, we started the winrm service so that the source computer could listen to the collector's requests.

- On the source computer, we put the collector's machine account into the source's "Event Log Readers" group so that when the collector asked the source for its events, then the source computer was already configured with permissions allowing the collector to request those events.

- On the collector system Vista1, we started up the Windows Event Collection service; we had to do that because wecsvc does the actual asking for the events from the source.

- On the collector, we configured the subscription. And waited.

The difference in setting up a subscription between two systems that are not members of the same Active Directory forest lies in the security part. We can't just put Vista1's machine account in Vista2 because the two systems don't have any kind of trusting connection between themselves, as they would if they lived in the same AD forest. So we'll have to do some security adjustment.

To try this out, set up two systems named, again, Vista1 and Vista2. They should not be members of the same AD forest. (They *can* be members of domains, but not domains in the same forest or in forests that trust each other.) Ensure that the two computers can resolve vista1.bigfirm.com and vista2.bigfirm.com in DNS properly.

Once that's done, enable the Administrator accounts on both systems and set the password of the Vista1 administrator to "bigpebbles1" and the password for the Vista2 administrator account to "bigpebbles2." Now we're ready to start.

Step One: Configure WS-Management on Vista2

Just as we did before, we'll start by getting WS-Management running on Vista2, the source computer. Log onto Vista2 as its local administrator account. Start up an elevated command prompt and type

```
winrm quickconfig
```

 Vista does not apply UAC to the default administrator account, so I don't actually have to explicitly raise the privilege on my command prompt when logged in as "administrator." But Vista can be configured to constrain the default administrator account as well and your system might be configured differently, so I'll keep reminding you to ensure that the command prompts are elevated.

Type **y** and Enter when it asks if you really want to set up WinRM, and you're done on Vista2.

Step Two: Tell the Collector to Trust the Source

Now move over to Vista1 and log on as its local administrator. Because Vista1 and Vista2 no longer share a domain relationship, we're going to have to see how to authenticate between Vista1 and Vista2. Open up an elevated command prompt on Vista1, the collector, and type this:

```
winrm set winrm/config/client @{TrustedHosts="vista2.bigfirm.com"}
```

That tells Vista1 that it's okay to, if necessary, attempt logging onto Vista2. This seems a bit odd to me—you'd think that you'd have to tell Vista2 to trust Vista1, rather than the other way around—but that's how `winrm` works.

That's something of a strange-looking command, so let's take a moment and understand it. winrm has a number of configuration parameters that you can examine and change. You can see them all by typing

```
winrm get winrm/config
```

You'll get about a screen's worth of output; here's what some of it looks like:

```
C:\>winrm get winrm/config
Config
    MaxEnvelopeSizekb = 150
    MaxTimeoutms = 60000
    MaxBatchItems = 20
    MaxProviderRequests = 25
    Client
        NetworkDelayms = 5000
        URLPrefix = wsman
        AllowUnencrypted = false
        Auth
            Basic = false
            Digest = true
            Kerberos = true
            Negotiate = true
        DefaultPorts
            HTTP = 80
            HTTPS = 443
        TrustedHosts = vista2.bigfirm.com
...
```

Notice that this information is presented with varying levels of indentation. That's intended to convey the hierarchical nature of these settings, which is referred to as the "WS-management schema." The first line, Config, is not indented because everything here is part of Config, the configuration information. The next line, MaxEnvelopeSizekb=150, clearly expresses that there's a parameter named MaxEnvelopeSizekb (and don't ask, because I have no idea what it does) with value "150." But then skip down a few lines to Client. That's a level down from Config and is a container or, rather, subcontainer of its own. Notice that TrustedHosts is a parameter within Config/Client.

You can use this hierarchy with a winrm get or winrm set command. For example, the winrm get winrm/config command showed the entire schema; to see just the items in config/client then you'd type **winrm get winrm/config/client**. That would look like this:

```
C:\>winrm get winrm/config/client
Client
    NetworkDelayms = 5000
```

```
    URLPrefix = wsman
    AllowUnencrypted = false
    Auth
        Basic = false
        Digest = true
        Kerberos = true
        Negotiate = true
    DefaultPorts
        HTTP = 80
        HTTPS = 443
    TrustedHosts = vista2.bigfirm.com
C:\>
```

You've already seen how to set a value in the winrm schema:

```
winrm set winrm/place-in-schema @{parameter="value"}
```

Where *place-in-schema* refers to wherever in the schema the parameter is stored. You can use "*" as a wildcard in the TrustedHosts value, and you can specify more than one item in the TrustedHosts parameter by putting a list of machines in quotes with commas between them. For example, this command would work fine to tell a system to trust both mypc.bigfirm.com and yourpc.bigfirm.com:

```
winrm set winrm/config/client @{TrustedHosts=
"mypc.bigfirm.com,yourpc.bigfirm.com"}
```

That's all one line and do not put spaces between the machine names in the list. (Wondering why I'm spending so much time showing you how to configure and control winrm? Because all kinds of things in Vista and Server 2007 are built atop winrm. Trust me, you'll end up using this stuff.) And while you probably don't want to do this in a production environment, here's an example of trusting everyone:

```
winrm set winrm/config/client @{TrustedHosts= "*"}
```

Reviewing, then, the first thing that we've seen that's new in setting up event forwarding between two systems who lack a domain relationship is that we've got to use the `winrm set` command to add the *source* computer to the TrustedHosts list on the *collector* computer.

Step Three: Test WS-Management Connectivity

This step is not absolutely necessary, but I'm a big believer in a little belt-and-suspenders work up front to avoid pain later. Open an elevated command prompt and let's try a winrm's ping-like command. As before, type

```
winrm id -r:vista2.bigfirm.com
```

This time, however, it won't work. Winrm needs to know how to authenticate between systems. Now, if you don't *tell* it how to authenticate, then it'll just assume that it can use Kerberos, which worked fine when both systems were in the same domain, and that's why this command worked fine in the earlier example between domain members. That's not true any more, so we've got to tell it how to authenticate. The simplest way is to just say, "don't use any authentication." That looks like this:

```
winrm id -r:vista2.bigfirm.com -a:none
```

The option -a: is short for "authenticate." It takes several possible options:

- -a:none means "don't authenticate." As the id command is pretty basic, the winrm service is fine with skipping authentication in this case, and the command will work. I mean, we folks with an interest in security are paranoid, but there are limits—I'm not ready for a "secure ping" or "authenticated ping" yet, although I fear that it may happen one day.

- -a:basic says to authenticate using a cleartext username and password. This will not work by default, as winrm forbids all unencrypted logon attempts. You can change that with this command:

```
winrm set winrm/config/client @{AllowUnencrypted="true"}
```

But I don't recommend it. You must follow a -a:basic command with a username and password that must be written as -u:*domain**username* -p:password. We'll see an example of that soon.

- -a:digest uses the same "digest" logon mechanism as the one that Internet Information Services has supported for years. winrm considers it an unencrypted logon method and digest logons will not work by default.

- -a:kerberos says to use Kerberos authentication. This is the default behavior and, again, requires a domain.

- -a:negotiate says to use a Windows NTLM-like challenge-response logon. It's encrypted and will work with winrm's defaults.

To make a negotiated logon work, add the -u and -p options. As we've set the Vista2 administrator's password to "bigpebbles2," we could make this winrm id work:

```
winrm id -r:vista2.bigfirm.com -a:negotiate -u:vista2\administrator -
p:bigpebbles2
```

(That's all one line, even if it did break on the page.) That should work, and at the same time we've verified that Vista2 can accept logons with its administrator account from Vista1. Armed with that knowledge, we're ready for the next step.

Step Four: Set Up the Subscription

Still working at Vista1, set up the subscription just as we did before, except for two changes. First, you'll have to establish a connection of some sort with Vista2, or the Event Viewer won't let you even punch in "vista2" as a source computer. My answer was to briefly create an exception in Vista2's firewall for "file and print sharing." Then, from Vista1, I typed

```
net use \\vista2\ipc$ /u:vista2\administrator bigpebbles2
```

That connected me to Vista2. I was then able to specify "vista2" as a source computer.

The second issue also concerned authentication. In the Subscription Properties dialog for the subscription that let Vista1 suck events from Vista2, there's a button labeled "Advanced…" Click it and you'll see a section in the resulting Advanced Subscription Settings dialog box labeled User Account. In there is a radio button Specific User. Click that radio button and you'll see a button labeled "User and Password…" Click it and you'll get a chance to punch in a username and password. Punch in **vista2\administrator** for the username and **bigpebbles2** for the password. Wait the requisite 15 minutes and you'll have events!

To summarize, setting up a workgroup-based event forwarding differs from a domain-based one in a few ways.

- You've got to add the source computers to the TrustedHosts parameter in winrm on the collector computer.

- You've got to temporarily open up file and print sharing on the source computers and then connect in some way—I used the IPC$ trick—to establish a session with those computers. Then it's possible to add the computers to the list of source machines in Subscription Properties.

- In Advanced Subscription Properties, you'll need to punch in the names and passwords of accounts on the source systems who are members of their local Event Log Readers groups.

In this chapter, I took you through a quick tour of some of what I call the Vista "small surprises." In the next chapter, we'll tackle our first big surprise—User Account Control.

2

Understanding User Account Control (UAC): "Are You *Sure*, Mr. Administrator?"

Vista includes many neat new features and I suspect that it includes something for everyone to love. Not *everybody* will love any given feature, but every feature will be loved by *someone*, right?

Okay, that's a lie. There's probably one Vista feature that *everyone* will hate: User Account Control or UAC. Although actually, that's not really true, not everybody hates it…I like it. Although truthfully when I met it, I probably hated it more than anyone.

In this chapter, I'll offer a quick summary of what UAC does for those who've not run into it yet, and why it drives everyone nuts. Then I'm going to explain why I think that UAC is a very significant step toward not only securing Windows, but making the average person more *aware* of Windows security—and that's a big part of what I like about UAC, because I think that if everyone becomes aware of Windows security, then I suspect that most of the problems with security in Windows will disappear. After that, we'll get into the heart of UAC. Explaining it, I hope, will win it some converts and, if you're not converted by then, at least you'll know how to turn it off.

Introducing UAC

UAC makes itself known pretty early on, and it's usually not a happy meeting—permit me to tell you about my early aneurysm-producing moments with Vista—which I've alluded to in the Introduction and in Chapter 1.

I installed my first copy of Vista. When it started up, it prompted me to create a local account, as the system that I was working on was workgroup-attached, and when I told Vista what to call this new account, Vista made that account a member of the Administrators group by default, just as XP did. (In other cases, I built a copy of Vista that was a domain member and logged onto the Vista machine as a member of the domain's Domain Admins group and that group, of course, is a member of the Vista box's local Administrators group.) Either way, I was logged onto Vista on an account *other* than the local Administrator account. (Remember, by default Vista disables the Administrator account.)

Once logged into Vista, my first task was to create a local user account named "Mark" with password "swordfish." As I'm a command-line kinda guy and, to be truthful, not really interested in having to figure out the GUI du jour, I clicked Start ≻ Accessories ≻ Command Prompt and the command prompt window appeared. I then I tried to create the Mark account by typing

```
net users mark swordfish /add
```

I was then surprised when told that System error 5 has occurred. Access is denied. Now, that's odd, I thought; I have successfully used this command on Windows NT–based systems since NT 3.1, and it's always worked. Although wait…it didn't say that the syntax was wrong; just that "access is denied." Aha! Maybe I forgot to log on as an admin? Just to be sure, I went so far as to log off and then back on so as to double-check that I was indeed logged on as an admin…and still the command failed.

Okay, I thought, I surrender, let's do it the GUI way. I clicked Start, then Control Panel, and I then noticed that they rearranged the Control Panel—but I was expecting that anyway—and I then saw a couple of people with heads but no faces, which has always kind of creeped me out every since those guys appeared in XP. Looks like something from an *Outer Limits*…or maybe a bad episode of *Sopranos*.

Next to the faceless people, I saw "User Accounts and Family Safety," "Set up parental controls for any user" (hey, cool, that must be a tool to allow me to control my father's spyware-collecting Web surfing habits—that would constitute "parental control," right?), and finally "Add or remove user accounts." Yup, that's gotta be the ticket, I thought, and so I clicked it. But, then the screen dimmed, and a dialog box appeared smack-dab across my once-colorful screen, a dialog box like the one you see in Figure 2.1.

FIGURE 2.1   Meet the "Consent UI"

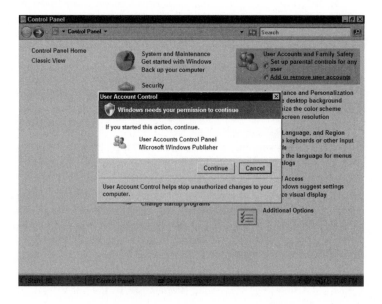

What *is* this, I wondered? After a moment's reading, I realized with a little annoyance that it's basically a mildly colorful "are you sure?" dialog box. (Its official name is, you may recall from the previous chapter, the "consent user interface" or "Consent UI.") For some reason, Windows was making absolutely sure that I did indeed want to do something administrator-ish. So I clicked the Confirm button, and Vista opened the user creation GUI. Once there, I was able to get down to the business of creating a user account.

As I used Vista more and more, I saw the Consent UI more and more. As time went on, it annoyed me more and more. (This, of course, was all before I had my insight that I referred to in the Introduction.)

Why UAC Is Good, after All

The basic point of UAC is simple: by raising the Consent UI every time we're going to do something that requires administrative powers, then we will be more *aware* of when we're doing administrative things. But, as I've already observed, being reminded of something that I already know can be blasted infuriating. So how does this *help*? Well, as I said in the Introduction, it wasn't until June of 2006 that I saw any value at all in the whole idea of UAC. As far as I was concerned, it was, again, nothing more than an "are you sure?" dialog box, and something that pokes a particular sore spot of mine. You see, for years I have only half-joked that if I could have just one wish for Windows, it would be a Registry entry in HKEY_LOCAL_MACHINE\SOFTWARE\ Microsoft\Windows NT\CurrentVersion called NeverQuestionMarksJudgment of type REG_ DWORD. In this fantasy, I'd just set that entry to 1, reboot the system, and never, ever, get any more confirming dialog boxes. Given that perspective, you can see that I wouldn't seem to be a candidate for liking UAC.

UAC Benefits for Users

Despite all that, I haven't really come to *like* UAC. Yes, clicking the Consent UI is irritating, although you get used to it. But to understand my point of view, think of UAC as having two very different kinds of benefits. First, there's what it can do both for veterans like myself (and, if you're reading this book, what it can do for you as well, more than likely), and, second, there's what it does for the less-technical Windows users.

The less-technical Windows users will, I hope, soon learn that the Consent UI is a "wake up!" call. When they're surfing around and some website says "click here to read your horoscope" or something like that and they click it, but that click triggers the Consent UI, then maybe they'll have learned enough to stop and say, "hmmm...clicking on a hyperlink doesn't *usually* cause Windows to gray out the desktop and put that dialog box thing up...maybe I'd better click Cancel," and thus avoid installing a piece of unwanted spyware. That'd be really nice.

UAC Benefits for Admins

But what about us techies? Isn't UAC pointless? No, I don't think so. When you first got started working with NT, or Unix, Linux, OS/X, or whatever OS you first worked with that involved user accounts where some accounts had little power and others had more power, someone probably told you a basic thing about keeping your computer secure: don't spend all day logged in as an administrator. Or, rather, someone might have *told* you that, but observing the behavior of others around you probably taught you that that was what we're *supposed* to do, but that we usually don't bother with. It's just too much trouble to run as a user and, in fact, anyone who's ever tried to use Window 2000 Professional or XP for a few days as a user has discovered that in many cases a regular old user just plain can't get anything done. Applications that are just plain get-a-job-done-not-manage-the-computer *applications*, what many call "productivity applications" rather than administrative tools, often fail if you're not running as an administrator, including such common tools as Internet Explorer, Outlook Express, and Outlook.

UAC as a Transition Tool

Most people who try to just log on as a standard user in XP soon run into so many things that don't work that they soon surrender and just spend all of their time behind a keyboard as an administrator—and that's been true for every other version of NT that I can recall. As a result, we're all just mentally "stuck" on the notion that we run as admins all of the time without even thinking about it; it's culturally embedded in the Windows world. The problem with spending all of your time logged on as an admin is that we all make mistakes; a few times I've clicked "delete" when I meant "rename" on some program file, or perhaps I might've inadvertently clicked "Yes" to that offer of installed spyware when I thought I was pointing at "No." In both cases, the operating system could have saved me from myself with its built-in protections, protections created with situations like this in mind, but it couldn't because when I'm logged in as an administrator, all of the safety features are off—the seat belts have been removed, the air bags shut off, and the roll bars taken out. Most of the time I don't have collisions or roll vehicles, but were I to, I'd be happy that I had those things.

With Vista, Microsoft has tried to remove the need to be an administrator in order to do day-to-day productivity activities like surfing the Net or reading e-mail. Whether they've succeeded or not is one that you'll have to decide for yourself, but I strongly suggest that you give living as a standard user in Vista a try before deciding to just chuck UAC "out the Windows," so to speak, and in the rest of this chapter I hope to give you the tools to be able to do that. Anyway, what I'm saying here is that we really need to change the culture of Windows techies and get us all running as standard users, and certainly I'm not the first person to say that.

Cultural change is difficult, but not impossible; the Unix folks went through this years ago. When you install Unix or Linux on a system, you get an account named "root" that acts like the Windows "administrator" account: it's all-powerful and that's great to use when configuring a system, but can lead to making mistakes that can cause real damage to a system that could have been avoided had you run as the Unix equivalent of a standard user. For years, everyone who used Unix spent their days logged on as root, but the folly of that soon became apparent. People *tried* to run as a standard user, but many Unix apps wouldn't run for standard users. Over time,

Unix developers learned to write applications that *could* run as standard users, and nowadays most people use Unix or Linux boxes from standard user accounts rather than root, and it works fine, but it *did* take time to retrain both the users and the developers. In fact, the Mac OS, which you may know is built atop a variety of Unix called "BSD," has a root account, but I'm told that Apple will void your warranty if you ever log on as root! Windows is undergoing the same sort of change, and there will be some growing pains in the changeover—but it's worth it.

But if they ever threaten to void my warranty if I ever log on as Administrator, I'm going to visit a neighbor of Microsoft's, Boeing, and purchase some aircraft equipped with devices to convince them otherwise. (Just kidding. Mostly.)

You know, looking back at the last few paragraphs, I'm reminded that I almost subtitled this chapter, "...Cod Liver Oil for Your PC." I've spent over two decades telling people about what their computers can do for them, revealing cool things that they might not know, and talking about how to work around annoyances; I'm not used to doing what feels like nagging people to be sure to wash behind their ears and floss—but in this case (UAC, not the ears and flossing), I think it's for the best, so please forgive me if I sometimes end up sounding a trifle like a finger-wagging preacher warning you of fire and brimstone!

I started this discussion by saying that while UAC might not be of all that much value to techies who are savvy enough to know not to click on those spyware-installing links and would never open up an unexpected attachment, it *might* help out in another way. That's why I've been talking about the process of cultural reacclimation from the current state of affairs to one where we spend most of our time logged on as an administrator; what's UAC got to do with that? Simple: you *will* still need to do things as an administrator now and then even in the bright future where we can spend our days as standard users, but it's a pain in the neck to have to log off the standard user account and then log back on as an administrator and back again. Windows 2000 tried to make that a bit less painful with the RunAs feature, but it was uneven and hard to make work for some programs. UAC, in contrast, acts as a kind of super-RunAs when you run as a standard user. We'll talk about how it works later in this chapter, but when you see it, then I think you'll agree that it makes the transition easier. Additionally, even if you still log on as an administrator all of the time, UAC has the effect of making you run as a standard user anyway—and I'll explain that too.

An Overview of UAC

I want to start out our exploration of UAC with a brief overview of UAC in action, but before I can do that, let's do a quick review of some Windows security basics. (For the security experts out there, apologies; the UAC's nature requires that everyone reading have a good understanding of Windows security fundamentals close to hand, so we'll have to do detours now and then to explain and review those fundamentals. For now, just skip the next two paragraphs and it'll all be over for the moment.)

When you log onto a computer, you normally get a piece of data identifying you that sits in that computer's RAM called a *token*. Tokens are important security-wise because they contain a list of your group memberships and privileges.

You use that token whenever you start up a program. When you run a command from the command line, double-click an icon on the desktop, start up a program from the Start menu or the like, Windows copies your token to whatever program you told it to start up. If you start up Microsoft Word and then tell it to go open a file named mydiary.doc, then Word asks NTFS, the file system, to let Word open up mydiary.doc for reading and writing. As the file mydiary.doc has NTFS permissions associated with it, NTFS needs to check to see whether or not Word's got the permissions to read and write mydiary.doc, so NTFS says to Word, "let's see your token." As Word's token is nothing more than a copy of *your* token, then NTFS ends up granting Word whatever access to mydiary.doc that you do. (Or, rather, the copy of Word that *you* started up has whatever access to mydiary.doc that you do.)

Note that Windows copies your token and gives the copy to a program *when the program starts*. Once you've started a program, you can't change the token; there's no way to pump the program's token up after the fact. If the program needs greater power to get something done, then you'll have to either exit the program, log off and log on as a more powerful account, and then restart the program, or, in any version of Windows after NT 4.0, use RunAs to start the program with the token of a higher-power account. As we'll see, Vista adds to those options.

Vista still works as Windows always has in that it's got file and folder permissions, and that when you log on you get a token that contains your group memberships and privileges. But where Vista varies from earlier versions of Windows is that Vista now has something called "Administrator Approval Mode," which allows you to let your administrators log on as administrators and in fact spend all *day* logged on as administrators, but without exposing their machines to the amount of risk that running all day as an admin did in pre-Vista versions of Windows. Microsoft called these administrative accounts that were essentially protected from themselves "protected administrators" or PAs for a while, but as I write this, the current term is —I'm not kidding—"administrators in Administrator Approval Mode." (Makes me want to just stick to "PAs" in this text.)

When you log on as an administrator in Administrator Approval Mode, you get not one but *two* tokens (Microsoft calls it a "split token," although some at Microsoft call it a "filtered token") when logging on:

- One token looks as it would before Admin Approval Mode, containing all of your groups, rights, and privileges. Microsoft calls that either the "administrator access token" or, in some places, just the "administrator token." If you've read earlier Microsoft texts about UAC then you might have seen the phrase "privileged administrator token," an older and now-unused term that still appears on a lot of Web pages. I'll just refer to it as the "administrator token" in this chapter.

- The second and new token, called the "standard user access token" or "standard user token," works as the words "standard user" suggest: the standard user token has been stripped of any administrative group memberships and privileges. (We'll get to the details of how a token gets "stripped" later, I promise; for now, I'm just laying out the basics.) Some texts use the phrase "split token" to refer to the whole notion that an administrator's token gets divided into two tokens; others use the phrase "split token" to refer to the lower-power, "standard user token."

 Recall from the last chapter that "standard user" isn't just a colloquialism, it's Microsoft's relatively new buzzword for users without any admin powers. They *were* calling it a "restricted user" for a while but the marketing guys thought that had bad connotations—"why are your restricting me on my own machine?"—and they were probably right.

Under Vista, Windows sees that you have two tokens. Which does it use when you try to do something? Well, basically, it ignores your administrator token and gives you whatever powers are conferred by your standard user token, which means that for pretty much all intents and purposes, Windows treats you like a regular old standard user even while you're logged on as an administrator. And, truthfully, that's not as bad a thing as you'd expect, as Microsoft has made a real effort in Vista to identify many things that unnecessarily required administrator-level powers in XP and reclassify them as available to standard users. (Making that call's not as easy as you'd think; what is to one person a solution to inconvenience is a horrific security hole to another.) As I suggested before, being a standard user is also a good thing when you unknowingly try to install some spyware as a result of some social engineering on the part of an evil website, e-mail attachment, or application.

Sometimes, of course, you *need* to run some program that requires administrator-level powers, and in that case you'll need Windows to recognize your administrator token when it starts the program. (Remember, programs get tokens *when started*, so Windows has to know which token to use at the time that it fires up the program for you. As I noted before, once a program has started, there's no way to switch tokens, and there's no way to inject more power into an existing token. One of the key things to understanding UAC is how it tells the "start up a program" part of Windows which token to use.)

In fact, however, Windows will *never* use your administrator token even if you *have* one unless either (1) you tell Windows to use your administrator token, or (2) Windows is smart enough to say to itself "hey, this sucker ain't gonna work without an administrator token, and this user's *got* an administrator token; let's see if she'll let me give it to the program." If either of those things happens, then you get the Consent UI that you saw back in Figure 2.1; the Consent UI is Windows' way of saying, "I *think* you want me to use your administrator token— may I?" Assuming that you click Confirm, then Windows can start your program with an administrator token rather than a standard user token.

That's a subtle point, but an important one that I can use to explain something that I said earlier. Remember my earlier description of what happened when I tried to create a new user account in Vista? In that scenario, I said that I logged onto a Vista system as an administrator, and started up a command prompt and tried to use the net.exe program to create the new user account. Vista rejected the attempt and said that I lacked the access to create a new user account, even though I was an admin.

Why did it fail? Because, in my scenario, I didn't *ask* Windows to run net.exe with my administrator token (I'll show you how to do that later) and because, for reasons I'll make clear later, Windows didn't know when it started up net.exe that it would require administrative powers, and so didn't think to ask my permission to attach the administrator token. *That* means that by the time net.exe needed to actually create the user account, net.exe had only the standard user token and lacked the ability to create a user account. Result: the whole thing failed.

In contrast, when starting to create a user account through the GUI, then Windows has been designed to *know* that anyone clicking the hyperlink "Add or remove user accounts" will require an administrator token to succeed. Thus, Windows knows that continuing with "Add or remove user accounts" would require an administrator token and that I *had* an administrator token. But that's still not enough to allow Windows to run "Add or remove user accounts," as Windows will never just use your administrator token without permission. So Vista raises the Consent UI. When I clicked Confirm, then the "Add or remove user accounts" process gave me my administrator token, and I could then create user accounts without error. That's UAC in a nutshell.

Digging Deeper into UAC

Let's recap what we've seen so far. By default Vista makes administrative accounts into *protected* administrators by splitting or filtering their logon tokens into a full-power *administrator token* and a low-power *standard user token*. When you kick off a program, Vista will, by default, attach the standard user token to that program. Alternatively, Vista may attach the administrator token to the program *if* you ask it to, or Vista may be smart enough to foresee that the program will need an administrative token, and attach that—but whether you ask or Vista foresees the need for an administrative token, you've got to confirm that it's okay for Vista to use that administrative token.

While that's a good start, it raises just about as many questions as it answers, at least in my mind. Let's add some more details to make User Account Control a bit clearer.

How Windows Creates the Standard User Token

As you've already read, logging onto an account that is an "administrator in Administrator Approval Mode" causes you to get a token with fewer powers than you'd normally get when logging on as an administrator. *How* many fewer powers? Here's the scoop.

How Windows Vista Tokens Are Structured

The token is, recall, a data structure in the RAM of a computer that you're logged onto. Vista tokens, which are very similar to pre-Vista Windows tokens, contain several items: your name, your group memberships, your privileges, and your Windows integrity level. Let's look at all of that in more detail. (And again, yes, some of this will be review for the security experts out there, but it's very important that everyone understand these fundamentals so as to understand what's happening under the hood in UAC and in Chapter 4's discussion of Windows integrity levels.)

Your "Name": Your Security ID (SID)

Your token doesn't really contain your name, as different people can have the same name, no matter how unique their names. (Amazingly, I learned a few years ago that there's another person named Mark Minasi, and he runs a telemarketing operation. So I started using my middle initial more often!) Instead, Windows needs some kind of guaranteed-to-be-unique way of identifying you, and so ever since NT 3.1, every user account has had a user account identifier called a Security ID or SID. User account SIDs and some group SIDs look like

`S-1-5-21-domainID-relativeID`

Where *domainID* is a 96-bit number that identifies the user account's location—either a particular domain or a particular machine where a local account might reside—and *relativeID* identifies the particular account in that location. More specifically, every time you set up Windows on a system, that system gets a (supposedly) unique 96-bit number that no other machine has ever had, or ever will. That also happens when you create a domain; that domain gets a 96-bit ID that no other domain or, for that matter, machine will ever get. So, for example, suppose I created a domain named bigfirm.com. The process of creating the domain causes a random 96-bit number to be generated; let's imagine that value turns out to be 12345. (It's unlikely but let's start with smaller numbers.) Every user account created on that domain would look like S-1-5-21-12345-*relativeID*, where the domain starts assigning relative IDs from 1000. The first user account created would have a SID of S-1-5-21-12345-1000, the second would have a SID of S-1-5-21-12345-1001, and so on. Meanwhile, bigfirm.com might have a member workstation that, of course, can have local user accounts, and that member workstation might have gotten a randomly generated identifier when built of 99999999999999999999999 (also unlikely), meaning that any local user account on that member would have a SID of S-1-5-21-99999999999999999999999-*relativeID*. Thus, if that were my workstation, then I might have a local user account on my workstation with a SID of S-1-5-21-99999999999999999999999-1000 ("1000" because, again, it's the first number used when creating user accounts, and I'm probably the only user account on the system), and a separate domain account with a SID of S-1-5-21-12345-1062.

Oh, and one more bit of terminology: the relative ID is often abbreviated "RID," and pronounced "rid." Thus, the RID on my local account would be 1000, and the one on the domain would be 1062. Some accounts have fixed RIDs and are called "well-known RIDs." The most well-known example of well-known RIDs is "500," the RID for the built-in Administrator account.

Again, as far as Windows is concerned, you *are* your SID. Yeah, you've got a name, but Windows cares about knowing that about as much as it would knowing your shoe size; it's just an attribute of your user account. Similarly, if you have an explicit permission on something like a file or folder, then that permission isn't stored as "Jane Smith has Full Control of

C:\JANESTUFF;" nope, it looks more like "S-1-5-21-9999999999999999999999999-1005 has Full Control of C:\JANESTUFF." Ever opened up the Security tab on an object's Properties page and expected to see the little icons of white-faced heads with blue eyes and black hair, only to face a bunch of empty head outlines with question marks in them? It's because of the fact that permissions store SIDs, not names. So when you open up a permission on a member server—which does not contain a copy of the domain's usernames and SIDs, as it's just a member—then the member server has to find and communicate with a domain controller, asking it "hey, can you tell me the names associated with these SIDs?," proffering the SIDs on the permissions that you're looking at. As this sometimes takes a few minutes, you'll sometimes see those empty heads with the question marks in them for a few moments; you're just seeing the results of a slow network or a slow domain controller. *Sometimes* you'll see empty heads that never go away; that's because someone gave a permission to a user or group account, and then subsequently deleted the user or group. The file and folder permission data is sitting on and is maintained by NTFS, which has no idea what the user account–maintaining part of Windows is doing at any moment, and so has no way to clean up permissions pointing to nonexistent accounts.

 A Resource Kit tool named subinacl can find and fix those problems, however.

Your Groups: A SID List

After your SID, your token contains a list of the groups that you're a member of, including

- Domain-based global groups
- Domain-based universal groups
- Domain-based domain local groups
- Built-in local groups like the Administrators and Users groups
- Normal local groups such as you or some application might create on your system

But the list in the token doesn't include the names of the groups; instead, it contains their SIDs. Some start with S-1-5-21- as did user SIDs, and in fact the Domain Admins and Domain Users SIDs look just like user SIDs—you can pick those two out with their well-known RIDs of 512 and 513, respectively. Built-in groups on a local system, in contrast, do not include the *domainID* part that I explained earlier; the local Users group on every Windows system around always has a SID of S-1-5-32-545, and the Administrators group is always S-1-5-32-544. There are also what Microsoft calls "well-known groups," groups whose membership is built on the fly like the Everyone (S-1-1-0) group or the Interactive (S-1-5-4) group, which you get to be a member of when you're physically sitting at a computer.

Your Privileges: What You Can Do

Windows gives you the power to do things besides having read or write access to a file, user account, service, or the like. It also lets you perform certain tasks that don't fit into the "permissions" way of thinking, like being able to shut down a computer or change its time. Windows defines the ability to do certain functions either as rights or permissions. "Rights" refers to the way that Windows controls whether you can or can't log onto something, so the ability to "log onto this machine locally" or "deny access to this machine across the network" are rights. All other abilities are called "privileges."

Now, you *could* argue that Microsoft could make the clock an object with permissions on it, and those permissions might be whether you could change the time or change the time zone; then you could control who can and can't change the time with a standard Security tab on a Properties page rather than by adjusting a privilege, and so perhaps the whole idea of privileges and rights versus permissions is an unnecessary distinction. But there are some abilities that probably wouldn't fit into the permissions model. For example, consider the "right to take ownership." This lets administrators take ownership of any object no matter how much they've been locked out of that object. There'd be no way to implement that as a permission without bending the whole permission model out of shape pretty badly. Essentially it could never be a permission, but instead an ability to seize a state (ownership) that would then grant the permission to set a permission! In any case, rights and privileges have been around for a long time in Windows and I don't think that'll change any time soon. Although there's always Vienna....

Se*What?*

Vista defines 34 different types of user privileges and 10 different types of rights for user accounts. When you see descriptions of privileges, then you may see them described in two ways. The first way is a short English description of the privilege, like "change the system time." As its name suggests, having this privilege gives you the power to reset a computer's clock. But when doing low-level security programming in Windows, developers needn't type out "change the system time"; instead, every privilege has a short name that looks like Se*something*Privilege. For example the short name for "change the system time" is "SeSystemtimePrivilege." Having a shorter, if more cryptic name is mostly for the convenience of coders, and, as Microsoft's CEO Steve Ballmer once famously explained, Microsoft's central focus is developers.

Actually, Ballmer—who's known for a flamboyant presenting style—did it by yelling "developers, developers, developers…" a few dozen times. He likes to do that kind of thing, although he *did* have to get his vocal cords operated on to repair them after a similar performance in 1991. He was chanting "Windows, Windows, Windows" a zillion times at a conference in Japan. My guess is that he probably did it in the hopes of making his audience forget that he had told the world fewer than two years before that the operating system that Microsoft was 110 percent behind, the one that would take us into the 21st century, was… OS/2. But he's a heck of an amusing guy to listen to. My personal favorite Ballmerism was when he explained to a crowd I was in that the new version of Office (I forget which it was) would let you create more "impactful" presentations. Imagine; there are 411,000 words in English, and Steve's still got to create some more.

I'll try to remember to use both the Se term and the English phrase in this text because while the English description is more descriptive, Microsoft has a tendency to use the short name for privileges in their documentation far more than the English description.

Your token includes your privileges, but for some reason does not include your rights—I guess declaring your ability to log onto a system after you've already logged onto it is sort of pointless. As I explained in Chapter 1, standard users under UAC get five privileges:

- The ability to shut down a system, `SeShutdownPrivilege`.

- The ability to manipulate a file or folder that they have access to, even if the file or folder are inside folders that the user lacks access to. This is known as "bypass traverse checking" and `SeChangeNotifyPrivilege`.

- The ability to undock a laptop from a docking station, `SeUndockPrivilege`.

- The ability increase a "process working set," the geeky phrase for "the amount of memory that a program uses." This is a new privilege that did not exist before Vista and I presume that Microsoft intends to *deny* this to some service accounts so as to make it harder for a service hijacked by some buffer overflow worm to start sucking up the computer's RAM. Its short name is `SeIncreaseWorkingSetPrivilege`.

- The ability to change a workstation's time zone. This is also a new-to-Vista privilege, and it's intended to solve an old problem. We don't want just anyone being able to change a system's clock because the clock needs to be in sync with the network in order for Active Directory to work, and in particular we wouldn't want bad guys being able to mess with a clock so that the Event Log items that document their evil deeds would show misleading times. But traveling folks want to make their system clocks match the clocks around them as they shift from time zone to time zone, so Microsoft split off this function into a new privilege. Its short name is `SeTimeZonePrivilege`.

But let's look at why Vista gives standard users those five privileges by default. It's *not* that Vista says, "standard users get these five privileges;" in fact, in this case, you were originally logged on as a member of the local Administrators group, and that group has all of those privileges. When Vista yanked your Administrators group membership, therefore, you lost all of those privileges.

But now consider the case of a standard user account to which some administrator has added some extra privileges. For example, what if an administrator were to grant your account the "change the workstation's clock" privilege—would you keep the privilege when logged on under the watchful eye of UAC? It's true that UAC doesn't want standard users to have some privileges, but "change the workstation's clock" isn't one. (That seems odd to me, given what I explained earlier about the new "change the time zone" privilege, but that's the way it is.)

There are 34 user privileges that any user or group account can possess. UAC only objects to nine of them:

- **Create a token object,** or `SeCreateTokenPrivilege`, lets you actually create tokens of the kind that we discussed just a few pages ago. You can see that this could be a pretty powerful ability, as it would let you "write your own ticket," so to speak!

- **Act as a part of the operating system** (`SeTcbPrivilege`) has been called "the Holy Grail of hackers." It was the basis of the forerunner to RunAs, a Resource Kit tool called "`su.exe`" and is an essential part of doing things but looking like someone else. It's useful if you're doing hardware debugging, but standard users don't need it.

- **Take ownership of files and other objects** (`SeTakeOwnershipPrivilege`) is probably familiar, but for those who've not heard of it, this privilege lets its possessor take not just ownership but *control* of files, folders, services, Active Directory components, and more. "More" in this case includes Windows integrity labels, which we'll cover in Chapter 4, and isn't really something that you want users messing with.

- **Load and unload device drivers** (`SeLoadDriverPrivilege`) is sinister because there's more to a device driver than simply making a piece of hardware work. Many applications depend on device drivers not because they're dependent on some special hardware but because a device driver can look anywhere in the system and often modify any data structure in the system. Want to peek at passwords? Write a device driver. But then you've got to install it, and that's what UAC's trying to keep you from doing.

- **Back up and restore files and directories** (`SeBackupPrivilege` and `SeRestorePrivilege`) are two privileges that have always kept security people up nights, believe it or not. Try this some time: create a file and deny yourself all access to the file, then run most of the backup programs out there. Your backup will succeed, even though the backup program is running as you. Why? Because `SeBackupPrivilege` and `SeRestorePrivilege` are "back doors" that let you read files (`SeBackupPrivilege`) and write files (`SeRestorePrivilege`) even if you lack the NTFS permissions to do so.

- **Impersonate a client after authentication** (`SeImpersonatePrivilege`) is similar to "act as a part of the operating system" in that it offers bad guys the opportunity to hide their identities while working on your system, so UAC blocks this privilege.

- **Modify an object label** (`SeRelabelPrivilege`) gives you the power to modify an object's mandatory integrity control level. We haven't discussed Windows integrity control yet, but it's an important new feature of Windows that we'll cover in Chapter 4. In short, it's a way to describe how "trusted" a file or user is, sort of like the government notion of things that are "classified," "secret," "top secret," and the like. People with this power can reclassify objects nearly at will, which is *not* a good idea.

- **Debug programs** (`SeDebugPrivilege`) does not, as the name suggests, let you debug programs; a debugging program lets you do that. But debuggers need to look into a program's processes and data structures, and those processes and data structures are essentially owned by whomever's running the program. Therefore you can run a debugger to examine your own programs without any trouble. But what if you wanted to examine programs running in the operating system that you *don't* own, like most of the operating system? Then you'd need somewhat higher privilege…and "debug programs" is the key. Remember, you needn't give this permission to the coders in your office unless they're rewriting the operating system for you!

You have probably run into `SeDebugPrivilege`, whether you realize it or not. If you've ever run Task Manager from a Windows 2000 or later system, you may have noticed a check box in the lower left-hand corner of Task Manager labeled "Show processes from all users." That check box is there because a standard user has complete rights to see and manage her own processes, but none to examine what other users or the system is doing. But if she happens to possess the SeDebugPrivilege, then she can check that box and monitor the entire operating system.

As UAC only blocks the Notorious Nine, there are potentially 25 user privileges that users can employ without requiring elevation.

Your Windows Integrity Level

The final thing that you'll see in a token on a Vista system is your current Windows integrity level. It's a completely new idea first appearing in Vista, and we'll cover it in Chapter 4. But here are a couple of basic notions that we'll need in this chapter. Windows integrity levels are a means of describing how much the operating system "trusts" you. There are six levels of Windows integrity, but we'll just look at two here: the "medium" Windows integrity level and the "high" Windows integrity level. Standard users get a medium Windows integrity level; administrators get a high Windows integrity level.

Windows integrity levels show up in your token as a SID. They look like S-1-16-*value*, where *value* is 8192 for medium Windows integrity level and 12,288 for high Windows integrity level.

Seeing Your Token Information

By now, you're probably itching to find out about your token. Fortunately, Vista gives us a nice command-line tool with which to explore tokens: the whoami.exe program. Open up a command prompt and type **whoami /user**. When I did that while logged on as a user named "mark" from a domain called "bigfirm.com," whoami returned this:

```
C:\mystuff>whoami /user

USER INFORMATION
----------------

User Name   SID
=========== =============================================
bigfirm\mark S-1-5-21-1592023571-1864867759-2423328773-1010
```

The first part of any token is, again, the user SID, and whoami /user shows that. Next, let's see what groups your user account is a member of. whoami /groups displays that information. If I run that command on my system, I get this result:

```
C:\mystuff>whoami /groups

GROUP INFORMATION
-----------------
```

Group Name	Type	SID
Everyone	Well-known group	S-1-1-0
BUILTIN\Users	Alias	S-1-5-32-545
BUILTIN\Administrators	Alias	S-1-5-32-544
NT AUTHORITY\INTERACTIVE	Well-known group	S-1-5-4
BIGFIRM\Domain Admins	Group	S-1-5-21...
Mandatory Label\Medium Mandatory Level		S-1-16-8192

Actually, yours will look a bit different; I had to edit the output a bit to allow it to fit on the page. In the process I deleted some interesting information, but in a bit I'll bring that back and explain it. What I want you to notice right now is that whoami displays group membership, so you can see that this account is both a local administrator (it's a member of BUILTIN\Administrators) and a domain admin (it's a member of BIGFIRM\Domain Admins); that looks like this account hasn't been reduced in power at all—but there's a catch that we'll see in a minute. Notice also that, as I said, my Windows integrity level shows up as a SID "S-1-16-8192." The OS doesn't exactly call it a "medium Windows integrity level," it refers to it as "Mandatory Label\Medium Mandatory Level," but perhaps by the time you read this they will have brought the various names for mandatory integrity levels into line with each other.

Now let's return to the fact that I've got an entry for BUILTIN\Administrators on my token, but if I try to do something admin-like then what I'm trying to do will either fail, or I'll get the Consent UI that will, recall, kick in a whole different token. whoami /groups produces some pretty wide output, and if I scroll over to the right a bit I see that I've skipped an entire column labeled "Attributes."

If you get tired of scrolling left and right, as I eventually did, you can tell whoami to just format the information as a list by adding "/fo list" to the command, as in whoami /groups /fo list or, if you'd like to pump it into an Excel spreadsheet, add "/fo csv."

The attributes for most groups are "Mandatory group, Enabled by default, Enabled group," which basically means "UAC didn't mess with this group." But a look at the attributes of the BUILTIN\Administrators group shows them to be "Group used for deny only." Huh? Whuzzat?

Well, usually when we put a permission on something like a file or a folder, those permissions tend to be what are called "allow" permissions. When we say that we gave someone "read access" to a folder, what we really mean is that we created an "access control entry"—a permission—*allowing* "read" permissions. But it's also possible to create an access control entry *denying* "read" permissions. We usually don't bother creating "deny" permissions because by default if you don't have any "allow" permissions on something, then you're denied access to it. But sometimes "deny" permissions make sense, so here's what UAC did: it kept my membership in the BUILTIN\Administrators group, *but only insofar as it lets someone deny me access to something*. In other words, if I want to do something administrator-like then I won't be able to, because any "allow" permission naming the Administrators group has been removed from my standard user token, but if I was previously unable to do something even as a member of the Administrators group because of an explicit "go away, Administrators!" permission, then I'm still subject to that. All of the bad things about being an admin, and none of the good!

We've seen that UAC removes membership in BUILTIN\Administrators from the standard user token, but that's not the only one that it'll block. To find out which groups get eighty-sixed from the standard user token, I tried creating a local user and joined it to every one of Vista's built-in groups, then ran `whoami /groups /fo list` to see which got the deny-only access control entry. The list of the Fearsome Four groups, then, is:

- BUILTIN\Administrators
- BUILTIN\Backup Operators
- BUILTIN\Power Users
- BUILTIN\Network Configuration Operators

All of the other built-in Vista group memberships are passed right on through to the standard user token. Additionally, I was surprised to see that my membership in the domain's Domain Admins group remained in my standard user token.

Summary: From Administrator to Standard User

Now that we've picked at a UAC standard user token, let's summarize exactly what happens when UAC creates a standard user token from an administrator account.

- You get the same user SID in your standard user token as you have in your administrator token.
- You lose all of the Notorious Nine "scary privileges": create a token, act as a part of the OS, take ownership of objects, load and unload device drivers, back up and restore, impersonate a client, modify an object label, and debug programs.
- Your Windows integrity level goes from High (S-1-16-12288) to Medium (S-1-16-8192).
- You retain all group memberships except for the Fearsome Four—BUILTIN\Administrators, BUILTIN\Backup Users, BUILTIN\Power Users, and BUILTIN\Network Configuration Operators. On those groups, you still have the group membership, but *only* if that group membership lets someone deny you access to some object. Even if a group confers on you one of the Notorious Nine privileges, you retain the group membership...you just lose any of the forbidden privileges unless you elevate. Thus, if you're a member of Domain Administrators, then you remain a member of Domain Administrators; you just lose the membership in the *local* Administrators group that you previously had as a side effect of being in Domain Admins.

How to Tell UAC to Use the Administrator Token

Now that we've exercised the standard user token a bit, let's take the full-power administrator token out for a spin. But how?

Using RunAs to Get an Administrator Token Command Prompt Window

With a variation on a tool that you may already know: the RunAs command.

Windows 2000, XP, and 2003 let you tell Windows when starting any command, "run this command, but don't attach *my* token to it—attach another account's token." You then specify the username and password of the account whose token you want the program to have. There's a command-line RunAs, but most folks will probably find it easier to right-click the Start menu item or program icon and choose "Run as administrator," as you see in Figure 2.2.

FIGURE 2.2 Running a command prompt as administrator

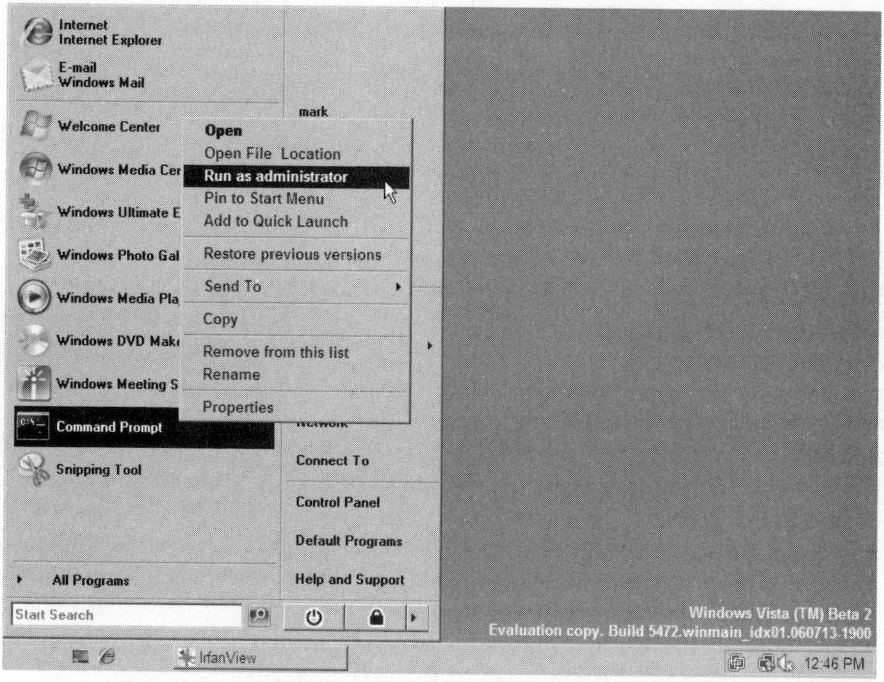

If you've used Windows 2000, XP, or 2003, notice the difference in this context menu. In those earlier Windows, you'd choose "Run as..." and then punch in the username and password of the account to run the program under; now, instead, there's the simpler "Run as administrator." This has disappointed some folks, because it can be quite convenient to test security in a newly configured or reconfigured system by being able to just fire up a client program under any account desired and then use that client-with-a-different-user-token to check whether something that you *think* you've just secured from some group of users is, in fact, secured. I wish they had offered both "Run as administrator" and "Run as...," but they didn't, so there's not much to be done about it. You can, however, still use the command-line RunAs tool to run any arbitrary program under any given user account, and its (ugly) syntax has not changed since XP and 2003.

Anyway, right-clicking something and choosing "Run as administrator" causes Windows to raise the Consent UI and, after you click Confirm, Windows runs the desired application and gives it the administrator token rather than the standard user token. We can see that in action if I log onto a Vista machine as a local administrator, start a command prompt with "Run as administrator," and try a `whoami /groups /fo list`. I'll spare you most of the output, but a couple of entries are interesting:

```
Group Name: BUILTIN\Administrators
Type:       Alias
SID:        S-1-5-32-544
Attributes: Mandatory group, Enabled by default, Enabled group, Group owner


Group Name: Mandatory Label\High Mandatory Level
Type:       Unknown SID type
SID:        S-1-16-12288
Attributes: Mandatory group, Enabled by default, Enabled group
```

The first item is interesting because note that the BUILTIN\Administrators group membership is, indeed, activated—none of that "Group used for deny only" stuff anymore. The second shows that the Windows integrity control SID is now S-1-16-12288, the "High" level for Windows integrity control.

If I were to try that `net user mark swordfish /add` command now, I wouldn't get an "access denied" message. (I *would* get an error message because now there's already an account named "mark," but that's another story.)

In case you're still a doubter, do a `whoami /priv` to see the privileges enjoyed by this command prompt. Still got that measly five privileges? Heck no. I count 23 on mine. I sure hope all of that power doesn't go to my head....

By the way, before I leave this section, there's a bit of terminology that I've mentioned before but wanted to underscore: "elevated." Instead of saying "run the command prompt with Run as administrator," you can instead say "run the command prompt elevated," or "run an elevated command prompt." "Elevated" here just means "run with an administrator token."

Making Elevated Windows Easier to Get To

But perhaps you'd rather not waste a lot of time right-clicking. Time to turn off UAC? Definitely not. Here are a few ideas to let you keep that standard user token around for your own protection, while getting to apps to run as with a full-power administrator token.

Keep a High-Power Command Prompt Handy

I find it extremely useful to start up a command prompt window with "Run as administrator" and leave it open so that I've always got an admin-level command prompt close at hand. Once you get it open, do yourself a favor and click on the control menu on the command prompt window, and then click Properties. Go to the "Colors" tab and give it a different-colored background; I always change the black background to dark blue. That way, I don't do regular standard user tasks from that command prompt window accidentally, exposing myself to some destructive error that a command prompt running as standard user would protect me from. That blue background always says "hey, don't use me unless you need to!" to me.

> Microsoft *did* add a feature to the Command Prompt window around RC1 whereby they prefix the Command Prompt window's name with "Administrator" to also clue you into that window's elevated status. They're not doing it for all apps unfortunately, though.

Make Any Icon Automatically Raise the Consent UI

Having an elevated command prompt around is okay, but it's still a pain to have to remember to right-click the Start menu item for "Command Prompt" and choose "Run as administrator." Isn't there a way to create icons and Start menu items that automatically *know* to ask to run with the administrator token? Sure.

First, create a new item on the Start menu as you would in Windows 2000, XP, or 2003, by adding a new shortcut to some part of the Programs folder in your profile. I'll create a new shortcut to Command Prompt that I'll call "Floating Command Prompt" (it *is* elevated) like so:

1. Right-click the Start menu, and choose Explore.

2. That opens an Explorer folder. In that folder is a folder called Programs. Open that up.

3. Inside Programs, you'll see a folder structure that mirrors the hierarchy of your Start menu. Find where you'd like to put Floating Command Prompt. (I put mine in Accessories.) Right-click wherever you want the icon and choose New ➤ Shortcut.

4. A wizard appears that asks you what you want this shortcut to *point* to. Command prompt points to cmd.exe in c:\windows\system32, so either type that into the field labeled "Type the location of the item:," or click the "Browse…" button to find cmd.exe. Once you've got that filled in, click Next.

5. The second wizard page asks, "What would you like to name this shortcut?" I'm filling in "Floating Command Prompt," but you're welcome to use whatever you like—it's just a label for our convenience.

6. Once you've got the prompt name entered, click Finish. You'll see the Accessories folder with icons in it, as before, but now you'll see an icon labeled "Floating Command Prompt." Right-click that and choose Properties.

Congratulations, you now have a new Start menu item. But it's not smart enough yet to automatically raise the Consent UI and get itself the administrator token. To do that, right-click the item and choose Properties, and then the Shortcut tab. You'll see a property page like the one in Figure 2.3.

So far, Vista's not doing anything that different from 2000, XP, or 2003. But now let's click the "Advanced…" button to see something like Figure 2.4.

FIGURE 2.3   Shortcut properties page, Shortcut tab

FIGURE 2.4   Advanced Shortcut properties

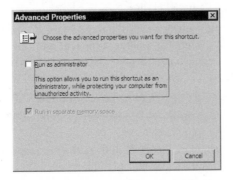

Notice the check box labeled "Run as administrator." Check out the Advanced Properties page for a shortcut under XP or 2003 and "Run with different credentials." Again, Microsoft has collapsed the "RunAs" infrastructure a bit. Check the "Run as administrator" box, click OK twice to dismiss the Advanced Properties dialog for the shortcut and then to dismiss the Properties page for the shortcut, and close the Windows ➢ Start Menu ➢ Programs ➢ Accessories Explorer. Now click Start ➢ All Programs ➢ Accessories and you'll see "Floating Command Prompt." Click it and the Consent UI will appear; click Confirm and you've got a full-power command prompt at your fingertips. (Don't believe me? Run `whoami /all` for the full story. Expect to have to scroll to see it all, though.)

You can do this for any program that you like; the command prompt's just the start. If you find that you're trying to run an older program that needs the full administrator token but Vista isn't smart enough to ask for the administrator token, then this is the way to easily bypass the need for right-clicking every time that you want to run the program.

> Before leaving this, though, you might want to finish up that "Floating Command Prompt." Click Start ➤ All Programs ➤ Accessories, then right-click the "Floating Command Prompt" item and choose Properties. Click the Shortcut tab and, at the end of the Target: field, which is currently populated with C:\Windows\System32\cmd.exe, add /T:1F without the double quotes. That'll tell the command prompt to start up with a dark blue background and bright white lettering. That way you needn't set the colors every time that you start the command prompt—the shortcut will do it for you if configure it in this tab. Honestly, I highly recommend putting together a special elevated command prompt menu item with a different color scheme; once I put this together I didn't find UAC nearly as annoying.

Now, what I just showed you works fine for Start menu items and shortcuts because they're basically the same thing, but if you tried to mark a particular EXE file as requiring elevation, then you'd see something just a mite different.

> When I say "EXE file," I'm referring to most of the files that contain programs. When you run Notepad, you're really telling the operating system to load and run a file called "notepad.exe." If you've never seen anything like that, just open up the Computer folder on your Vista box and navigate to the Windows\System32 folder. And be sure that you've told Vista not to hide file extensions, or you'll just see "notepad" rather than "notepad.exe."

For example, I have a program simple.exe written a long time ago in the pre-Vista days. To mark it as requiring elevation, I right-click it and choose Properties, and then the Compatibility tab to see a page like Figure 2.5.

Notice the check box "Run this program as an administrator." *That's* where you check in order to get this elevated every time that you run it, as there's no Shortcut tab here.

> The reason that I mentioned that this application was not Vista-aware was that if you *do* try to look at the Compatibility tab on a Vista application, then you'll see the tab and the entire page will be grayed out.

Note that if I *did* check that box so that UAC tries to elevate simple.exe, then that setting would only apply when *I* was running simple.exe. Someone else with an account on my machine would not get the UAC elevation prompt, and perhaps their attempt at running simple.exe would fail because it wasn't elevated. To fix that, click the box labeled "Show settings for all users." That brings up a similar-looking page that lets you check the "Run this program as an administrator" box for all users.

FIGURE 2.5   The Compatibility tab for a pre-Vista application

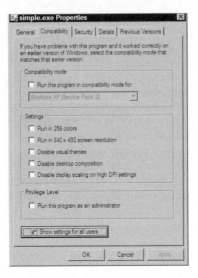

Sometimes Elevation Doesn't Work

Once I got comfy with creating shortcuts that had the "Run as administrator" embedded in them, I soon realized which program I *really* wanted an elevate-me-without-the-right-click icon for: Windows Explorer. I figured that I'd save all kinds of time navigating the much-tighter default permissions on my Vista hard disk with such a thing.

Unfortunately, it's not possible.

Yes, you *can* fiddle around with the Windows Explorer icon and check the "Run as administrator" box, but nothing will happen. You see, you start up a copy of Explorer when you log on; it's an essential part of the logon process. Now, when you try to run a second copy of Explorer, you don't really *get* a second copy of Explorer. When Explorer is asked to start up, it looks around to see if there's already a copy of Explorer running. If there is, then Explorer *doesn't* run a second time; it just opens up a new window into the same copy of Explorer. The copy of Explorer that starts up when you log on gets, as you'd guess, your standard user token and, because starting a second copy of Explorer doesn't really start a new program, there's no way to get an Explorer running with an administrative token.

Now, it was once possible to run multiple independent copies of Explorer on a system, but apparently Microsoft's removed the capability due to some low-level philosophical security reason. So sadly there's no way to create a "floating Explorer." Bummer.

You *Can't* Get Past the Consent UI

One tip you're probably looking for is "how can I create an icon that I can just click so that it'll start up with an administrator token?" You can't, not without turning off UAC altogether. The whole point of UAC is, again, to make you stop and be aware that you're doing something administrative before you do it.

What Tells Windows to Use the Administrator Token

As you've read, one way to convince Vista to give your application the administrator token rather than the standard user token is the right-click and "Run as administrator." But a little work with Vista will show that Vista raises the Consent UI quite a bit without any right-clicking involved. How does Windows Vista know before even running a program that it'll need the administrator token? In four ways:

- If Vista guesses that the program is installing an application, as installers pretty much always need to write to protected places in the Registry and on the disk, then it'll ask to be elevated.

- Developers can warn Vista that an application requires elevation by embedding something called a "manifest" into the EXE file itself, or putting a "manifest file" into the same directory as the EXE file.

- Vista's Explorer and Internet Explorer includes something called the "Program Compatibility Assistant" that looks for pre-Vista programs and then examines them for "compatibility issues," according to Microsoft. (That's all they've said.) If it detects them, then it'll pop up a box asking the user if it's okay to mark the application as requiring elevation. If the user agrees, then PCA stores that pre-Vista program's elevation needs in the Registry and from that point on, whenever the user runs the program, the Consent UI will appear.

- Vista contains a large database of information about older applications in something called the Application Compatibility Database. In that database, it's got a list of applications that will fail unless elevated. If you run one of those apps, then UAC will pop up the Consent UI.

That's not as complicated as it all looks, and understanding it may allow you to solve a passel of problems getting pre-Vista apps to work more smoothly. Let's take each point in turn, with a couple of side trips to see how Vista uses the GUI to offer feedback about what does and doesn't need elevation.

Vista Looks for Installers

You very rarely run across an application installer that doesn't need administrator-level privileges. Badly designed installers write things to Windows\System32, and standard users only have the permissions to read, execute, and list the contents of things in the System32 file, so you'd need to be an admin to install an app that did that. Better-designed installers still need to write to Program Files, which gives standard users the same permissions that System32 does, and to write to some subkey of HKEY_LOCAL_MACHINE\SOFTWARE or HKEY_LOCAL_ MACHINE\SERVICES, neither of which let standard users write to them. So, instead of letting an installer blithely try to do one of those things and fail, UAC tries to guess when you're running an application whose job is basically to install another application.

Now, in the computer business we don't actually *say* "guess"; that sounds sort of flaky. Instead, we say that an application evaluates probabilities based on "heuristics." Now, I'll save you the trip to the dictionary: heuristics are just what most of us would call "rules of thumb." UAC's rules of thumb for smoking out an installer? Two main approaches: look at the name of the EXE and recognize popular installer types.

Rule number one: if the phrases "setu," "instal," or "update" appear in the name, then raise the Consent UI. Yup, it's just as simple as that, and it's a good set of guesses. Wait, you may be thinking, doesn't that mean that bad guys can just rename their setup programs and slip past UAC? No, not at all—this isn't a feature to deter bad guys, it's a feature to save good guys some trouble. Again, if I were to rename "setup.exe" to "bananas.exe" then sure, I wouldn't get the Consent UI, and Vista would happily run bananas.exe…and then watch it crash when it tried to poke around Program Files, System32, or the Registry.

Rule number two: most installation packages were created with either the Wyse installer or the Installshield installer. In case you don't recognize those names, they're very popular third-party applications that simplify the process of creating a program that installs an application. Both Wyse and Installshield's setup programs have very distinctive "looks" to them and are easy for UAC to detect.

Rule number three: if a suspect application is marked with a UAC-aware "manifest" (which we'll cover soon), then don't bother applying either the first two rules, and just let it run as a standard user.

You can see the first rule in action. Just take any innocuous and pre-Vista EXE file that runs without needing an administrator token; rename it to setup.exe and all of a sudden it'll start popping up the Consent UI every time you run it.

For example, try this.

1.   Copy the `calc.exe` program from a copy of Windows XP to a Vista box.

2.   Run calc.exe; you will see no Consent UI and XP's Notepad will start right up.

3.   Now, rename the XP `calc.exe` to "setup.exe. *Now* run it. You'll see, the Consent UI pops up every time you run the XP Calculator. In contrast—and in keeping with rule 3—try copying the *Vista* calc.exe somewhere and rename it as setup.exe, then run it; no Consent UI, and it runs just fine.

 You can, if you want, tell Vista not to try to automatically detect and elevate installation programs with a group policy setting, "User Account Control: Detect application installation and prompt for elevation," as you'll read later in the section "Reconfiguring User Account Control."

UAC and the Vista GUI

By the way, if you tried that, then you might have noticed something like Figure 2.6.

It's just one example of how UAC uses the Vista graphical user interface either to signal you how closely to examine a Consent UI prompt, or to warn you that a particular app will require elevation.

FIGURE 2.6   The Consent UI in another guise

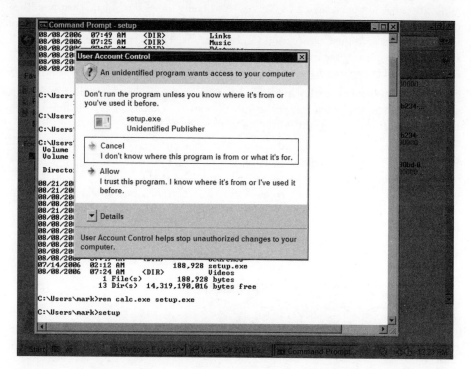

Vista's "Alertness Warnings"

First, let's look at what I call the "alertness warnings." There are actually four different dialog boxes used by the Consent UI in response to different levels of how cautious Vista thinks you should be about elevating a program, using different colors to provide more visual cues to the amount of "alertness" that Vista recommends. Inasmuch as our publisher prints this book in black and white, you can see a change in the Consent UI's dialog box, but you can't see a change in color. The Consent UI that I showed you in Figure 2.1 has a bar across the top that is teal (a blue-green). The one in Figure 2.6, in contrast, has a bar across its top that is orange. The colors work like this:

- If the program is signed and from a publisher that you've blocked via group policy, then the bar across the top of the dialog box is red, and the bar contains a red copy of the little shield icon that Microsoft's been using since XP SP2 to designate security matters. It does not offer you a "confirm" button, just an "OK."

- If the program that needs elevation is digitally signed by Microsoft as an integral part of Vista, then you'll see the Consent UI that you saw back in Figure 2.1, with a teal bar across the top and a red, green, blue, and yellow shield icon.

- If the program that needs elevation is digitally signed and the signature checks out, but the application has not been signed by Microsoft as being integral to Vista, then you'll see a dialog like the teal one, but instead of teal on the top bar you'll see gray. It has a gray shield icon and both the Confirm and Cancel buttons. This is the Consent UI dialog that you'll most commonly see from third parties and even from many things at http://www.microsoft.com/downloads.

- Otherwise, you'll see the dialog in Figure 2.6, with an orange bar across its top and a red shield icon. There aren't buttons per se, just the new-to-Vista tile-like "big buttons" that pretty much offer Confirm or Cancel, but with more verbiage.

It's probably a good idea to add "introduce users to the different Consent UI dialog boxes" to your "things to tell users when introducing Vista." And I guess it was a good idea for Microsoft to include it in Vista...I just wonder how color-blind folks will feel about it?

By the way, if you ever walk away from a Vista box when the Consent UI is raised without responding to it, then after two minutes, the Consent UI will close with a dialog box like the one in Figure 2.7.

FIGURE 2.7 UAC timed out!

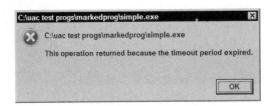

The theory behind this is a simple one. If the Consent UI is up, then whoever's logged on is an administrator. If no one's responded to the Consent UI after two minutes, then the operation is either unimportant or, more disturbing, this machine that an admin's logged into is unattended...yikes! So Microsoft basically "times out" the UAC prompt.

UAC's Clues: Will This Need Elevation?

A big part of the whole idea behind UAC, it seems, is to clarify when we do and do not have to act as administrators. As I observed earlier in the chapter, a big part of moving away from the point of view that we need to be logged in as admins all of the time stems from the fact that, well, I don't know about *you*, but I'm often not quite sure what does and doesn't require administrative permissions and privileges. For example, do I need to be an administrator in order to shut down a system? Well, the answer is "it depends." If we're talking about a workstation, then anyone can shut it down. But if we're talking about a domain controller, then you've got to be a member of any one of a few groups to be able to shut it down. Or how about being able to adjust power management settings? I'd have assumed that anyone could do that sort of thing, but the fact that Microsoft specifically reprogrammed Vista in Beta 2 to allow standard users to change power management means that my guess would have been wrong.

To help us become more "admin-aware" and, I guess, to warn standard users about what they can't do so as not to deliver unpleasant surprises, Microsoft has begun suggesting that developers add the four-color shield icon to any button or other graphic that will, if clicked, do something that will require elevation. For example, take a look at Figure 2.8.

FIGURE 2.8   The Administrative Tools folder, with and without shields

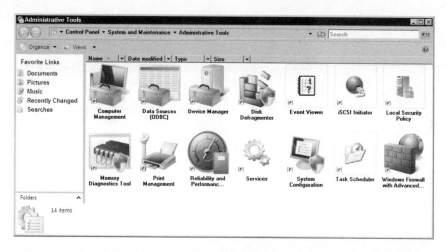

Here, I've taken the Administrative Tools folder from Control Panel and cranked up the icon size to "Large" and, in case you're wondering, there *is* an "Extra Large" in Vista. Notice that on the Disk Defragmenter, Memory Diagnostics Tool, and System Configuration icons there are smaller icons of the four-color shield superimposed on the larger icons. These are intended to be the visual cue—or warning, depending on how you see it—that Beyond This Place Standard Users May Not Go.

Now, while it's a good idea, there's no guarantee that you'll actually see a shield where there ought to be one. For example, looking at the Disk Defragmenter icon on the Start menu at All Programs ➤ Accessories ➤ System Tools shows—well, looking *very* closely shows, anyway—that the little shield icon is, indeed, still there, although I don't imagine that many will notice or even be able to see it on the small Start menu icon. Similarly, look again at Figure 2.8. Don't you need to be an administrator to mess with Windows Firewall, or Print Management, or other items in this group in order to do anything? Sure; clearly that's why it's called the "Administrative Tools" group, and in fact a quick double-click of everything there will show that each of those items causes the Consent UI to ask for elevation. But there are only shields on three of the 14 icons in this group...why? Probably because the three icons with shields point to EXE files, and the other 11 point to MMC snap-in files. You see, Vista is smart enough to sniff around a program and, if Vista guesses that it'll need elevation, then Vista adds a shield icon automatically.

You can see this by just doing the exercise that I referred to in the earlier section where I suggested copying calc.exe from a copy of any version of Windows prior to Vista to a Vista machine and then renaming `calc.exe` to "setup.exe." That causes a Vista heuristic to kick in, and Vista's Explorer will add a shield icon to the `setup.exe` file icon.

Vista *can't,* however, detect a need for elevation in an MMC snap-in. That's because Explorer doesn't directly run MMC snap-ins—MMC.EXE does. *It's* got a shield icon, but that doesn't really help much, as the curious user usually wouldn't open MMC.EXE to explore MMC snap-ins; instead, the curious user would just see icons in Control Panel and the Start menu. Perhaps that'll change in later Vista builds or later versions of Windows.

A third place where you'll see shields is in Control Panel applets. Open up Control Panel and you'll see something like Figure 2.9.

FIGURE 2.9 Opening Control Panel window

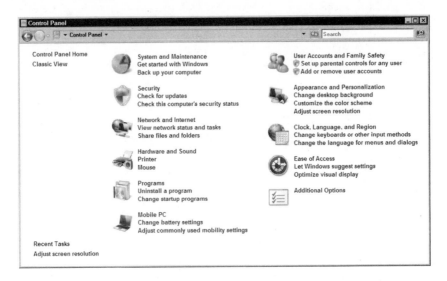

Look in the upper right-hand corner of the Control Panel window, under User Accounts and Family. You'll see two hyperlinks, "Set up parental controls," and "Add or remove user accounts." Notice that they've both got shields next to them. As far as I can see, those aren't automatic.

Summarizing, then, Vista tries to alert users to which programs require an administrator token to run by superimposing a shield icon on the icon associated with that program. That works sometimes either because Vista sensed that the icon needed it and added it, or because the developer remembered to put the shield on the program's icon. But you can't count on it being there. Nevertheless, it's a good start at making people more aware of what they do that's administrative in nature.

Vista Requests Elevation if a Manifest Requests It

Let's return to our examination of what causes Vista to request elevation and learn about the most surefire way to tell Vista that an application needs elevation. You will sometimes *really* want Vista to know that an application needs elevation because while those UAC prompts can be annoying, it's even *more* annoying when you try to run something, only to get "access denied" halfway through the process. So if we're going to use UAC, we may as well ensure that it does the right thing, and the simplest way to ensure that UAC does the right thing is to *tell it what to do*. Developers (and we admin types, once you know a few tricks) can do that with something called *manifests*.

What Manifests Are and What They Do

Manifests are small text files associated with an application that tell the operating system how to load and run that application. They can be embedded inside an executable, or they can exist as separate, external text files of the kind that you can edit with Notepad. I wouldn't claim to be a coding expert—I'm not—and so I may be explaining this incompletely, but three things that I know that various versions of Windows have done with manifests have been to

- Tell the operating system which version of a dynamic link library (DLL) the application needs,

- Tell the operating system whether or not it's okay to build the application's windows using the rounded-edged XP windows theme, and

- Tell the operating system which token an application needs: the standard user token or, if one's available, the administrator token.

The original manifests appeared in XP, which also introduced a thing called "Windows Side by Side," which was the first big user of manifests. Side By Side was supposed to alleviate the problem known as "DLL hell." But first, a little background....

When developers create programs, they tend not to put all of the program in one big file. The reason that they don't create one big file is that anyone who writes more than a couple of programs soon finds that very different programs often share the same code challenges: both word processors and games may need to print things, or sort a list, or encrypt data, to name a few possibilities. Programmers make their jobs easier by taking those often-reused program parts and putting them in what is essentially a library of programs. As these library routines might be shared by a number of programs, it'd be silly to copy and paste the library routines into every program that uses them. Instead, these libraries of useful programs live in separate files of their own called "dynamic link libraries" or DLLs. Their file extensions are usually ".DLL" as well.

To make programmer's lives easier, Microsoft packages a bunch of DLLs right in Windows. For instance, have you ever noticed that the File Open dialog box looks pretty much identical on every program that you run? That's because it'd be a pain for every single programmer to have to cook up her own File Open dialog box, and so Microsoft ships a file called "comdlg32.dll" that contains the pre-built code for a number of commonly used dialog boxes, including File Open. Lots of apps not ever written by Microsoft rely on comdlg32.dll to get anything done.

But in order to keep improving, fix bugs, and keep up with new operating systems, DLLs change. That can be a good thing, as it was for most developers when XP came around. Recall that XP introduced the notion of "themes" whereby you could have window frames with rounded edges. Microsoft built rounded-edge dialog boxes into the XP version of comdlg32.dll, with the interesting side effect that running most NT 4.0 or Windows 2000 applications under XP would give those older apps an immediate "facelift."

Not every application, however, liked the new look, and the new comdlg32.dll blew up some older apps. By default programs find their DLLs by their names, and so comdlg32.dll has been called "comdlg32.dll" since NT 3.1, if I recall right. Now, most folks thought that the rounded window edges were pretty neat, but, again, some didn't, as those rounded window edges broke some important apps, and so those folks wanted Windows to leave their window edges square—to run with the old `comdlg32.dll`, in other words.

How, the question arose, could you have two copies of `comdlg32.dll` on the same computer without one clobbering the other? The answer was "Side by Side." Suppose you've the unlucky developer of an application that didn't like XP's `comdlg32.dll` dialog box. With Side by Side, you could ship your application with the old version of `comdlg32.dll`, and either rename the DLL so it didn't try to overwrite the one shipped with XP, or you could put it in another folder; either approached worked. But now how does your app that needs the older Windows 2000 version of `comdlg32.dll` know where to find it? Answer: a manifest. When the OS sees your application needs `comdlg32.dll`, then it looks for a manifest to see *which* `comdlg32.dll` to pick up. If there's no manifest, or if the manifest is silent about `comdlg32.dll`, then the app goes to the default; if not, then it gets hooked up with the `comdlg32.dll` that it needs, the older version.

You can either embed a manifest right into an EXE (or, for that matter, a DLL) file using code development tools, or you can just write up the manifest in Notepad and save it as a simple text file. If you do that, then you tell the operating system to associate a given manifest file with a particular application by doing two things.

- First, the manifest file goes in the same directory as the EXE file.
- Second, the manifest file must be named *something*.exe.manifest, where *something* is the name of the EXE that it applies to.

So, for example, if I'd written a program called greatgame.exe and that file lived in `C:\Program Files\MarkSoft\Coolgame`, then the manifest would have to be called greatgame.exe.manifest, and it, too, would have to be located in the `C:\Program Files\MarkSoft\Coolgame` folder in order to take effect. If your app has both an embedded and an external manifest (that is, one stored in a separate text file), then Windows ignores the external manifest.

You can see also how manifests might solve problems arising from Microsoft's monthly hotfixes. Consider what would happen if you'd written an application dependent on some Windows DLL, but then Microsoft detects a security problem with the DLL and fixes it, *but* the fixed DLL breaks your code. You could tell clients to store the older version of the DLL in some directory and give them a manifest to use the old DLL, assuming that there weren't an embedded manifest in the file already. That way, they can install the patch instantly, be protected from the vulnerability when running 99 percent of their apps but still be able to run your app until you get it revised to work around the new problem. (Microsoft's Knowledge Base article 835322 discusses this.)

Over time more and more things got stuffed into manifests, but it is still Windows Side by Side that manages manifests, so any error messages relevant to manifests show up in the Application folder of Vista Event Viewer as errors whose source is "SideBySide."

Examining Manifests

Let's take a look at a working manifest. We'll examine an embedded one, the one in net.exe. But before we do that, we'll need something that lets us look at manifests; for that, we'll need something called a "resource editor." (When you embed a file inside a program, as we do when embedding manifests, they are said to be "resources.") There's a nice free one called the XN Resource

Editor that you can find at `http://www.wilsonc.demon.co.uk/d10resourceeditor.htm`. If it's not there anymore as you read this, then just Google "XN Resource Editor." (To paraphrase Heraclitus, "you cannot search the same Web twice, for links go dead and new junk is added to it all the time.")

Install the XN Resource Editor on your system and start it up. It'll look like Figure 2.10.

FIGURE 2.10   Opening screen on XN Resource Editor

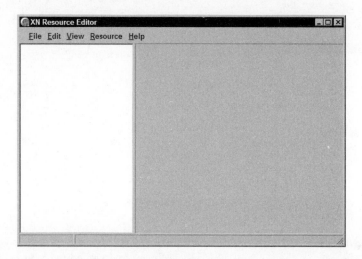

To work this, you just point it at an EXE file. It opens the EXE file and looks for any resources and, if it finds any, then it shows them as numbers "1" through however many resources are in the file. To look at net.exe, click File ➢ Open, and then in the field "File name:" fill in `c:\windows\system32\net.exe`. XN Resource Editor will then look like Figure 2.11.

FIGURE 2.11   XN Resource Editor with net.exe loaded

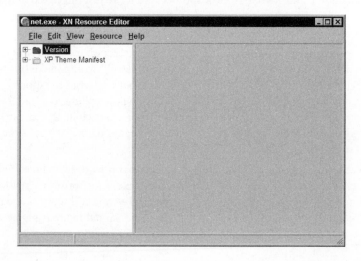

Click the plus sign to the left of "XP Theme Manifest" to reveal a folder labeled "1"—there is only one resource in net.exe—and click the plus sign next to *it* to expand the folder to reveal the manifest, as you see in Figure 2.12.

FIGURE 2.12   net.exe's manifest

The manifest is written in XML, which looks a lot like HTML. Most of it we can ignore; I want to focus on the part on the bottom, which I've reformatted and edited a bit here:

```
<requestedExecutionLevel
level="asInvoker"
uiAccess="false"
/>
```

You don't have to understand XML to follow this because we're just interested in that line:

```
level= "asInvoker"
```

Now, there *is* one thing about XML that you've got to understand: it cares about case. Changing "requestedExecutionLevel" to "requestedexecutionlevel" would make this manifest erroneous and you'd get one of those SideBySide errors that I referred to before.

That level= is the place where a developer (or an admin who's willing to do a bit of resource hacking, and you'll see how soon) can signal UAC that a particular application needs to be elevated. level=—remember, that lowercase l at the beginning is essential—can take three possible values:

- **asInvoker** means "just give me the same token as the person who started me." That works for net.exe because if all you want to do with net.exe is just browse your workgroup—which anyone can do—then you can type **net view** and it'll work fine with a standard user token. If, on the other hand, you want to do something that requires the administrator token, like creating a user account, then you need to first have an elevated command prompt running, and *then* you can issue the `net user` command, as net will inherit the token that the command prompt's already got, the administrator token.

- `highestAvailable` means "please give this process the highest token the user possesses, and if necessary please raise the Consent UI to get me that token."

- `requireAdministrator` means the same thing as "highest available," except that it adds "but if the user isn't a member of the Administrators group, then don't bother, I need an administrative token and if this guy isn't an admin, then he can't help me; just fail this application."

What's the difference between the last two? It's possible that an account may have a split token, *but* that neither token possesses administrator-level power. (It's *possible*; offhand I can't think of why that'd happen.) So to mark an EXE file as requiring an administrator-level token, then ensure that its manifest includes `level="requireAdministrator"`.

I know, there's that other parameter `uiAccess="false"` that I've not explained here. I'll get to it later, but here's the short version. There is a special class of applications that need to work *with* the Consent UI called "UI automation" applications. They use the uiAccess parameter to alert UAC to their UI automation-ness.

Adding a Manifest with a Resource Editor

Armed with this information, we could equip an older application without a resource with a UAC-aware one. In fact, there are three ways to do it.

First, we can use our resource editor to put a manifest with a `level="Administrator"` instruction right into an EXE file. Before we start, we'll need an EXE file without a manifest. If you can't find one handy, then do this:

1. Open a command prompt. (Do not elevate it.)

2. Create a folder `c:\mystuff` by typing **md c:\mystuff** and press Enter.

3. Navigate to `c:\mystuff` by typing **cd c:\mystuff** and, as always, press Enter.

4. Open up Internet Explorer and visit my website at `http://www.minasi.com/vista/vistafiles.zip`. It'll let you download a ZIP file containing files and programs that you can use to experiment with UAC, file virtualization, and Windows integrity control. Download the files to `C:\mystuff`.

5. In Explorer, navigate to `c:\mystuff`. Right-click `vistafiles.zip` and choose "Extract all..." and tell Vista to extract files to `c:\mystuff`.

6. One of the files will be a program called "simple.exe," which is the world's simplest C++ program. It's a command-line program that you run by just by typing `simple`. It prints on the screen `This is a program that just puts this text on the screen` (and yes, I'm fully aware that I do not have a future in high-tech commercial programming). When prompted where to put it, tell IE to put it in `C:\mystuff`.

7. Give it a try just to verify that it does not cause the Consent UI to pop up in its initial form.

8. Type **copy simple.exe mansimple.exe** so that we've got a copy of simple.exe around without a manifest—we'll embed a manifest into mansimple.exe.

Then follow these steps to add a manifest to simple.exe:

1. Start up XN Resource Editor.

2. Click File ➤ Open, navigate to c:\mystuff and open mansimple.exe.

   You'll notice that the pane on the left, which showed you net.exe's resources before, is completely empty now. That's because simple.exe has no resources.

3. Click Resource ➤ Add Resource.

4. In the "Add Resource" dialog that appears, choose "XP Theme Manifest" and click OK.

   On the left-hand pane, you'll see "XP Theme Manifest," "1," and "Language Neutral." On the right-hand side, you'll see some XML.

5. Mark the text in the right-hand side pane and then press Del to clean it all out.

6. Notice that in c:\mystuff\manifests is a file named "example.exe.manifest." It's the world's simplest manifest file.

7. Open it in Notepad.

8. Copy the text from Notepad to the right-hand pane of XN Resource Editor.

9. Click "XP Theme Manifest" in the left-hand pane.

10. Click File ➤ Save.

11. Exit XN Resource Editor.

When you next run mansimple.exe, it'll cause the Consent UI to pop up.

Adding an External Manifest

The second approach is even easier. Take the simple.exe.manifest file that you got from my website and copy it into the same directory as simple.exe. *If* simple.exe *does not have an embedded manifest,* then Vista will read and use that external manifest. In other words, you add an external manifest for a given program, call it example.exe like so:

- Create the manifest for example.exe. If the manifest's only purpose is to cause UAC to elevate the app, then open Notepad and just type this in:

```
<?xml version="1.0" encoding="UTF-8" standalone="yes"?>
<assembly xmlns="urn:schemas-microsoft-com:asm.v1" manifestVersion="1.0">
<assemblyIdentity version="1.0.0.0" processorArchitecture="X86"
name="Anyapp" type="win32"/>
<description>Basic manifest</description>
<trustInfo xmlns="urn:schemas-microsoft-com:asm.v3">
<security><requestedPrivileges>
<requestedExecutionLevel level="requireAdministrator"/>
</requestedPrivileges></security></trustInfo></assembly>
```

Be absolutely sure to follow the case of the commands when typing this manifest. Alternatively, simple.exe.manifest will work fine as something to copy when you need to create a manifest.

- Name the manifest file `example.exe.manifest`.
- Place the manifest file in the same folder as `example.exe`.

This manifest will now affect how Vista runs example.exe, *provided* that there is not a manifest already embedded in example.exe. You can find out if an executable file contains a manifest by examining the file with a Windows resource editor, as described earlier.

WARNING   As late as RC2, Vista did not always notice external manifests; putting a valid example.exe.manifest file in the same folder as example.exe didn't always work. *Embedded* manifests always worked, but including an external didn't always work. So here's a workaround that seems pretty reliable, using another program from `vistafiles.zip` as an example.

It can be infuriating trying to get Vista to notice that there's an external manifest for a file, at least in RC2. I seem to have found a workaround, though: create a folder and then copy both the EXE file and the manifest into that folder, then run the EXE from there. Here's a step-by-step example. Notice that one of the files extracted from vistafiles.zip is named "`show.exe`." It displays a file's contents on the screen, like the `type` command. We'll create an external manifest for that. As before, work from the unelevated command prompt in the `C:\mystuff` folder.

1. Create a folder called "test" in `c:\mystuff` by typing **md c:\mystuff\test** and press Enter.

2. Copy `show.exe` to that folder by typing **copy show.exe test** and press Enter.

3. Copy the example manifest to test, but rename it to `show.exe.manifest` by typing **copy example.exe.manifest test\show.exe.manifest** and press Enter.

4. Change to the `C:\mystuff\test` directory by typing **cd test** and press Enter.

5. Type **show** and press Enter.

6. You should see an "Open File - Security Warning" dialog asking if you really want to run `show.exe`. Click Run.

UAC should then raise the Consent UI, so we've proven that the Vista noticed the external manifest. Click Cancel and let's look at one more thing that Vista does when it detects a manifest that requests elevation. Open up Explorer and navigate to `c:\mystuff\test`. Click the Views button until you can see the icon for show.exe. Notice that Vista's given it a shield!

Embedding a Manifest with Manifest Tool

The third approach uses a command-line tool to stuff an external manifest into an EXE. (It'll even overwrite an existing one if there's one there.) It's "Manifest Tool," a command-line tool `mt.exe`. You can get it from Microsoft, although you'll have to download a lot of stuff to get it. (There are other ways to download it, but they're all fairly complicated; what I'm going to show you seems the easiest way.) Manifest Tool ships with the Windows Platform SDK. I find that it's easiest to get with Visual Studio 2005's free version, Visual Studio Express 2005. Here's how to get the free version.

1. Open your Web browser and surf to `http://msdn.microsoft.com/vstudio/express/`, which is the home page for Visual Studio Express. If that URL doesn't work—there is someone at Microsoft whose job is apparently to rearrange their website every week or so—then Google "download visual studio express" and you'll find a link to wherever Microsoft's got Visual Studio Express 2005 that week.

2. You have several choices of versions of Visual Studio 2005: a Web developer edition, one for Visual C++, one for Visual Basic, and one for Visual C#.

> If you're not a coder, "C#" may not have an obvious pronunciation; as a would-be successor to C++, Microsoft opted to use the octothorpe (#) symbol, which kind of looks like two plus signs engaged in unnatural acts. If you're musically inclined then you may know that the music world uses the octothorpe to designate a sharped note, which explains why that particular variety of C is said "C sharp." This falls in the category of "programmer humor."

3. I found that "Visual C# 2005 Express Edition" did not deliver `mt.exe`, but "Visual C++ 2005 Express Edition," did, so let's go with that one in our quest for the Manifest Tool.

4. Under the hyperlink for "Visual C++ 2005 Express Edition," which is under the heading "For Windows Development" in the middle of the page, click the Download hyperlink.

5. That'll bring you to another page, which will instruct you first to remove any previous versions of various things, and then offers a Download link. Click that.

6. At the "File Download - Security Warning," click the Run button.

7. If you're doing this on a Vista system, then you'll get a UAC confirmation box; confirm that you do indeed wish to run the setup program by clicking Continue. (Notice that the banner is gray because while it's signed and even from Microsoft, it's not an essential part of Vista.)

8. You'll finally come to a Setup wizard. Click Next to go to the next page.

9. Accept the "License Agreement." (I guess they capitalize it so that you know that they mean *business*, buster, so you'd better not go around redistributing their program which is, ummm…free.) Click Next.

10. The next Installations Option page will offer to download even more stuff to your computer. Leave the SDK and SQL boxes unchecked and click Next.

11. Check that you're fine with the destination folder and click Install. That'll kick off the actual download of Visual Studio C++ 2005 Express Edition, which is about 35 MB.

12. Once the download's done, click Exit and close the Web page that you downloaded Visual C++ from.

If you let the installation wizard put the files where it wanted to by default, then you will now find mt.exe in C:\Program Files\Microsoft Visual Studio 8\VC\Bin on a 32-bit version of Vista, or, on a 64-bit version, you'll find it at `C:\Program Files (x86)\Microsoft Visual Studio 8\VC\Bin`. Copy that somewhere and you've got your Manifest Tool. If you want to recover that disk space that Visual Studio burned up, just uninstall all of the Visual Studio components. (Why you can't just download mt.exe is a puzzle to me.)

You can now tell `mt.exe` to insert a manifest file into an existing EXE file with this command:

```
mt /manifest NAMEOFMANIFEST /outputresource:EXEFILENAME;#1
```

For example, you could embed simple.exe.manifest into simple.exe like so:

1. Ensure that `mt.exe`, `example.exe.manifest` and `simple.exe` are all in c:\mystuff.

2. If you don't have a command prompt open, open one and navigate to c:\mystuff.

3. The files in `vistafile.zip` all get a "read only" attribute, so let's get rid of that by typing **attrib -r *** and pressing Enter.

4. Copy simple.exe before we manifest it, so we've got a manifest-less simple program to play with later by typing **copy simple.exe nomanifest.exe**.

manifest example.exe.manifest /outputresource:simple.exe;#1.

command should be typed as all one line. Notice that mt's syntax is a bit irregular, here's just a space between /manifest and simple.exe.manifest, but there's no space between /outputresource: and simple.exe;#1—that wasn't a mistake, that *is* the syntax.

we embedded the manifest into simple.exe, then you'll always get the Consent UI run it, regardless of whether or not simple.exe.manifest is in the same directory .exe; as a matter of fact, now that simple.exe has an embedded manifest, then Vista will ignore any external manifests.

Embedding Manifests Can Break Digital Signing

Now that you've seen two ways to embed a manifest in an existing EXE file, *should* you? Not always. Embedding a manifest changes the content of the EXE, and that renders any existing digital signatures invalid. Not everyone understands exactly what's happening with signed program files, so here's a quick review.

When Windows starts up a driver, program, or whatever, it identifies that executable by its file name. But what if a piece of malware infested your operating system by erasing some important piece of Windows code like, say, RPCSS.DLL and replacing it with itself? As Windows starts up RPCSS.DLL (the thing that provides Remote Procedure Call, the thing that lets, among other things, Outlook talk to Exchange) automatically, that'd be a great way for a piece of malware to ensure that it got started up every time you started the computer.

To combat that, many operating systems use *digital signing* to allow developers to prove cryptographically which developer created a piece of code. Here's how it works.

A developer finishes work on a particular program, whether it be an EXE, DLL, driver file, or whatever. (Let's say for this example that it's an EXE file.) He then uses a cryptographic function that takes megabytes and megabytes of data and boils it down to a single unique 128-bit key. (Most code signing approaches that I've seen either employ MD5 or SHA-1, two popular hashing algorithms.)

The basic idea at this point is that you can verify that it is indeed the program that he wrote whenever you'd like. You just take the EXE file and use it to create an MD5 or SHA-1 hash from that file. Then compare it to the hash that the developer says he computed. If they're the same, then you can feel pretty sure that the copy of the EXE that you've got is identical to the one that the developer created—so it wasn't damaged in transmission and, more important, you don't have a copy that someone infected with some kind of malware. And I said "pretty sure" rather than "completely sure" because there is a tiny, tiny, minuscule chance that someone modified that EXE file but the modified file generated the same hash as the unchanged one, but that's a pretty long shot.

Well, that's the idea behind signing, but you can probably see the flaw here. Who wants to have to go download a hash value from a developer, then compute a hash for the downloaded EXE, and compare them? Sounds like too much work and, even then, someone might have successfully spoofed the developer's website, and you'd be getting some kind of bad data— either a bum EXE or a bum hash, or both—anyway. So we add a few steps to the process.

First, the developer goes to a digital certificate vendor like VeriSign and buys a kind of certificate called a "code signing certificate." He asks his computer to generate a public/private key pair and sends that along to VeriSign. VeriSign checks him out and verifies that he is who he claims to be, collects a few hundred bucks (repayable annually to VeriSign) and generates a certificate for him with his public key embedded in that certificate. Now, when he computes the hash on an EXE, he can take that hash value and encrypt it, using his private key. He then embeds the encrypted hash and the certificate the VeriSign created for him into his EXE...and now things can get automatic.

When you get a gray or teal banner on a Consent UI, it means that Vista looked at the EXE that seems to need elevating and saw the certificate and encrypted hash. (If there wasn't one, then you get the orange-banner Consent UI.) Vista computes a hash based on all of the EXE file except for the certificate/encrypted hash combination. Then it uses the public key embedded in the certificate to decrypt the hash that Vista found in the EXE. If the computed hash and the newly decrypted hash match, the EXE has been properly signed. If so, then the Consent UI offers a gray or teal banner. If not, it's orange-banner time.

Digital signing is not a panacea. Signed code could still offer a couple of problems. First, digital signing is not a guarantee of high-quality code. Lots of code signed by Microsoft and other large vendors has horrendous bugs. But at least you know for sure who wrote the code, and so you can be reasonably sure if it's a firm like Microsoft, IBM, Adobe, or whomever that they didn't deliver you malware on purpose! Further, digital signing is not a guarantee that there is no malware in the code. If the coder built his application on a system that was infected with some kind of malware, then the malware might have infected his newly built application as well. But, again, you can feel pretty certain that it wasn't his *intent* to send you infected stuff. But that's not necessarily so, as VeriSign doesn't check out a person to see if he or she has created malware in the past or has a criminal record before issuing him or her a code signing certificate.

There are two great strengths to digital code signing. First, you know with a very, very high degree of certainty who released the code. (Not a certainty because a vendor could have its code signing certificate keys stolen.) That's important because while it's entirely possible that a bad person might take the time to write some bad software, get a certificate, sign the software, and give it away, he'll only get away with it once. (And perhaps not even then, as the authorities may be able to locate and apprehend him based on information he had to provide to get the certificate.) From that point on, he'd have a reputation as a criminal and the prospect of convincing someone to install software signed by him would be nil. Second, and more important, the operating system can use code signatures to verify that the files containing vital operating system components haven't been modified since they were created. This is a big advance in security in the Vista world, as Vista checks the code signatures on every low-level piece of software every time it boots. (You'll read more about that in a later chapter.)

Well, that was a fairly long (but, I hope for some, valuable) side trip, but here was the point of it. As an embedded manifest is part of an EXE, modifying it with a resource editor would have the same effect as infecting that EXE with a piece of malware: it would cause the digital signature to fail. Once that happens, the "Digital Signatures" tab goes away, and the program would not pass a signature verification.

What would that mean in practice? Well, remember that the reason we'd consider adding a manifest to an EXE would be so that operating system would know to request elevation whenever someone ran that EXE. Such an EXE is likely not to have either a digital signature or a manifest in the first place, and so has nothing to lose by getting a manifest. (Certainly none of my small example programs are signed.) Still, keep that in mind before *manifesting* your desire for automatic elevation requests!

Creating signed programs is a bit more work, but in the long run we'll probably see all new applications signed. At that point, you may consider enabling the group policy setting "User Account Control: Only elevate executables that are signed and validated." I'll discuss that in more detail in the later section "Reconfiguring User Account Control."

The Program Compatibility Assistant Tells UAC to Elevate

You read earlier that UAC uses heuristics like words in a program's name, or telltales that a program was generated by popular installer makers, and when it sees those heuristics then it assumes that it's dealing not just with any old application—it's working with a Setup program. But Vista takes things a bit further to ensure compatibility. It reasons that if that *was* a Setup program of some kind, then there must be a record of the program's having installed something, the kinds of traces left behind that allow you to use the Control Panel's Add/Remove Programs to see what programs have been installed, and, further, how to remove them. If Vista doesn't think that it ran correctly, then it raises a dialog box called the "Program Compatibility Assistant" that basically says "hey, did everything come out all right here, or should we try it another way next time?," as you see in Figure 2.13.

FIGURE 2.13 The Program Compatibility Assistant

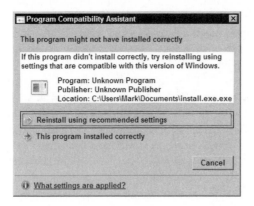

What exactly will happen if you click "Reinstall using recommended settings?" To see, look back at Figure 2.5. That's the "Compatibility" tab that you'll find on pretty much any EXE that hasn't been specially marked as an essential Vista program—that is, any program that wouldn't get a teal bar across the top of its Consent UI. It lets you quickly and easily solve a number of the most common solutions to "hey, this program ran fine on Windows 95/Windows ME/XP/ whatever and it won't run under Vista." For example, since the dawn of computing, there's always been applications hard-coded to only run on, say, Windows 95, even though they'll run just fine on Vista. The "Compatibility" tab includes a drop-down list box labeled "Run this pro-gram in compatibility mode for," and offers Windows 95, 98, Me, NT 4.0, Windows 2000, XP SP2, or Windows Server 2003 SP1; checking the box and choosing "Windows 95" would make that hypothetical I-require-95 application to run fine on Vista. The Compatibility tab will also let you tell your Vista Desktop to simplify both the screen and the way that it refreshes the screen, as you can check boxes to hold Vista to 256 colors, 640 × 480 screens, rescaling and desktop composition (that thing that lets Vista allow you to drag windows all over your Desktop without leaving those "skid marks" behind), or disable visual themes altogether. If some of that sounds familiar, it should: XP also had a "Compatibility" tab, although it offered fewer options.

> You actually have many more options in terms of compatibility fixes, hun-dreds in fact that you can explore with the Application Compatibility Toolkit (ACT). ACT's a much bigger story than can fit here, though, so the Compati-bility tab is basically "ACT lite."

When the Program Compatibility Assistant thinks that an attempt at installing a program fails, it will make some educated guesses about what setting it might make on the Compati-bility tab. Then it'll rerun the setup program with its guesses; that's what happens if you click "Reinstall using recommended settings."

The Program Compatibility Assistant could become sort of annoying if it popped up every time that you ran a given program, so it's designed to remember what applications it has already examined and to ignore them from that point on. It keeps its list of applications that it has examined in HKEY_CURRENT_USER\Software\Microsoft\Windows NT\CurrentVersion\ AppCompatFlags\Compatibility Assistant\Persisted. In that key, it creates an REG_ DWORD entry for every application that it has examined in the past, setting the entry name equal to the full path of the application's EXE file, and sets that entry to 1. If the Program Compatibility Assistant ends up also checking some of the options on the Compatibility tab for that application, then they're stored nearby in HKEY_CURRENT_USER\Software\Microsoft\ Windows NT\CurrentVersion\AppCompatFlags\Layers. Once again, it creates a separate entry for every application (although this time it's a REG_SZ rather than a REG_DWORD), with that entry's name equal to the full path name of the application's EXE file. In the value, it fills in the names of the compatibility modes applied. For example, if it decided to select the XP SP2 compatibility mode, then the phrase "WINXPSP2" appears in that Registry entry. In addition to those Registry settings, I've found that there's a key corresponding to the Layers key, but in HKEY_LOCAL_MACHINE rather than HKEY_CURRENT_USER.

I know, that was a lot of yackety-yack and, God willing, you won't have to deal with the Program Compatibility Assistant. But if you'd like to see it just once in action to see the dialog box and verify what goes in the Registry, try this.

1. Open a command prompt and navigate to c:\mystuff.

2. We'll need a copy of simple.exe without the manifest to play with, so type **copy nomanifest.exe installer.exe**. As you see, we're creating a simple program that will raise UAC's hackles and cause it to raise the Consent UI.

3. Type **installer**.

4. UAC, true to form, will raise the orange Consent UI dialog box. Click "Allow/ I trust this program..." and the c:\mystuff prompt will appear after another command prompt window—one with elevated privilege—will briefly appear and disappear.

5. In a few seconds, the Program Compatibility Assistant dialog will appear. Click either option, it doesn't matter as we're not really installing anything.

6. Next, verify that the Assistant does indeed remember which programs it has tried to help in the past. Type **installer** and you'll still get the Consent UI, that's expected, but afterward you will not get the Assistant. Now take a peek in the Registry at HKEY_CURRENT_ USER\Software\Microsoft\Windows NT\CurrentVersion\AppCompatFlags\ Compatibility Assistant\Persisted and you'll see something like Figure 2.14.

7. Delete that entry, then go to HKEY_LOCAL_MACHINE\Software\Microsoft\Windows NT\CurrentVersion\AppCompatFlags\Layers, where you'll find an entry for installer.exe and a REG_SZ value of "WINXPSP2," which seems to be the catch-all value when the Assistant knows that *something* happened, but it's not sure *what*. Delete this entry too.

8. Close Regedit.

9. Once more, run installer.exe, let UAC elevate it, and you'll see the Assistant return.

FIGURE 2.14 Half of the places where the Assistant remembers applications

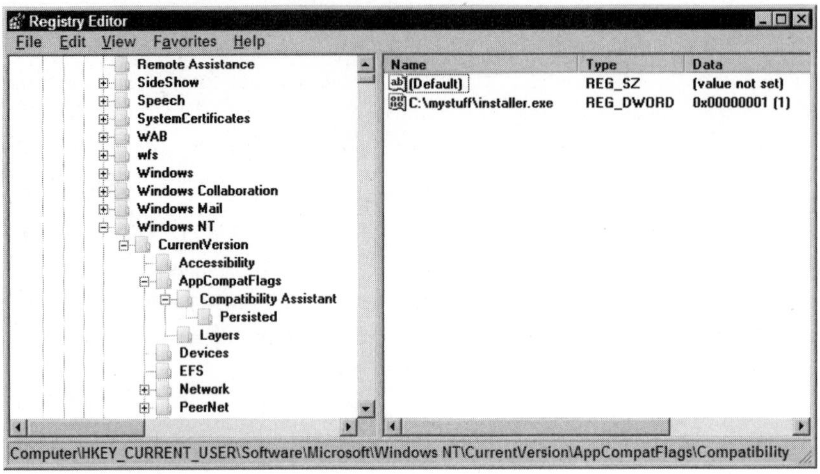

That's how the Program Compatibility Assistant works, except for one thing: I said that it could cause UAC to request elevation on a program, but we didn't see that; when might it happen? Well, as you've seen, it isn't the Program Compatibility Assistant's job to tell UAC to request elevation, but it *is* the Assistant's job to analyze what it thinks are troubled programs and adjust the settings in the Compatibility tab as necessary. In some cases, I am told—I've honestly not seen it, but then I've only had time to run a few dozen pre-Vista programs on Vista—that the Assistant may check the "Run this program as an administrator" box. In that case, you'd see an elevation prompt every time that you ran that program from that time on. Notice, however, that the Assistant is very specific in its help. If you had a separate but identical copy of installer.exe in another folder, then the first time that you ran that copy, the Program Compatibility Assistant would have no memory of the fact that it's already seen and analyzed this program, but in a different directory. In contrast, adding a manifest to a file that requests elevation will work no matter what folders you copy or move that file to.

Don't confuse the Program Compatibility Assistant with the Program Compatibility Wizard. The Wizard is the icon that appears on the left-hand side of your desktop the first time that you start up Vista. The Program Compatibility Wizard is basically a wizard that you point at any program. Once you do that, the Program Compatibility Wizard basically asks you a few questions and then automatically checks boxes in the Compatibility tab for that program. Not very impressive, you say? I agree, and wish that it didn't clutter the desktop when just about anybody can right-click a program and bring up the Compatibility tab.

Application Compatibility Toolkit "Shims" Tell UAC to Elevate

The final thing that might lead to Vista's requesting to elevate a process is something called a "shim" created by something called the Application Compatibility Toolkit. You just read about the Program Compatibility Assistant, which is basically a process that pops up under certain circumstances and follows a set of rules to modify the Compatibility tab on EXE files for programs that are having Vista compatibility problems.

Now, it's nice that choosing, say, "XP SP2 compatibility mode" and "Run as administrator" on a given program's Compatibility tab can take a pre-Vista program and make it useful under Vista—great, in fact, given that I sometimes use programs that I don't trust but that I'd prefer not to have to upgrade because while the current version is a pain, at least it's a pain that I'm sure runs well enough for my needs. (Like, say, Quicken.) But suppose I need to deploy those settings to 1,200 computers or, further, what if I need fixes for more than the handful of compatibility solutions offered by the Compatibility tab?

Then you're in the market for the Application Compatibility Toolkit. The Application Compatibility Toolkit is a set of programs that apply what are sort of "online fixes" to programs with compatibility problems, fixes that make Vista happy *and* the old program happy. What I've called an "online fix" is officially called a "shim." The Application Compatibility Toolkit's shims are different from the Compatibility tab's shims in that you can create a package of necessary shims for any application and deliver that package of shims from a central location with group policies. Additionally, where the Compatibility tab has about a dozen possible fixes, the Application Compatibility Toolkit had over 210 the last time that I looked at it, although in truth many of them are now irrelevant because some of those features now live in Vista and kick in automatically.

The Application Compatibility Toolkit creates databases of fixes, and you can recognize them by their .SDB ("System DataBase") file extensions. For example, you'll find a big one called sysmain.sdb that ships with every copy of Vista. By default, Windows stores SDB files in \Windows\AppPatch. There are no tools built into Vista that will let you look at that database, and I wonder if they're very serious about supporting ACT on a 64-bit platform, given that the Vista-specific ACT 5.0 will not run on 64-bit Vista. But, if you're running a 32-bit version of Vista, then you can download the current version of the Application Compatibility Toolkit from Microsoft and take a peek at sysmain.sdb. I am not exaggerating when I say that there are literally thousands of applications in that database, and I would bet every cent that I have that you've never even heard of a tenth of them...so I can't, in any practical sense, tell you which applications sysmain.sdb will cause UAC to request elevation for. The Application Compatibility Toolkit is a separate download from Microsoft, and it's a big, big topic—too much to take on in this chapter.

Reconfiguring User Account Control

We've been looking at how UAC examines and reacts to applications, and we've looked at how you can reconfigure applications to control how UAC reacts to them. Now let's look at reconfiguring UAC itself.

Unlike far too many Windows technologies, UAC does a nice job of giving you control over it in group policies. There's a nice panoply of options for UAC control there, but little in the GUI and command line, which isn't optimal but, if I had to choose between GUI control, command-line commands or group policy settings, I'd take the group policy settings, mostly because I have a sneaking suspicion that User Account Control's the kind of thing that enterprises are going to want to control centrally.

All User Account Control-specific group policy settings are in group policies under Computer Configuration / Windows Settings / Local Policies / Security Options. They're all prefixed with "User Account Control:," and there are nine settings that let you loosen or tighten UAC in various degrees.

Turning UAC On, Off, or in Overdrive

The first question everyone always asks about UAC is "how do I turn it off?" Well, I *hope* I've convinced you to give UAC a serious try, but if you can't live with it, then the place to turn it off or, as you'll see, crank it up is "User Account Control: Behavior of the elevation prompt for administrators in Admin Approval Mode." It takes three possible options:

- No prompt
- Prompt for credentials, and
- Prompt for consent, which is the default value.

"No prompt" means "when you need to check with the administrator to see if a requested elevation should happen, then don't bother the administrator—just elevate the process." Not "bothering" the administrator, of course, is the almost the same thing as not running User Account Control (I'll explain the minor differences in a minute), and in fact if you enable "No prompt" for this setting then a balloon will appear suggesting that you "Check your User Account Control settings; User Account Control is disabled."

"Prompt for consent" leaves UAC in its out-of-the-box configuration. When an administrator running under Administrator Approval Mode runs an application that requests elevation to use the administrator's administrator token, then that administrator gets one of four possible Consent UI dialog boxes, as we've seen, and in most cases he'll get the chance to give UAC the yea-or-nay about allowing the elevation. But if you want even *more* interaction by the admin when asked whether or not UAC can elevate a process, then you can choose... "Prompt for credentials," which takes consent a step further by asking an administrator not just whether he consents or not but goes beyond that, as you see in Figure 2.15.

That's the orange Consent UI screen, except that, as you've probably noticed, it isn't asking the same questions that it did before; now, it just wants me to punch in my password and click OK to consent to elevating the application. Do you need to crank up the Consent UI so that it requires entering a password rather than just clicking "Confirm" or the equivalent? Probably not, but I could imagine a scenario where your administrators were a little sloppy about locking their workstations before walking away from those workstations. Speaking sternly to the admins about this behavior and, if the behavior didn't change, then assisting them in finding new lines of work might be the best answer, but if that's not possible then making any elevation impossible without a human sitting at the system typing in an administrator's password would ameliorate the problem. Or you might just plain work in a place with an obsession for security. (Personally, I'm guessing that Microsoft added this option to make some large aerospace company happy. Probably one that's physically situated near them in the Seattle area. One that does a lot of defense contracting. It's just a guess, of course.)

FIGURE 2.15   A somewhat more demanding Consent UI

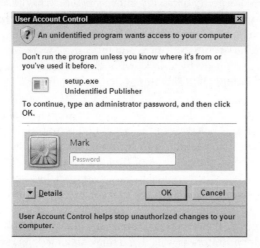

You just never know how quickly a group policy setting will take effect, so I tested them all to see what you've got to do to make them happen. When I modified the local Group Policy Object on my Vista machines, the new setting took effect as soon as I clicked OK; no reboots or `gpupdate /force` necessary.

 Now, I know I've said that this is the on/off switch for UAC, but that's not 100 percent correct. This has the effect of nearly eliminating UAC, but not entirely. There is a different setting, "User Account Control: Run all administrators in Admin Approval Mode," and will discuss it later, but not immediately, because I can't explain the subtle differences between that setting and this "User Account Control: Behavior of the elevation prompt for administrators in Admin Approval Mode" setting until we've seen some of the other settings.

Configuring UAC Junior: UAC for the User

With all of this talk about how User Account Control affects the *administrator*, I've inadvertently overlooked what may be UAC's most convenient aspect. Thus far, you've seen UAC in it's sort of "cranky" mode, the "are you sure?" mode. But now meet its friendlier part.

Suppose you're doing what I suggested in the beginning of the chapter by following that old security practice of spending most of your day logged on as a user account with only standard user powers. But now you want to do something that requires administrative powers. You can usually just right-click whatever icon you're going to run and choose Run as administrator, but with UAC, you needn't. If you do many things—not all, but many—that require powers beyond your account's and you try an administrative action, then in most cases you'll get a dialog box allowing you to type in the name and password of an administrative account, saving you the step of doing Run As. It looks pretty much the same as Figure 2.15 did.

As I said, not everything's smart enough to raise the Consent UI to give you the chance to punch in some admin credentials, but a lot of things do. Most EXE files that need privilege will cause UAC to prompt for credentials, and of course "Run as administrator" works in a pinch. Browse around the Control Panel and you'll see hyperlinks with the shields, as before, and double-clicking one of them gets the prompt. The only things that are troublesome are the MMC snap-ins.

In any case, if you *don't* want UAC to behave this way, then there's a group policy to make it stop. The setting "User Account Control: Behavior of the elevation prompt for standard users." Like the previous setting, it offers "No prompt" and "Prompt for credentials," but not "Prompt for consent." By default UAC sets this to "Prompt for credentials." But "No prompt," which meant "skip most of UAC" when applied to administrators, has a completely different meaning here: "No prompt" means "don't ask the user for admin credentials; just refuse the request."

I'm not sure why you'd do that, although I'm certain that someone will find it useful. The default setting is actually of value to administrators as well, if you think about it. Suppose you're standing over a user's shoulder trying to troubleshoot a problem that she's having and you need to do something that requires elevation. It's quite convenient to think that you needn't have her log off so that you can log with an administrative account—just do click whatever icon you need and chances are good that you'll just get a prompt for username and password. And you can even fix those pesky MMCs, if you need to: just find MMC.EXE in System32, right-click it and choose "Run as administrator" and you'll then have a privileged MMC. Just add whatever components you need and, as the snap-ins will run within the MMC, they'll inherit its administrative token.

Like its sibling setting, this setting takes effect immediately. No reboots or logoffs necessary although, of course, you've got to do a bit of jiggery-pokery to change the setting while logged in as a standard user!

Side Point: How "Administrator-ish" Must You Be to Get UACed?

That previous section reminds me that I've been oversimplifying just a bit, so let me back up and fill in a little. I've sort of been painting a picture of a world with users who have only two sets of credentials: those with a full-power administrator token, and those with restricted "standard user" tokens, and I've said that UAC splits the token for any user with administrative powers.

But let's ask: how many "administrator powers" are enough to get UAC's attention? A standard user doesn't get a split token, and a member of the Administrators group definitely gets one. But what if I were a standard user who had been granted just one extra privilege, something like the power to change a workstation's time. Would *that* constitute enough power to cause me to get a split token whenever I logged in? Here are the details needed to answer the question.

Building on some things that I explained earlier, UAC wakes up and decides to split a user's token if it finds that *any* of these things are true:

- You are a member of any of the Fearsome Four local groups (Administrators, Backup Users, Power Users, or Network Configuration Operators), or

- You have any of the Notorious Nine privileges that UAC forbids.

So, for example, let's suppose that I create a user called LPA ("low-power administrator") who is not a member of any of the Fearsome Four groups but has just *one* privilege above that of a standard user—she might, for example, have the privilege to restore files and directories, and that would be the *only* above-standard user privilege that she enjoyed. In that case, whenever she logged on, UAC would create two tokens for her: her "standard user token" that includes the five user privileges, all of her group memberships, and a "medium integrity level" token. She would have an "administrator" token that she could access by right-clicking any program and choosing "Run as administrator," at which point she would get an administrator token that differed from her standard user token in just two ways: it would have the Restore permission and a "high integrity level" token.

But what if she needed to do something that required a real honest-to-God full-power administrator? UAC knows of that possibility and so does something interesting whenever she right-clicks a program and chooses "Run as administrator." Instead of just offering her the "Confirm" button on the Consent UI, UAC offers her the choice of running as her elevated self, or some other account that can do everything that a local administrator can do.

Excluding the Built-in Administrator

To be honest, I sometimes find UAC's prompts a bit intrusive and I wish I could just say to Windows, "hey, make all of the other admins do that UAC stuff; honestly, I don't need it, so don't bother with the elevation prompts." In other words, I want the *first* group policy setting that we looked at here, but I want it to be *user specific*. (After all, I'm in good company. Wasn't it Augustine who, in his raucous youth, prayed to the heavens above and asked something along the lines of "please, take away my bad habits and show me the right way…but not just yet, okay?" And yes, I know, that's not an exact quote.)

Well, UAC answered my prayers but, as is so often the case, sometimes they don't get answered quite the way we expect. There's a group policy setting "User Account Control: Admin Approval Mode for the Built-in Administrator account" which can be either enabled or disabled, and it's enabled by default. Basically this setting is a "Get out of UAC free" card for the Administrator account, and just the Administrator account—this card is *not* transferable.

By default the Administrator account never sees User Account Control prompts, which makes that account a bit troublesome—as it's always been—but that's tempered by the fact that, as we covered in the first chapter, the built-in Administrator account is disabled in Vista by default.

Telling UAC to Skip the Heuristics

We saw earlier that UAC's got an interesting feature whereby whenever you run a program and do not request elevation, UAC tries to sense whether or not the program is actually a program that installs another program. As installing programs often requires actions that will fail without elevation and that'd be annoying, UAC tries to avoid that by guessing whether or not any of the EXEs that you run are actually setup programs. Recall that it can recognize installers created with the Wyse and Installshield products, and guesses that any programs with "instal," "setu," or "update" in their names are setup programs.

If for some reason you don't want Vista to do that EXE examining, then you can tell it to skip the setup heuristics with the setting "User Account Control: Detect application installations and prompt for elevations." It's enabled by default, but can be disabled if you like. Unlike most of the other UAC-related settings, this one requires a reboot to take effect.

Controlling Secure Desktop

If you've actually seen the Consent UI in action, then you may have noticed that in addition to putting a dialog box on the screen, UAC grays out the rest of the screen. Furthermore, you can't interact with anything else on your now-grayed-out desktop. Things still go on underneath the gray, but you can't see anything change on the desktop. For example, if you were running a video on the desktop and decided to look at your local group policy settings by clicking Start ≻ All Programs ≻ Run and then filling in gpedit.msc and clicking OK, then you'd see the desktop gray out, the Consent UI appear, and the video freeze. But if you wait a few seconds before clicking Confirm, then you'll see the gray disappear from the screen and the video will begin moving again—but you'll have missed some of it. Clearly it was playing; you just couldn't see it while the desktop was gray.

Understanding the Secure Desktop

So what's with the desktop going gray? It's called the "Secure Desktop." It's a feature of Vista that User Account Control and at least one other Vista app, CardSafe (an online identification system), use to, as the name suggests, secure some sort of interaction on the Desktop.

The key to understanding Secure Desktop's whole purpose is in analyzing an important question about UAC: how could a bad guy compromise it? How could an imaginary future piece of malware get around UAC and either fool you into clicking "Confirm" when you intended "Cancel," or just click the button *itself*?

Well, a piece of malware built with Vista and UAC in mind knows full well that when it'll need to be elevated before it can do any damage. So it would have to kick off an EXE and request elevation, and the user will have to click "Continue" or a similar button. So suppose our malware waits for the Consent UI to appear, and then creates an image of your desktop and the Consent UI that's been modified just enough to cause you to click what you think is the "Cancel" button but is actually the "Continue" button.

Or recall that it's possible to replace the mouse pointer with a different, custom pointer, like the ones that ship with Windows itself. Thus, it is quite possible (if generally useless) to create a custom mouse pointer that shows the pointer 40 pixels to the left of the actual place that the mouse is pointing to. If you actually *wanted* a mouse pointer like this, then you'd have to get used to pointing not exactly *at* the button that you wanted to click, but instead to position the mouse about 40 pixels—not an easy distance to estimate—to the right of where you wanted to click! As I said, not very useful for *you*. A piece of malware, however, might anticipate that it was going to do something that would cause the Consent UI to raise, and that you'd wisely click the "Cancel" button when that happened, because you hadn't done anything that made you expect to see the Consent UI. So the malware silently installs a custom mouse pointer like the one that I've just described, and, let's just say that the Cancel button is 40 pixels to the right of the Continue button. You *think* you're clicking the Cancel button...but you're really clicking the Continue button.

The weak link in both cases was the human-to-computer interface; it's too easy under the standard Windows desktop for a bad guy to fool you and me into doing things that we don't want to do. So what's the answer? Well, Microsoft could remove the possibilities for custom mouse cursors, greatly restrict what sort of graphics an application could show on the screen, and a bunch of other new changes that would (1) render an awful lot of applications—like nearly every game I can think of—unusable on Vista, and (2) make the range of "look and feel" possible in the Windows world a lot smaller, making Windows a much less-attractive platform for development. Clearly that's a bad idea, so they came up with the Secure Desktop. When it's running, it'll only show just one program window at a time, and the things that program can do *are* very, very restricted. (Sorry, game designers: no Secure Desktop implementations of Tetris. Bummer.) For the few moments that Secure Desktop is up, you actually *have* that limited Windows that I just described. In fact, the only applications that can run atop the Secure Desktop are ones digitally signed to be part of Vista itself, like consent.exe, the program that pops up the various Consent UI. No malware's going to be signed with the "intrinsic part of Vista" cert and, if a piece of malware *is* signed with that cert, then at least we'll know who wrote it...Microsoft.

Disabling Secure Desktop

Thus, when UAC asks for elevation, two things happen. First, Vista raises the Secure Desktop, and then it raises the Consent UI dialog boxes. Those *are* two different operations and, if you want, you can turn off the first operation. Skipping the Secure Desktop means that in theory you could be fooled by some piece of malware into agreeing to install it, which seems like a bad idea.

But who knows, you might have some application that breaks whenever the Secure Desktop runs, and that app needs to run continuously on your system. (I'll talk about a class of those apps in the next section.) In that case, you might either fix or upgrade the app, or tell UAC not to raise the Secure Desktop. You do that with the group policy setting "User Account Control: Switch to the secure desktop when prompting for elevation," which can be set to either "enabled" or "disabled" and is enabled by default. I found it useful for one reason: to get screen captures of the Consent UI, because otherwise the Secure Desktop kept me from using a screen capture program to grab the screen. (That was to be expected; otherwise, Secure Desktop would have failed in its mission.) This setting takes effect immediately when changed in gpedit.msc. If you choose this option, then it doesn't affect other things that use Secure Desktop, like CardSafe.

Enabling Applications with Secure Desktop

You just read that Secure Desktop, when working with the Consent UI, ensures that Vista knows that it got an answer to its question "elevate or not?" by temporarily converting Vista's rich range of programming possibilities into a very narrow focus: click with the mouse or choose a hotkey on the keyboard. Like a browbeating lawyer cross-examining a witness in a movie, Vista says, "all I wanna hear out of you is a mouse click or a keystroke, and it had better be fast, because you've got two minutes!"

But there are situations where that's just not going to work: accessibility technologies. Vista comes with some of them, like its On-Screen Keyboard and its Narrator screen reading software...so clearly Secure Desktop's got to be able to accommodate alternative input methods. They are generically known as "UI automation tools."

Some, like On-Screen Keyboard and Narrator, are part of Windows and so are signed, and signed by a vendor that Microsoft trusts—Microsoft, that is. So Secure Desktop's notion of "what's an acceptable form of input and output?" will extend to Narrator and On-Screen Keyboard. But what about if some third party comes up an extremely reliable voice input system, or a mouth stick for people unable to move their bodies below the neck, or one of my dearest wishes, something that would let me just *think* at the computer—how would something from a third party connect in a secure way with Secure Desktop?

UI automation tools must do three things in order to work with Secure Desktop. First, they've got to warn UAC that they need access to the Secure Desktop user interface. They do that with a parameter in their manifests. You may recall that we can embed a manifest into any EXE file to alert UAC to the fact that the EXE needs to be elevated, and that the portion of the manifest that lets you mark an EXE's UAC needs looked like this:

```
<requestedExecutionLevel
level="asInvoker"
uiAccess="false"
/>
```

At the time, I explained what the `level=` `"asInvoker"` referred to, but skipped `uiAccess="false"` so I can amend that now. *This* is where the creator of an application that is a UI access application—that is, one that does some sort of input/output *and* that needs to do it atop the Secure Desktop—alerts Vista to that fact. Marking a manifest with `uiAccess="true"` is the syntax that accomplishes that.

The second thing a UI automation developer must do is to sign their code and get it approved by Microsoft. As I mentioned in Chapter 1, other vendors can have their signed drivers cross-signed by Microsoft as part of Microsoft's Windows Hardware Quality Testing Labs program after meeting some criteria and paying Microsoft some money.

Finally, once a vendor marks its code `uiAccess="true"`, then signs its code signed and gets it cross-signed by Microsoft, it's got a third criterion to fulfill in order for its UI automation tool to avoid rejection by Secure Desktop. All of the UI automation code must be stored in a small set of folders that Microsoft calls "secure locations." There are three of them:

- \Windows\System32 and its subfolders,
- \Program Files and its subfolders and, on 64-bit Windows,
- \Program Files (x86) and its subfolders.

 In case you've never had a chance to run one of the 64-bit versions of Windows, the Program Files (x86) folder acts just like the usual Program Files folder, except Windows puts the 32-bit applications in the x86 folder. It stores the native 64-bit applications in the "Program Files" folder.

Can any of those requirements be relaxed? Well, there's no wiggle room about the manifest marking or the signing and cross-signing, but there's a group policy setting "User Account Control: Only elevate UIAccess applications that are installed in secure locations" that tells Vista that it's okay to accept a signed, marked bit of UI automation code that isn't in one of the two or three secure locations. It's enabled by default, but can be disabled. Unfortunately I was unable to test it to find out whether it required a reboot or not, as I didn't have access to any third-party UI automation applications.

Sign or Go Home: Requiring Signed Applications

I really like the idea of signed code for reasons that I've already stated. So long as the people who sell digital certificates for code signing do a decent job checking that the certificate that they sold in the name of Joe Blow did, indeed, go to a guy named Joe Blow, then, as I've said, we haven't removed the chance that Joe's creating and distributing malware, but we *are* in a position to be able to say that Mr. Blow did indeed produce that piece of code. No, it's not the whole ball of wax when it comes to security, but it's an important step. In some ways, the worst part of the Internet and the best part about the Internet is its anonymity: as the old New Yorker cartoon said years ago, "on the Internet, no one knows you're a dog." That's good in some circumstances, but it's quite bad in others, and that bad is in large measure one of the important factors in creating a world of as much malware as we deal with today. Knowing who wrote a piece of good or bad code helps establish what I have strongly felt for years was something that the Internet desperately needs: a method of maintaining "reputation," a way to be able to say, "oh, this is an app from Joe Blow; he's a good guy." I mean, reputations are a fundamental part of how we interact with *people* and it's fairly useful. Why not do the same thing for code?

That's why it amazes me how few vendors actually sign their code. Open up Program Files and poke around to find some of the EXE and DLL files on your computer; right-click them, choose Properties, and look for a "Digital Signatures" tab. You won't find many, even among the files that *Microsoft* puts in Windows, much less third parties.

That's a shame, because digital signatures do more than just establish who wrote a piece of code. The hash encrypted in the signature lets the operating system quickly verify that the code hasn't been modified since the time that the developer signed it. Thus, when looking for malware, properly signed files can be overlooked, as they're going to be clean assuming, again, that we trust the particular individual who signed it. On the other hand, I can see one reason why a lot of things aren't signed: the process of getting a code signing certificate costs money and time, and people don't demand it. I can see that for free or low-cost programs, but it's still hard to believe that all of the larger software vendors don't sign their code.

The 64-bit version of Vista incorporates a bit of this reasoning in that it is hard-wired to check digital signatures on every single driver and program involved with Windows startup, as I've mentioned before. But Vista x64 stops insisting on signatures as soon as it's up and running. Want to take that a step further? You can with another group policy setting, "User Account Control: Only execute executables that are signed and validated."

If enabled, this group policy setting changes how UAC works just a bit. Recall that to this point, once UAC's gotten the okay from you to elevate an application, it elevates it: the rule has been "if the administrator with the split token wants to give her administrator token to ABC.EXE, then let's do it." But this setting adds to the rule that not only must the administrator approve of the elevation, but the EXE must be signed.

This setting does not require that *all* executables be signed, just ones for programs that you want to run with your administrator token. Microsoft probably did that because malware running under a standard user token would not be able to do nearly as much damage as malware running with an administrator token.

If you *do* try to run an unsigned application that requires elevation, then Vista will tell you that it won't run the app, but, as you see in Figure 2.16, the dialog's not very clear.

FIGURE 2.16   Vista dialog explaining that it can't run a program because it's not signed

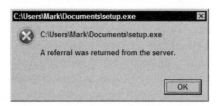

Before I move on to the next group policies setting, let me clarify what I think that you should do with this group policy setting.

On the one hand, I've given the impression that I'd like to see this happen sometime, but let me again leaven that with some reality. The fact is that most developers do not sign their executables currently, and so requiring signing all of a sudden might seriously affect your admins' abilities do to their jobs.

For example, I recently looked over the applications that I use in my small network to see how much I'd miss if I required signed executables. Virtually all of the programs that I run that do not require elevation are not signed with the exception of the Office apps: my digital photography applications aren't, Adobe Reader isn't, nor is Quicken. Those probably aren't problems except for Quicken, because Intuit has been on everyone's Top Ten Most Wanted—and here I don't mean "wanted" in a good way—for their inability to write simple accounting software that standard users can run. Yes, that's right: if you number among the millions of us poor fools who entrust our personal accounting to Quicken, then you may as well just go mark that Quicken executable as "Run as administrator." But if you turn on "User Account Control: Only execute executables that are signed and validated," then you'll be in some trouble, as Quicken's not digitally signed, either. That's an important point: if you're thinking about being the first on your block to require digital signatures, then don't just look at your administrative tools to see if they're signed—remember that there are still plenty of simple productivity tools that have no good reason at all to require your administrator token but do anyway.

On the administrative tool side, I use the stuff that's built into Windows, as well as many of the utilities that you can download from their site. Unfortunately, however, while many files in Windows are signed (although incomprehensibly not *all* of them), most are not, and a substantial number of utilities that I've downloaded from the Microsoft site do not have signatures. The other site that I get useful utilities from, Sysinternals—which I guess has become a Microsoft site recently when Microsoft purchased Winternals—seems to sign most but not all of their utilities.

There's one more reality that we can't ignore here, and that's the cost of signing. If I were to start creating terrific little command-line tools and give them away, what's the chance that I'd invest hundreds of dollars in getting a code signing certificate just so that I could give utilities away? Not very good.

So the bottom line is this: unless you rely on a set of administrative utilities that are signed and use productivity applications that do not require elevation to run, then it's probably a bit early to click on "User Account Control: Only execute executables that are signed and validated."

Working around Apps That Store Data in the Wrong Places

For many years, applications thought it was just fine to store user data in places where users aren't supposed to be writing. With Vista, that's not going to work anymore, as folder locations \Program Files, \Program Files (x86), and \Windows are locked down, as is the Registry hive HKEY_LOCAL_MACHINE\SOFTWARE. But older applications that still try to write to those locations may not fail after all, thanks to a Vista tool called "file and Registry virtualization." This topic is covered in a later chapter, but while we're here looking at the group policy settings for UAC, let me mention in passing that you can disable file and Registry virtualization with the group policy setting "User Account Control: Virtualize file and registry write failures to per-user locations." This appears to require a reboot to take effect and, again, we'll take up this interesting subject in more detail in a future chapter.

The Big Switch: Turning Off UAC Altogether

Okay, despite reading all of this chapter, you've decided that you really *hate* UAC, can't live with it, and want it *gone*. You want things as they were in the old days: when standard users try to do something administrator-ish, things just fail, and when administrators do something, it *happens*, and let the chips fall where they may. (Just think; perhaps in 2026, some old timer will be waxing poetic to a youngster, telling him of "the good old days, when administrators were *administrators*...and almost nobody was a *user*." Maybe the kid will reply with a smirk, "yeah, I bet those were the days...drive-by downloads, root kits, malware using your mailbox as a broadcasting site; sure sorry I missed it.")

Seriously, you may decide that UAC doesn't work for you, or perhaps you're trying to figure out why some pre-Vista application doesn't work on your Vista system, and you want to immediately test whether UAC's getting in the way, or perhaps you just forgot something when you installed and configured the system. Setting "User Account Control: Behavior of the elevation prompt for administrators" to "no prompt" is not the same as shutting UAC off altogether. To do that, you need the group policy setting "User Account Control: Run all administrators in Admin Approval Mode." Set it to Disabled, reboot, and UAC's gone in all of its forms, even including file and Registry virtualization.

Will UAC Succeed?

As I said in the beginning of this chapter, it's been odd acting as a champion of a feature that I think that most people's initial reaction to UAC mirrors what I first experienced: ugh. "It may be good for me, but *I* say it's spinach, and *I* don't like it!" That sort of thing.

But, as I've already explained, I had a road-to-Damascus moment back in early June, when I was helping what seemed like the millionth friend, family member, or random acquaintance in removing 10—I'm not kidding, it was 10—different pieces of spyware off of her computer. Here's an intelligent person, not a dummy at all. Someone who works in a technical field other than computers, and yet she'd not only opened Pandora's box, she'd put a addition on the house to make the box's former occupants feel right at home.

I think we need UAC because while on the one hand almost everyone nowadays uses a computer, on the other hand the vast majority of them aren't technical enough to understand the dangers that networked computers face. Regular folks have a vague knowledge that they should have antivirus software and maybe a personal firewall and that Bad Things Can Happen, but they really don't understand what computer activities can potentially endanger their privacy and their property. Furthermore, almost none of them understands which of those might cause their systems to become infested with enough worms and bots to make their computer the cause of some seriously slow Internet availability for the rest of us. Now, don't misunderstand me on this: I'm not patronizing anyone who doesn't know the geeky internals of computer security, nor do I expect that the normal Internet user should become a security expert, but there *is* a need for the average bear to at least become aware of when he's doing things that might put him at risk. There is a serious problem out there that calls for serious medicine.

Yes, as I've said, UAC has annoyed me sometimes, although I've gotten used to it and I suspect that others can as well. But heck, for that matter, I find *seat belts* irritating. As a guy who got his driver's license in 1974—a mere six years after the U.S. government required seat belts on all cars—I remember driving without them and am a bit annoyed that I've got to use them. Similarly, I love getting the maximum miles per gallon out of my car—not to save a buck or two, but just out of the sheer joy of optimization: I used to own a Volkswagen Beetle that got about 50 miles to the gallon, and that seemed pretty cool. As a matter of fact, however, nowadays it's hard to match the fuel efficiency of that 1962 vehicle, given that every modern car has to carry around hundreds of pounds of bumpers, side impact beams, air bags, and extra 1986-and-later rear brake lights…and that messes with my mileage.

What's that got to do with User Account Control? Simple: all of that junk that slows down my car and makes it cost more money is there for one reason: to make me safe whether I want it or not, even though I'm a safe driver. It's logical, therefore, that as someone who understands how to operate a computer safely that I'd chafe a bit at UAC.

But, oddly and sadly enough, Microsoft doesn't make operating systems just for me; they make 'em for the average Joe and Jane. And Honda doesn't make cars just for me (even though my 67 MPG 2000 Honda Insight is pretty near what I'd design), they've got to make them for a mass market. A mass market regulated by the *government*. Car manufacturers put that safety stuff on their cars mainly because the government requires them to because, while the government knows full well that most people drive pretty safely, the amount of highway injuries, fatalities, and property damage years ago was unacceptable. No one's *making* Microsoft put UAC into their operating system, but it's clear that the risk factor in using computers is orders of magnitude worse than it was a decade ago, when NT 4.0 Workstation hit the shelves.

In other words, I've never actually *needed* my seat belts, thank heavens, but that doesn't mean that I won't eventually need them, and after that I suspect I'll feel more warmly toward them. Similarly, I don't *think* I could be gulled into installing some malware on my system, but it's possible. So having UAC flash the "warning: entering biohazard zone, please don protective gear" light may turn out to be quite welcome one day.

The number of bad guys out there is growing daily, and that's no exaggeration. UAC may help keep them at bay. (Or, as I sometimes fear, UAC prompts may become so common that we'll click them without thinking.)

Summary

Let me wrap up this chapter with a few final suggestions to the UAC haters in the crowd. First, I strongly recommend that you give it a try, a serious try. In my experience it really does become innocuous after a while. And take the time to help out your friends and family by showing them what it does and what it's intended to do. Please don't let your first answer to a UAC question be "oh, that's a stupid feature, let me show you how to make that go away forever," particularly to a nontechnical user. Second, before you say that UAC should work in some other way—"it should remember that I'm an admin for X minutes before prompting me again"— remember what you know about malware and how it works. When you consider that they had to install Secure Desktop because the bad guys might trick you into installing something that would fake out your mouse and perhaps keyboard, causing you to confirm when you intended to cancel, then you can see that the competition is tough, which means, as the saying goes, Microsoft's got to be tougher. Remember, malware gets smarter all the time! Worst of all, creating a UAC that catches only 80 percent of the common types of malware would be the worst of all things—something that annoys us but that does not protect us. (As we all know, only the airport security people get to do that kind of security *and* get paid for it.) Finally, remember that in the end analysis you can always turn it off, either from the GUI or group policies. If you find that you truly can't live with it then it's a moment's work to shut it off, but by making UAC the default behavior, Microsoft may save one of your friends or family members a heap of trouble!

3

Help for Those Lame Apps: File and Registry Virtualization

I've previously mentioned nonadministrative applications—so-called productivity applications and games, mostly—that require elevation to run despite the fact that they aren't intended to do anything administrative. Part of the reason why something like a personal accounting program or a technical drawing program or an e-mail client (to name three that come to mind offhand) would require elevation is because those applications are, to put it baldly, defectively built. Some write user configuration data into HKEY_LOCAL_MACHINE rather than HKEY_CURRENT_USER. Others install their applications to Program Files, which is perfectly fine, but then store user-created data files right in the same directory as their programs, in Program Files, which is quite bad, as the NTFS permissions for Program Files don't let users write files. It's frustrating to see third-party independent software vendors produce this kind of software, but they're not the only culprits by any means—one of the worst offenders here has been Microsoft itself, although they say that's changing. Nevertheless, Visual Studio Express puts projects in its Program Files directory by default, and SQL Server 2000 and 2005 both put databases in their Program Files directories as well. Arrgh.

I've mentioned System32 and Program Files, but they are not the only verboten areas in the file system. XP changed things by disallowing the Everyone group from creating files in the root directory of a computer; Vista continues that trend.

 In fact, Vista locks down the Windows directories so much that it's a major job to enable an administrator to change anything in those directories, but that's a story for the next chapter.

File and Registry Virtualization Basics

What does all of this mean? Well, essentially, the fact is that some of the most basic, simplest programs in the world may stop working under Vista. Of course, Microsoft knows full well that if Vista were to break a lot of applications, then folks might decide not to use Vista. So they added an interesting fix that catches the bad behavior of some applications and amends that behavior on the fly. They call that fix "file and Registry virtualization."

In short, here's how file and Registry virtualization works. When an unelevated application tries to write to one of three folder locations—Program Files, Program Files (x86), and \Windows—then that file write is automatically redirected to a folder in the user's profile, *and*, best of all, the application has no idea that it's happened. A similar thing happens whenever an application tries to write to the HKEY_LOCAL_MACHINE\SOFTWARE key in the Registry, as any such writes get automatically redirected to another key in HKEY_CURRENT_USER. The old application has no idea that it hasn't written to some protected folder or Registry key, so it's happy, and the data's not in a protected system area, so those of us wanting to keep standard users from writing data to those areas are happy.

Hmmm...that sounded good for a *write* operation, but what about a read? When the application goes to read the data that it *thinks* it wrote into, say, C:\Windows, then what happens? Clearly the data file isn't in C:\Windows, it's in some alternate location, so won't the read attempt fail? No, fortunately. When a pre-Vista application tries to read from a protected location, then Vista quietly *first* checks the place that it stashes virtualized data and, if it finds the file that the application's looking for, then it delivers it, saying "here it was in C:\Windows, just like you told me." If the file isn't in the virtualized data area, then Vista looks in the protected location to see if the file *is* in the protected location and, again, the application is blissfully unaware of all of this. As far as it's concerned, it asked for the file or Registry entry, and it got it.

Seeing File Virtualization in Action

I find it easier to understand things when I see them work, so let's try out some file virtualization. Now, to do this, we clearly need a Vista-dumb legacy application, and I don't know about you, but I'm fresh out of them. So I wrote a few "legacy" applications that we can use to put file and, later, Registry virtualization through their paces. To try out this demonstration, you'll need to grab two program files from my website and save them to C:\mystuff, the folder that I had you create in the previous chapter. The files to download are located at http://www.minasi.com/vista/show.exe and http://www.minasi.com/vista/createfile.exe.

The createfile.exe program takes just one argument, a file name. It then creates a file by that name and puts the text "Hello, World!" in it. We'll use that to simulate what happens when a legacy program tries to write to a protected space, as we'll try to write a file to C:\Windows. Then we'll use show.exe, which is a "legacy" application that takes just one argument, a file name, and shows the contents of that file on the screen. In essence, show.exe just duplicates the function of the command-line tool type, which has been around since DOS 1.0.

So why don't we just use the type command? Because Vista knows that the type that came with Vista is made for Vista. Vista never does file and Registry virtualization in combination with Vista apps. We'll see later that most applications will not enjoy the benefits of file and Registry virtualization, when I explain how Vista decides when to enable that virtualization and when not to. Microsoft calls applications that Vista monitors to see if it should automatically redirect reads and writes to "virtualized" applications, so we could say that createfile is virtualized and type is not.

Make sure that you're logged on either as a standard user or an administrator in Administrator Approval Mode; this won't work if you've disabled UAC or if you try these commands from the default Administrator account. Open a command prompt, navigate to C:\mystuff by typing **cd c:\mystuff**, and then type these two lines:

```
createfile c:\windows\testfile.txt
show c:\windows\testfile.txt
```

You should get a response of Hello, World! indicating that both createfile and show succeeded. Then try this:

```
type c:\windows\testfile.txt
```

Remember, Vista knows that type isn't a legacy app, and so doesn't bother with virtualizing it. So type responds not with Hello, World! but instead with a grumpy The system cannot find the file specified. Why did type fail? Simple: because we told it to go looking in the Windows folder for a file named testfile.txt and there isn't anything by that name in the Windows folder!

But don't believe *me*, friends—let's look in C:\Windows and see what we find. Before we do, however, we're going to need to be able to see hidden folders in order to observe the *true* location of testfile.txt, so if you haven't done it yet, tell your Vista system to show hidden files and folders and, while we're at it, tell it not to hide file extensions. In case you're still figuring out Vista's interface, here's how:

1. Click Start ➤ Computer.

2. In the upper left-hand side of the Computer folder, there's a rectangular icon-like thing labeled "Organize." Click that, and a menu will drop down.

3. In that menu, click Folder and Search Options.

4. That brings up a property page Folder Options; click the View tab.

5. In the Advanced Settings box, find the "Hidden files and folders" item, and click the radio button labeled "Show hidden files and folders."

6. Right under that, uncheck the box labeled "Hide extensions for known file types."

7. Click OK to dismiss Folder Options.

It's times like this that I *really* hate GUIs. We ought to be able to just type folderview hidden=yes or the like from the command line, press Enter, and be done with it. Or, better, to be able to just show hidden things with a group policy.

8. Back in the Explorer window, open up C:.

9. Navigate to C:\Windows.

10. Look around, and you will see that there is no testfile.txt in C:\Windows, just as promised.

So where *is* it?

1. Still working with Explorer, look in `C:\Users` for a folder whose name matches your username.

2. Open that folder. Inside it, you'll see a folder named `AppData`. Open that.

3. Inside that, open up the Local folder. Inside that you'll find a folder named `VirtualStore`. Inside *that*, you'll find a folder named `Windows`...and that contains `testfile.txt`.

Still skeptical? Edit `testfile.txt` with Notepad and put some different text in it than `Hello, World!` and then return to the command line and type **`show c:\windows\testfile.txt`** and you'll see whatever text you just put into `testfile.txt`.

File and Registry Virtualization Considerations

Now that we've verified that there is indeed something interesting happening under the hood here, let's understand it more specifically. Thus far, I've said that file and Registry virtualization works by sensing that some apps are pre-Vista apps without a clue and then, once Vista decides that the app should be "virtualized," then Vista spies on their file reads and writes to detect attempts to store user data in protected operating system folders and Registry keys. Then, when Vista sees one of those attempts, it silently redirects the reads or writes elsewhere to places in the user's profile. That's a nice high-level explanation, but now let's consider some specifics, like:

- Exactly *where* does User Account Control store the virtualized data?

- Vista doesn't spy on *every* application; how does it know which ones to virtualize, and which not to? And what happens when a *Vista* application tries to write to a protected area?

- Exactly what folders and Registry keys are protected by file and Registry virtualization? Can we add to that list?

- How can we monitor file and Registry virtualization?

- Can we halt folder and Registry virtualization altogether?

Now we're ready to start examining those things, and, of course, along the way I'll show you a few more demonstrations of how file and Registry virtualization works.

Which Areas Are Protected and Where They Are Virtualized

I've been writing "file and Registry virtualization" all in one breath as if it were one uniform operation but, as you'll see, it isn't—they're two somewhat different animals. File virtualization has a lot fewer details about it than does Registry virtualization, so we'll start there.

How Virtualization Handles Files

File virtualization protects just two folders on the x86 version of Vista, and three folders on the x64 version:

- `\Windows` and its subfolders
- `\Program Files` and its subfolders
- `\Program Files (x86)` and its subfolders

As before, "Program Files (x86)" only appears on systems running the 64-bit versions of Vista. (Note that's 64-bit *Vista*, not just a 64-bit chip: you can run any of the 32-bit versions of Vista on a computer equipped with a 64-bit chip, and they'll run just fine. But you won't see the "Program Files (x86)" folder on your system.)

Notice that the list of folders that file virtualization protects almost exactly matches the list of "secure locations" that User Account Control refers to in the "User Account Control: Only elevate UIAccess applications that are installed in secure locations," but the match isn't perfect; for some reason, that group policy setting considers only `\Windows\System32` secure, where in comparison file virtualization protects all of `\Windows`.

File Writes under Virtualization

Any time a virtualized application tries to write to one of those two or three folders, file virtualization redirects those writes to an area in a user's profile, `\Users\`*username*`\AppData\Local\ VirtualStore`. Thus, if I were logged into my system with a username of "Mark," then my redirected files would all end up in `\Users\Mark\AppData\Local\VirtualStore`. Within Virtual-Store, file virtualization creates folders whose names correspond to the folders that the legacy application was trying to write into—Windows, Program Files, or whatever. So, for example, if some legacy application tried to write a file named `appsettings.ini` to `\Windows\System32` on my computer, then `appsettings.ini` would actually end up in `\Users\Mark\AppData\Local\ VirtualStore\Windows\Settings\appsettings.ini`; take a look back at the exercise that we did earlier in this chapter and you'll see that Vista behaved as expected there.

 Of course, if for some reason the virtualized application's token actually *has* the permissions to write to the protected location, then file virtualization stays out of the way and lets the application actually write to the protected location.

File Reads under Virtualization

When a "virtualized" application tries to read a file from one of the protected locations, then Vista assumes that the same application tried to *write* to that location and was redirected. That's why legacy file read attempts cause Vista to always look in the VirtualStore folders *before* checking the actual locations. So, for example, if a user named Mary were to run a legacy application that asked Vista to open a file named `\windows\system32\appsettings.ini`, then Vista would *first* look for a file with the file specification `\Users\Mary\AppData\Local\ VirtualStore\Windows\System32\appsettings.ini` and, if that file exists, then Vista would deliver that to the application. If Vista *doesn't* find a file with that specification, then it checks to see if `\Windows\System32\appsettings.ini` exists and, if it does, then Vista gives *that* to the application.

Notice that the fact that Vista's rule for locating files means that Vista doesn't have to have any kind of "memory" about what files it has stuffed into VirtualStore in order to locate them when it needs to read them. Its "how to write files" rule just says "if it's a virtualized application making the request, and the requested location is protected, then actually write the file in VirtualStore," and its "how to read files" rule says "if it's a virtualized application making the request, and the requested location is protected, then first look for the file in VirtualStore and, if it's not there, then look in the protected location."

Can you change the list of protected folders from the two or three that Vista ships with? No, unfortunately not. Microsoft sees file and Registry virtualization as something that's a short-term bridge that people can use to continue to use legacy apps for just a little while longer before getting up-to-date applications, and doesn't want to encourage people to become dependent on it. Making it more flexible would do that, I guess.

How Virtualization Handles the Registry

Vista virtualizes the Registry as well, but only the HKEY_LOCAL_MACHINE\SOFTWARE key. Its basic approach is the same:

- If a legacy application without the proper Registry permissions tries to write to a location anywhere in the HKEY_LOCAL_MACHINE\SOFTWARE key, then Registry virtualization writes the data instead to an alternate location and tells the application that the write operation succeeded.

- If a legacy application tries to read anywhere in HKEY_LOCAL_MACHINE\SOFTWARE key, then Vista first looks in the alternate Registry location for that data. If it finds the data that it's been sent to get, then Vista returns the data from the alternate location. If the data isn't in the alternate location, then Vista looks in the originally requested location and, if it finds it, gives that data to the application successfully.

Registry virtualization is, however, a bit different in a few ways. First, the alternate location clearly isn't a folder in the user's profile. Instead, it's a new key, HKEY_CURRENT_USER\Software\Classes\VirtualStore\MACHINE\SOFTWARE. So, for example, if an application tried to create a new key HKEY_LOCAL_MACHINE\SOFTWARE\Mynewkey, that key would actually end up as HKEY_CURRENT_USER\Software\Classes\VirtualStore\MACHINE\SOFTWARE\Mynewkey.

You can try this out with another of my homemade legacy applications, which you can download at http://www.minasi.com/vista/regwritekey.exe. Save the file, as before, in c:\mystuff. Then open a command prompt, navigate to c:\mystuff, type **regwritekey**, and press Enter. That application tries to create a new Registry key named HKEY_LOCAL_MACHINE\SOFTWARE\Testkey. To see what it *really* did, start up Regedit and look in

HKEY_LOCAL_MACHINE\SOFTWARE; you won't see a Testkey folder. But now open up HKEY_CURRENT_USER\Software\Classes\VirtualStore\MACHINE\SOFTWARE and you'll see a key Testkey, as you see in Figure 3.1.

FIGURE 3.1   The virtualized Testkey folder

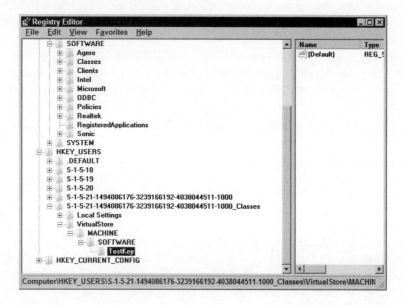

As with file virtualization, you can't extend the range of Registry keys protected but, unlike file virtualization, you can fine-tune which keys are protected by virtualization. For any given Registry key in HKLM\Software, you can specify whether or not Vista should virtualize for that key. You do it with the reg.exe application that you may recognize from earlier Windows versions, but in Vista it gets a new parameter, "flags." You can tell Vista not to virtualize a key like this:

```
reg keylocation dont_virtualize [/s]
```

Where the optional /s means "make this change to this key and its subkeys as well." For example, to tell Vista not to virtualize the HKEY_LOCAL_MACHINE\SOFTWARE\Microsoft key and its subkeys, type (from an elevated prompt):

```
reg hkey_local_machine\software\microsoft\ dont_virtualize /s
```

That's all one line, even if it broke on the printed page. It's important to understand that "Don't virtualize" doesn't mean "let the low-privilege legacy application modify this key"; it just means "ignore the application's attempt to modify this key."

What Does "Legacy" Mean, Exactly?

Thus far, we've seen that Vista virtualizes when an application (1) tries to write to a protected area, (2) lacks the NTFS or Registry permissions to do so, and (3) is a legacy application. We've covered the first two conditions; now let's look at the third.

Vista will virtualize any application's read or write requests *unless* the application does one of several things.

- **Runs with an administrator-level token.** Vista assumes that if you're logged in as an administrator and are running a legacy application of some kind, then you must know what you're doing. In that case, Vista will allow the app to try to write to the file or Registry key. If the administrator lacks the permission to write to the file or Registry key, the operation will fail.

- **Runs with a token that has write permissions to the file or Registry key.** We've already covered this.

- **Running in kernel mode.** In the Windows world, programs either run as "user mode" or "kernel mode." Almost every program that you've ever installed on Windows runs in user mode: word processors, Web browsers, e-mail clients, games, spreadsheets, databases, and so on all run in user mode. The beauty of user mode is that each user mode application is placed in its own little "memory compartment" that it cannot write outside of. It is, then, impossible for a bug in a copy of Notepad to cause Notepad to overwrite some of the memory space allocated to, say, Calculator; when Notepad tries, it will trigger an error that will cause Windows to close down Notepad and ask you if Vista can send a trouble report to Microsoft about it. Kernel mode code, in contrast, *can* mess with whatever part of memory that it wants to, so buggy kernel mode programs can do a lot of damage. Basic operating system components, device drivers, and a lot of malware are three examples of commonly encountered kernel mode programs. (That's why one of the easiest ways to make your system unstable is to install a buggy driver. Or, I suppose, some malware!) The bottom line is that about the only kernel mode code you're ever going to be aware of installing is a device driver, and I can't see why a device driver would want to write to any of the protected locations. Virtualization would be fairly unnecessary for device drivers anyway, as they typically run with the token of the LocalSystem account, which has permissions to do just about anything anyway—it may be powerful, but it doesn't fall under Administrator Approval Mode. (If it did, you'd have to respond to about a thousand Consent UIs just to get a computer booted up!)

- **Has a manifest with a `level=` parameter in it.** If an application has a manifest, then Vista figures that it's been given the once-over, and doesn't need virtualization. (I should point out, however, that as of RC1 I found that the effect of manifests behaved differently for external manifests as opposed to embedded manifests when it comes to deciding whether or not to virtualize. That may be fixed by the time that you read this.)

- **The user token is derived via impersonation.** In the Windows world, "impersonation" essentially means that the application's token comes from a user logged on from across the network. In other words, in order for an application to enjoy the benefits of virtualization, then whoever's running that application must at least appear to be logged on locally rather than from across the network.

- **The application is a 64-bit application.** Virtualization is intended by Microsoft to be a mere bandage for temporary use. They reckon that any application built to be a 64-bit application is modern enough that its developer would understand what standard users can and can't do, and so would not need virtualization.

- **The application seeks to modify a Registry key that has been marked "dont_virtualize."** We've already covered this.

So long that an application does not meet any of these criteria, then it will get the benefits of file and Registry virtualization.

Seeing Virtualization in Standard Versus Administrative Users

By now, we've covered enough about virtualization to give it a really good run through its paces, so I think you'll find this upcoming section a useful demonstration of how it works. In this demonstration, I'll have you create a file named "testfile.txt" in both the Program Files directory and the VirtualStore directory. But I'll have you put different text in the two files so that we can differentiate them. Then we'll ask `show.exe` to show us `c:\program files\ testfile.txt` under varying conditions: as a user, as an administrator, with a manifest, without one, and so on. Here are the steps to making this demonstration work:

1. Log onto Vista as an administrator, but be sure to use an account that gets a split token— one that works in Administrator Approval Mode. (So by default the account actually named Administrator wouldn't work.)

2. Open a command prompt, but not an elevated one; just click Start ➤ All Programs ➤ Accessories ➤ Command Prompt.

3. If your system doesn't currently have a `c:\mystuff` directory, then create one from the command prompt by typing **md c:\mystuff**.

4. Change your default directory to `c:\mystuff` by typing **cd mystuff**.

5. Copy the program `show.exe` to `c:\mystuff`, if it's not there already. If you haven't downloaded `show.exe` yet, it's at `http://www.minasi.com/vista/show.exe`.

6. Set your folder options so that you can see hidden files, and so that Windows does *not* hide file extensions. Also, check the box next to "Display the full path in the title bar (Classic folders only)."

7. Open up an Explorer window and navigate to `c:\users\yourusername\AppData\ Local\VirtualStore`. This is why you needed to see hidden files, as AppData is a hidden folder.

8. In VirtualStore, create a folder named "Program Files." Spell it exactly the same way that Windows does, including the space between the two words.

9. In VirtualStore\Program File, use Notepad to create a file named "testfile.txt." In the file, place the text "Hello from the virtual store!" Save the file and close Notepad.

10. Open up an elevated command prompt.

11. In that, type these lines:

```
cd \mystuff
copy con "c:\program files\testfile.txt"
Welcome from Program Files!
```

12. After pressing Enter after the "Welcome from Program Files!" line, press the F6 function key. You'll get the response 1 file(s) copied.

13. From the elevated command prompt, type **show** "**c:\program files\testfile.txt**" and press Enter. You will see the message "Hello from Program Files!" That means that the request to read c:\program files\testfile.txt was *not* virtualized because you ran the program with your administrator token.

14. Now move to the *non*elevated command prompt and run the show command again. This time you'll see "Welcome from the virtual store!" because you ran show.exe with a standard user token.

15. Next, let's see what a manifest does to virtualization. If you haven't done it yet, grab my sample manifest at http://www.minasi.com/vista/simple.exe.manifest. It's a small text file; save it to c:\mystuff. Then edit simple.exe.manifest with Notepad and change the line

```
level="requireAdministrator"
```

to

```
level="asInvoker"
```

and be absolutely sure to type that with the capitalization as you see it here, with the capital "I" in the middle of "asInvoker." We're doing this because this manifest will *not* trigger the Consent UI, but it *is* clearly a Vista-aware manifest and should cause Vista not to use file and Registry virtualization.

16. Rename simple.exe.manifest to show.exe.manifest. Remember, in order for an external manifest to affect a program, the manifest's name must be the program file's name with ".manifest" on the end.

17. Working from the *non*elevated command prompt, once more type **show** "**c:\program files\testfile.txt**" and press Enter. You should see "Hello from Program Files" because the manifest's presence should tell Vista not to virtualize.

WARNING   If you don't, and instead see the VirtualStore, then don't panic; it seems that this was a bit flaky even in RC2. But embedded manifests seem to always work, so you can always go that route. You can also do what we did in the last chapter, where you create a new folder and copy both show.exe and show.exe.manifest into that folder. "Introducing" both files to a folder together seems to make Vista notice a manifest whereas adding one later doesn't.

So we see that if you've got an application that you don't want Vista to virtualize with, then just create a manifest for that app. Or, better yet, embed it in the EXE and from that point on wherever you put the application, Vista won't virtualize.

Tracking Virtualization

As I've mentioned a couple of times already, Microsoft's stance on file and Registry virtualization is that it is just a patch, a bit of baling wire and bubble gum that Vista has because it unfortunately *needs* it, and that virtualization should be very clearly seen as a short-term patch rather than a long-term feature.

Given that, it would be nice to be able to find out after some time just how important file and Registry virtualization *is* to my network and my users. Fortunately, Vista offers some logging information, if not as much as we might like.

The first way that we can retrospectively determine the importance of file and Registry virtualization is simply to examine the \Users\username\AppData\Local\VirtualStore folder and the HKEY_CURRENT_USER\Software\Classes\VirtualStore\MACHINE\ SOFTWARE key in the Registry. As developers store their application information in keys that sit inside keys bearing their company names, finding a folder named "JoeBlowSoft\myoldapp" would immediately tell you that one of your users clearly uses some application named "myoldapp" from a firm named "JoeBlowSoft." You can then contact the vendor to see if there's a new version and, if not, then you've got a five-year warning that come the next version of Windows, this application may no longer work.

Besides looking in the virtual folders and Registry keys, you can discover who needs virtualization with a log file. The Event Viewer includes a log *dedicated* to file virtualization. You can find it like so:

1. Open up the Event Viewer.

2. Under "Event Viewer (local)" in the left-hand pane, open up "Applications and Services logs."

3. Inside that, open the Microsoft folder.

4. Inside that, open the Windows folder.

5. Inside *that*, open the UAC-FileVirtualization folder.

Inside there, you will see events, typically event ID 4000—one for every case where file virtualization has occurred. There is not, for some reason, a similar log for the Registry, but you can glean some useful information from these events about those apps that need file virtualization. Figure 3.2. shows one such event.

Notice that it's a pretty simple, clean event, but it might be more useful. Clicking the Details tab offers some more valuable data, as you see in Figure 3.3.

FIGURE 3.2   A typical file virtualization event

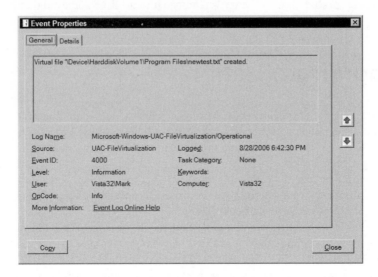

FIGURE 3.3   Details of the file virtualization event

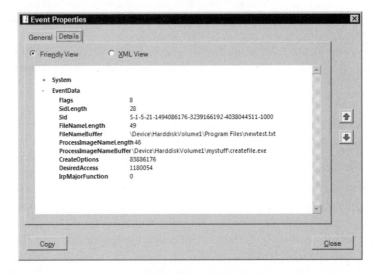

Aha! Not only do we find out what file must be virtualized, but we also discover what application required it. Now, add the existence of these useful events to the new ease of telling the Event Viewer to generate some action based on a particular event, and I could imagine a not-too-difficult-to-construct tool that built a database of "troubled" apps automatically.

A Possible Virtualization Problem

While virtualization looks to be a pretty good online fix for legacy applications, it may introduce altogether new problems of its own. Suppose, for example, that you used a pre-Vista application we'll call "Oldapp." Oldapp is so old or so badly written that it stores user settings in a text file called oldapp.ini rather than the Registry, and it stores that file in `C:\Program Files\OldSoft\oldapp.ini`. Thus, every user who's running Oldapp has an `oldapp.ini` file in the same place in their Program Files directory.

Of course, under Vista virtualization, that'd change. Instead of writing to `C:\Program Files\OldSoft`, Oldapp's file would end up in `C:\Users\`*username*`\AppData\Local\ VirtualStore\Program Files\OldSoft`. How could this be a problem? Well, Oldapp probably doesn't allow for any kind of centralized administration tool like group policies, so companies using Oldapp might be doing central control by regularly distributing an `oldapp.ini` file that contains company standard settings to every desktop via a login script, SMS, or something of that variety. Now, when everyone ran Oldapp on XP, then they all had their `oldapp .ini` files in the same place. Now, however, someone trying to centrally control Oldapp by distributing standard oldapp.ini files would have a somewhat more complex task ahead of her, as she'd have to write distribution code that would be smart enough to

- Detect the operating system the user is running, as all pre-Vista OSes will have `oldapp.ini` in `Program Files`;

- Detect the user's username, so as to be able to construct the directory path to the VirtualStore; and

- End up looking in both places for `oldapp.ini` anyway, as Vista users of Oldapp will *still* have `oldapp.ini` in their `Program Files` folder if they run as Administrator, or have disabled virtualization or UAC in general.

Now, understand, none of this is insurmountable, but it may cause some headaches.

Controlling Virtualization

If for some reason you don't want file and Registry virtualization to work, then you may recall that in the last chapter we met two group policy settings that can shut it off:

- "User Account Control: Run all administrators in Admin Approval Mode" will, if disabled, shut off all UAC-related code, including and file and Registry virtualization.

- "User Account Control: Virtualize file and registry write failures to per-user locations" will, if disabled, shut off file and Registry virtualization.

Both group policy settings require a reboot to see any changes take effect.

The Future of Virtualization

Well, according to Microsoft, there *isn't* one. As I've mentioned before, Microsoft sees this as a short-term fix that won't last beyond Vista. As I also suggested before, there were five years between XP's release and Vista's release, and I wouldn't be surprised if we didn't see Vista's replacement for another five. That means that file and Registry virtualization is, as I've already suggested, basically a five-year warning to start inventorying your software's application compatibility needs, because Windows Vienna—Microsoft's current code name for the post-Vista, post-Server 2007 brand of Windows—may not run that old code or, if it does, it'll only run the code if you strip Windows of most of its security features.

Yes, the notion that a future Windows is going to force you to get rid of software that you've been using for years is frustrating, but in the end it's really for the best, believe it or not. Windows desperately needed to get more secure, and doing that required structural changes that unavoidably means that some applications won't work anymore. Besides, the things that applications are doing that Windows doesn't like are things that Microsoft has been telling programmers not to do since April 1992; enforcing the rules after 14 years doesn't seem all that unreasonable. There just comes a time when that old Model T just isn't safe to drive on a superhighway, and the same might be said of "Module Ts" on the information superhighway.

But what if you really *do* need to run an old program? Use a virtual machine. VMWare gives away their VMWare Server as I write this, and Microsoft is giving away both Virtual Server and Virtual PC. In case you've never played with anything like these, here's how they work. Virtual machine managers are programs that let you create imaginary computers inside your computer—pieces of software that nearly perfectly emulate real computer hardware called "virtual machines." You can then install operating systems on these virtual machines, and at that point you've got an imaginary computer isolated in its own little sandbox, able to run just about any application that you'd like. Virtual machines even have virtual network cards, and so these systems can interact with real computers over your network if you like. Virtual machine technology is a powerful way to build and maintain systems for testing and to run older applications.

File and Registry virtualization is an extremely useful part of the User Account Control software that will, I think, make running older software a heck of a lot easier.

 I should note, however, that Vista isn't the first time that we've seen file and Registry virtualization in Windows, believe it or not. The Application Compatibility Toolkit has offered file and Registry virtualization as an option, one of its "shims," for as long as I can recall. But it was, at least in my experience, a bit hard to understand under ACT, and adding it right into the OS will make it more useful.

Summary

Give some of your old applications a try on a Vista box and then use the UAC-FileVirtualization event log and the contents of your VirtualStore to quickly get a look at what software needs work. I think in the end you'll find that file and Registry virtualization is both useful as a compatibility tool *and* as a way to inventory your software to determine the "problem children"!

4

Understanding Windows Integrity Control

As I've said before, the Internet drives Microsoft security people crazy, and you can see why. XP's a pretty stable and secure operating system...just so long as you patch, don't install any bad applications, and if you *do* install one, don't give it administrator-level powers. Of course, however, that's *just* what we do all of the time because getting anything done in XP and earlier versions of Windows requires running ourselves and our applications as administrators. As you've seen so far in this book, Microsoft is trying to administer some strong medicine to Windows and, to extent, to the way that we use our computers in order to keep the worms, bots, and Trojans away.

Now, if you thought that User Account Control (UAC) was a real change in the way that Windows works, get ready for Windows integrity control, WIC for short. With WIC, Microsoft introduces a piece of Windows infrastructure that is as important and ubiquitous as NTFS file permissions and that has appeared in other operating systems in the past—but those operating systems were all *military* ones!

During Vista's development process, Windows integrity control was called "mandatory integrity control" and then "Windows Integrity Mechanism." As I write this in late September 2006, Windows integrity control seems to be the final name, but that could change by the time that Vista releases to manufacturing.

In short, WIC's job is to define several different levels of what might be called "trustworthiness" but that Microsoft calls "integrity." Processes of the same level of integrity interact with one another as they always have in Windows. But where WIC changes things is when a *process* from a lower integrity level (IL) tries to read, write, or execute an *object* (for example, a file) with a higher integrity level. At that point, WIC steps in and may—just *may*, it's configurable if you know how—block that attempt. That may *sound* like a small change but, as you'll see in this chapter, it's got some big effects for how Vista works.

Windows Integrity Control Overview

Microsoft's primary approach with WIC is to basically put the Internet and anything downloaded from it into its own little universe or, in WIC-speak, "integrity level," separated from your user data and the system's files. There are six integrity levels in Windows Integrity Control, as you'll read later in this chapter. Things from the Internet go into the second lowest of the six levels, a level named "low." Microsoft put standard users, in contrast, into a different, higher integrity level named "medium." That way, anything downloaded from the Internet can't start deleting things or modifying your system without either at best just failing or, at worst, waking up User Account Control, which will start asking you whether you actually *wanted* that lovely game that you just downloaded to start emailing your passwords to a server in China.

WIC is one method of implementing a notion in security called *process isolation*. The whole idea with process isolation is that if we can't make the Internet a safer place, then we can at least watch more closely what things from the Internet do. Processes and objects in different integrity levels can communicate, but in a way that you can restrict and monitor or, more likely, you'll just let Windows' default behavior monitor for you.

For example, suppose you've clicked a hyperlink on some web page that causes Internet Explorer to download and run a program from the Internet. Suppose further that that program is some—insert minor chord from the lower end of the scale—malware. Now, the first thing that most malware needs to do is to ensure that it gets loaded every time that you start the operating system. That means writing something to the Registry. As it's been downloaded from the Internet, then, as you just learned, the malware's running at the Internet's integrity level—low, that is. About 99.9 percent of the Registry, however, has the higher medium integrity level. Thus, when the malware tries to modify the Registry to ensure that the malware gets run every time you boot, the write attempt will either fail or cause User Account Control to raise the Consent UI, depending on how the malware was written.

Thus far I've talked about WIC as a way to keep an eye on the Internet, but that's only Microsoft's *first* use of it so far. As we examine how WIC works you'll probably see many ways to use it to secure your systems. In brief, here are the big concepts in WIC, all of which we'll cover in greater detail in the rest of this chapter:

Six levels Windows Integrity Control defines six different levels of integrity, described in detail in the section "WIC's Six Integrity Levels" below.

They're mandatory, not discretionary An object, process, or user's integrity level is very much like the sort of permissions that we've known in NT ever since version 3.1, but not exactly so. Traditional NT permissions are technically known as "*discretionary* access controls" because they're intended have values set at the discretion of their owner, who can be a standard user. Integrity levels are, in contrast, based on a notion of *mandatory* access controls because in general integrity levels aren't set by the user, but instead by either the operating system or an administrator, or in some cases both.

Thus, in a mandatory access world controlled partially by the operating system, as is Vista, you end up with the uncomfortable notion that you might have a file on your computer's hard disk that you might own and have NTFS full control permissions on...but that you're unable to delete, even if you *are* an administrator. It's a good concern, but Vista doesn't create files with integrity levels too high for administrators to delete.

Objects "trust up, not down"   Windows Integrity Control's main job is as a protection structure activated whenever a lower-integrity process tries to read, write, or execute a higher-integrity object. (By default, WIC only tracks writes, but you can tell it to watch reads and executes, as you'll see later.) When that happens, WIC will typically send the process an "access denied" error, although the developer of a Vista-aware application could keep that error from occurring by requesting elevation for his low-integrity process. That would raise the Consent UI, offering the user the chance to allow or deny the elevation. Either way, the higher-integrity object—database, file, folder, Registry key, or whatever—is protected from the lower-integrity process. WIC's Prime Directive is "in order for you to act on me, you must have an integrity level that is greater than or equal to mine."

Integrity levels supersede normal permissions   Recall the example where, a few paragraphs back, I laid out what would happen if you were to accidentally click a link in Internet Explorer 7 under Vista. In that example, I said that when the malware tried to write to the medium-integrity Registry key, it would be rebuffed because of the malware's lower integrity level. But let me take that a step further and highlight a point that might not have been obvious when I first explained it. When the malware tries to write to the Registry, that attempt will fail *even if for some reason the malware has a Full Control permission on that Registry key.* Integrity levels "trump" regular NTFS and Registry permissions, essentially. The integrity checks that I've been talking about happen before and override any checks on more traditional permissions on NTFS, Registry keys, and so on. In other words, if the NTFS permissions say "sure, let the process do whatever" but WIC's comparison of integrity levels says "no, don't let it!" then Windows Integrity Control always wins.

Mandatory Controls Versus Discretionary Controls

I've already noted that the idea of integrity levels was taken from something called "mandatory access controls," which are different from something called "discretionary access controls." Those aren't Microsoft's terms, they're standard phrases in the IT security industry for describing different methods of securing things in operating systems. To see where they came from, permit me to set the dials on the Wayback Machine to the early 1980s. Disco's dead, Reagan's in office, they were still making good *Star Trek* movies occasionally, no one has yet heard of Martha Stewart, and it seems like *everybody* in the government's buying computers....

The Orange Book

In the late 1970s and early 1980s, government offices started buying computers. Compared to 10 years earlier, the government was buying *lots* of computers, partially because they were getting cheaper and partially because the government, like the rest of the world, was growing more and more dependent on number-crunching in large volumes. They bought mainframes from folks like IBM, CDC, Burroughs, and Univac. They bought minicomputers from DEC, Data General, and Harris. They bought stand-alone word processing systems from Wang and Four-Phase and, yes, as the 1970s became the 1980s, then even began to buy desktop computers from Apple, IBM, and others. Information security managers soon started saying that, hey, maybe those computer buyers should be thinking about security on these widely varying systems—but how much security did they need, and how would they know that they had it?

Some people might reflexively answer the question "how much security did those computer buyers need?" with "top secret" or "as good as possible," but that would honestly be a waste of money. Sure, military and intelligence agencies need a high amount of security, but most government facilities don't. For example, around that time I worked as a contractor for the Department of Energy, where I helped build economic models for forecasting short-term supplies and prices of various sources of energy. The group that I was in all worked on an IBM mainframe. We each had our own space on the mainframe's hard disks, but there was no security, and anyone could look at or modify anyone else's data. Eventually the IT managers there installed a package called ACF/2 that allowed us to secure any or all of our files, but the general consensus was "why bother figuring out to set up a 'who can use my files' list ?" I would do analysis based on data collected by the government for public use, and then I would write computer programs that did publicly available forecasts based on those data. The code, the data, and the forecasts were paid for by the U.S. taxpayer, so in theory if any citizen were to ask to see my files, I couldn't see a reason why I wouldn't just hand them over. (No citizen ever did, in case you're wondering.) My analysis wasn't exactly right, however, because putting all of the data created and maintained by several dozen people into a pool that anyone on the team could modify or delete was potentially dangerous. An unscrupulous team member looking to discredit another might change a file in a manner that would render the work useless and make his rival seem to be the culprit. The result? The unscrupulous character might get away with it, but the taxpayer gets to pay for the lost time as the data and code are reconstructed. Now, let me clarify that nothing like that ever happened, but it *could* have, so having *some* level of security seems like a good idea. But Top Secret, Pentagon-ish levels of security? It'd just cost money and offer no return to the agency or to the taxpayer. Most of us wouldn't find installing titanium doors, bulletproof glass, and gun turrets on our houses cost-effective security-wise, and making the Energy analysts spend the time and money to jump through the Top Secret hoops would have been as unrewarding.

But there *are* folks in the government who need Top Secret or similar data protection. Clearly, then, different places in the government needed more or less security in their system software; no one size would fit all.

Following this reasoning, some folks at the NSA decided that it might be a good idea to make life easier for government managers evaluating and buying computer software if there were a range of predefined standards that describe multiple levels of more or less secure computer systems. These would be a collection of sets of requirements, basically lists of what features a piece of software needed in order to satisfy the need for a given level of security. That way, the person running, say, the FBI's National Crime Information Center (NCIC) or the person running the online public records of the proceedings of the Congress in the THOMAS system needn't sit down from scratch and each try to cook up a complete set of security requirements that work for their particular operation. Instead, the NCIC person might be able to look at that list of features required for each level of security and say "aha, I see that there are seven defined levels of security and oh, heck, I don't need the top two levels; they'd cost a fortune to implement and we're not holding the keys to the nukes anyway, but the third level sounds just right" and the THOMAS manager could say "let's see, we need to make this open and easy to get to but we can't have the public modifying the content, so maybe we'll go with the second-to-the-lowest level of security."

The NSA group, named the "National Computer Security Center," laid out four "divisions" of trustworthiness in operating systems, each with subdivisions called "classes," of which there are seven in total. These divisions and classes were described in a document usually called the "Orange Book" because of the color of its cover, but its actual name was *Trusted Computer System Evaluation Criteria*. The National Computer Security Center released it in December 1985. (Isn't it strange to think that some standards that we work with are old enough to drink in every state in the United States?)

C2 Certification and NT

NSA called their four "divisions" of security D, C, B, and A in increasing order of security, and then defined seven "classes" of software requirements called, in increasing order of security, D, C1, C2, B1, B2, and A, and described them all in the Orange Book. That, however, was only the beginning. Once our imaginary FBI or THOMAS manager decides to go with a particular level of security, how will he or she know whether or not a product meets that level?

NSA then took on the job of evaluating systems to certify them for particular levels. Thanks to their certification efforts, the government computer buyer's job is a bit easier, as she can just say "let's see, I think we need something that meets C1 or C2 specifications…which operating systems can do that?"

Now, I'll bet that "C2" rings a bell for some of you, as it was often bandied about when discussing NT in the 1990s. Admittedly I'm simplifying when I say that a given operating system can be certified as B1, C2, or whatever as NSA actually evaluates entire systems, taking the hardware, applications , and so on into consideration. Informally, however, it's common to hear people say that such-and-such operating system is "C2 compliant," as has been said of Windows for quite some time, as NSA certified several specific NT configurations as C2. You won't hear the phrase nowadays, however, as the whole Trusted Computer System Evaluation Criteria program has been folded into an international set of standards called "Common Criteria."

C and B: Discretionary Versus Mandatory

Of the four divisions, most people only talk about B and C because D just means "this operating system has no security" and A is like B3, but requires formal proofs of security that are hideously expensive to acquire. The main difference between C and B is that C involves what *Trusted Computer System Evaluation Criteria* called "discretionary protection" and B involves something more stringent called "mandatory protection."

Discretionary Access Overview and Terminology

As I've already said, back when I was working at the Department of Energy, we needed *some* security, but not much. We all created and maintained certain data and program files, and so we might have benefited from a system that would let each of us provide our files to the common projects on a read-only basis. That way, the data or programs could contribute to the analysis that the project needed but we each could be sure that the files that we were responsible for wouldn't be tampered with. Again, we never needed to do that, but if we had, we'd have been using a *discretionary access control* security model. But note that none of us were system administrators for the mainframe on which we worked and, honestly, I don't remember ever even *meeting* any of the system administrators on that system. That's an important part of discretionary access systems: they give a lot of control to just regular old users over their own resources, without having to make them system-wide administrators.

Parts of a Discretionary Access System

The ingredients to a discretionary access control system are user accounts, a logon procedure, objects, owners, and permissions. In C2 certification, the idea with discretionary access is that every object, like a file or folder, has an owner. The owner is usually the person who created the object, but not necessarily. An object's owner has the power to create a list of user accounts and groups who are granted or denied access to the object. C2 requires user accounts so that the owner can name specific people or groups to allow or deny access, and therefore logons are a "must" so as to prove that someone claiming to be someone with access to an object does indeed have that access.

Sound familiar? It should. Microsoft used the C2 framework as the basis of what was initially a system of access controls for files and folders and that they later expanded to many more types of things. They adopted the C2 framework because they sought C2 certification for Windows. The central notion in a discretionary system is that the owner—again, just any old user who happens to be the owner, he needn't be an administrator to be a file's owner—gets to grant and deny access. If a file's owner wanted to grant Full Control to the Guest account, making it available to anyone on the planet, then nothing would stand in his way.

In a "pure" discretionary model, then, each user would store all of her documents in some folder that she owns, like a profile folder in Windows, but no one would have the ability to control who can access that folder but her, the owner. In Windows, of course, that's not exactly what happens, as the LocalSystem account and the local Administrators group typically get Full Control permissions applied to all folders on the computer by default. Nevertheless, Windows up through XP and 2003 offers something quite similar to the C2 notion of discretionary access.

In addition to requiring object owners, discretionary permissions, user accounts, and logon procedures, C2 also requires audit mechanisms to track use of discretionary powers, and of course Windows offers that via its security auditing functions.

"Securable Objects": What Discretionary Access Can Protect

Let's take a moment and look at the sorts of objects that Windows can secure. Even though Windows uses a discretionary model, not *everything* in Windows can have permissions on it. For example, could I grant you the power to change *just* the IP address on my computer, without also giving you the power to change my subnet mask, default gateway, and the like? (I have no idea why I'd want to, but it's a simple example.) No, I can't, because Microsoft has chosen to build support for discretionary permissions into some things in Windows and not bother for others. Microsoft calls types of objects that can get permissions "securable objects." A complete list of those objects includes, according to the Microsoft MSDN article "Securable Objects" (`http://windowssdk.msdn.microsoft.com/en-us/library/ms723270.aspx`),

- Files and folders

- Named pipes, a method for one process to communicate with another process

- Processes

- Threads

- Access tokens, the data that systems receive once you're authenticated to them

- Windows-management objects; also known as "WMI namespaces," they are currently the most important tool for programmatic control of almost anything in Windows

- Registry keys

- Windows services

- Local and remote printers

- Network shares

- Interprocess synchronization objects (the way that one program taps another on the shoulder and asks it to do something)

- Job objects (a tool that's been around since Windows 2000 that allows you to tell Windows, "run such-and-such set of programs but if they require more than some specified amount of CPU time or requires more than some specified amount of RAM, then kill the job)

- Directory service objects (user accounts, machine accounts, group policy objects, domains, and so on)

An object's permissions tend to be stored on the object itself. For example, if you configure a given file on an NTFS file system as having a file permission giving you full control of that file, then that permission itself is stored in an area that every file has called its "metadata." More specifically, every permission that you create, every *discretionary* permission, is technically called a "discretionary access control entry" or DACE, pronounced to rhyme with "face." The entire list of discretionary access control entries is a "discretionary access control list" or DACL, pronounced "dackel" to rhyme with "crackle." But in the Windows world we tend to drop the "D," and refer to an *ACL* that contains *ACEs*. Note that many people tend to simplify things even further and use the phrase "ACL" to refer to both ACLs and ACEs. When someone says, "I put an ACL on `accounts.dat` so that the Accounting group could read it," what he really means is "I added a discretionary ACE to `accounts.dat`'s DACL to grant the Accounting group read access." (You probably knew that, but I figured the reminder wouldn't hurt, because soon we'll be talking about corresponding terms for mandatory access control systems.)

Mandatory Access Overview and Terminology

But now suppose we didn't quite trust just any old user to set permissions. Suppose, for example, we found a few users setting the permissions on their profile directories to allow the Guest account full control of those directories. Argh! In that case, we might want to restrict just how much discretion we offered in our discretionary access control system, and impose some constraints on our users' abilities to open our systems to the world. In that case, we'd want some sort of *mandatory* access controls. To get a "B" certification under Orange Book specifications, operating systems required some kind of mandatory access control system.

The idea with a mandatory access control is that an organization draws up some enterprise-wide security policy with rules like "passwords must be at least 7 characters long" or "no permissions may allow the Guest account to do anything," and then some feature of the operating system keeps the user from doing anything contrary to that policy. It's called "mandatory" rather than "discretionary" because where in the theoretical discretionary model the user is king, the mandatory model demotes him to a sort of a local viscount.

We know that Windows implements discretionary access; does it do mandatory access as well? Well, yes, sort of; I suppose you could say that it should get more than a "C,"—something more like a "C+" or a "B–" rating. For example, here's a way to accomplish something of a mandatory access control that keeps users from granting access to the Guest account: ever since Windows 2000, a domain administrator could just create a group policy object applying a permission to every C:\ drive in the domain explicitly denying the Guest account any access to C:\. That would count as a mandatory access control, as it is imposed on the user from the outside and limits her power.

In the Windows world, though, the reality is that this wouldn't really constitute a "mandatory access control" of any real value. For one thing, the sad fact is that in the Windows world we often don't have the kind of separation between users and administrators that I saw in the mainframe days, as most machines are used by just one person, and that person spends her whole day logged on as an administrator. Furthermore, in Windows prior to Vista, the administrator can do anything that he or she wants, and so could undo the "mandatory" effects of most domain-based group policies. In order for any kind of mandatory access control to be effective in helping protect people from malware, it'll have to be imposed not by the administrator (who may not be security-conscious enough to restrict himself), but by the operating system itself, and in general that's how Vista's Windows Integrity Control system works.

Vista's "Windows Integrity Control" system, then, is an implementation of the standard notion of a mandatory access control system.

Strictly speaking, it's not really a mandatory *access* control, as it lacks the flexibility and richness of Windows's DACLs. Its goal is mostly to keep low-level processes from damaging higher-level objects, so Microsoft uses the phrase "integrity" rather than "access."

WIC's mandatory nature comes from the fact that by default it is the operating system, not the administrator, that sets the integrity levels, and it is possible for the operating system to create objects with integrity levels so high that no administrator could ever access them.

Conceptually, an object, like a file, stores its integrity level pretty much the same way that it stores its discretionary access control list and, for that matter, the name of its owner: in the file metadata. I figured that the piece of data on a file that says, "I have the medium integrity level" might be called a mandatory access control entry or MACE, but the Orange Book guys refer to that information as a "sensitivity label" or, sometimes, just a "label." Microsoft calls theirs "mandatory labels" although I would have thought that "integrity labels" would have been a better name. In any case, remember:

- "Integrity level" refers to a process, user, or object's level of trustworthiness.

- "Mandatory label" is just the name for the thing stuck on the process, user, or object to announce its integrity level.

WIC Components

Okay, thanks for sitting through the theory; time to get down to the details. Stringing together terminology and concepts, you have thus far seen that *Windows Integrity Control* applies *mandatory labels* to *securable objects* to declare their *integrity levels*, a measure of their trustworthiness. I've also said that the main effect of integrity levels is that you can configure anything to ignore attempts to read, write, or execute it when those attempts come from a process with a lower integrity level.

WIC's Six Integrity Levels

Microsoft chose six integrity levels. As far as I can see, they all get some use in Windows by default, but honestly the big one is the low integrity level. I'm simplifying, but at the moment it seems to me that most of WIC's work is in maintaining the border between "low" and everything higher than it. That's not to say that there isn't any difference between the levels or that you can't exploit them once you know what they are, so let's take a look at the six levels. Any process, user, or object can, in theory, hold any one of the following six levels, arranged in increasing order of trustworthiness:

Untrusted   According to Microsoft documentation, this is the setting given to any process logged on anonymously. I've not found a way to really try this out, except in one way. As I'll demonstrate later, if you give an untrusted integrity level to a program file, any EXE, and try to run it, Windows will tell you "access denied."

Low   This is the integrity level given by default to anything from the Internet. Internet Explorer runs in low by default, although you can change that by disabling a new feature of Internet Explorer 7 called "Protected Mode." When setting up your profile, Vista creates several folders with low integrity—for example, your Temporary Internet Files folder. It also sets up a few Registry keys with low integrity because the new Internet Explorer wouldn't be able to save your settings otherwise.

Medium   Standard users run in this integrity level. In fact, almost every file on your computer has a medium integrity level because anything that hasn't been explicitly labeled gets the medium integrity level. That's useful because recall that WIC's first job is to protect your files from malware collected from the Internet. As "unlabeled" means "medium," that means that most malware's attempts to modify your files or folders will be rebuffed. (Well, the malware you get from the Internet. Any malware you bring into the office on a CD will run at medium or high, depending on how you're logged in when you accidentally install it!)

High   Administrators run in this integrity level. Without a high integrity level, administrators probably couldn't get their jobs done, or at least it probably seemed that way when WIC first appeared. In its first incarnation, I'm told that you needed a *higher* integrity level than an object had to write to it. Thus, admins needed a higher integrity level than what users had.

System   Humans don't run in this integrity level or, rather, there's no way to make them do it that I've figured out. System services and in fact most of the kernel seem to run in the system integrity level. That's no problem and in fact it'll serve to make services more impervious to an administrator accidentally elevating some bad malware. The worrisome part is that perhaps some day some bad guy will figure out how to write malware onto the system with the system integrity level. Just think: malware that even an *administrator* can't uninstall.

Installer   Jumping off from a previous point, Microsoft needed the installer system to be higher in IL than anything else so that it could *uninstall* it due, again, to the original spec on WIC that said that a process needed a higher IL than an object in order to modify the object. (In practice, I'm not aware of any instance where you actually see anything operating as "Installer.")

Under the hood, though, you're going to see that integrity levels usually aren't as simple as "system," "high," and so on. Every integrity level can be expressed as a SID that looks like S-1-16-*number*, where the number varies from 0 to 16384. Each level also gets a name that looks like "Mandatory Label*Level* Mandatory Level," where *Level* is Untrusted, Low, Medium, or whatever. Most levels *also* have a two-letter code used for things encoded in something called the Security Descriptor Definition Language or SDDL.

I know that's a lot to see all at once but I promise, it'll be clearer when we see some real-live mandatory labels, SDDL strings, and the like—I promise, I'll cover all of that stuff in this chapter. For now, though, let me just offer Table 4.1 as a reference to the many guises that a given integrity level takes on—guises that we'll meet in this chapter.

TABLE 4.1   Summary of Types of Integrity Levels

Name	Account Name	SID	Hexadecimal Value	SDDL SID string	Notes
Untrusted	Mandatory Label\Untrusted Mandatory Level	S-1-16-0	0	None	Anonymous
Low	Mandatory Label\Low Mandatory Level	S-1-16-4096	1000	LW	"Protected Mode Internet Explorer" runs in this, and any objects automatically downloaded from the Internet into Temporary Internet Files get this level's label.
Medium	Mandatory Label\Medium Mandatory Level	S-1-16-8192	2000	ME	Users run here and anything without a label (i.e., system files) have an assumed IL of ME. Files that standard users download from the Internet with "save as" get this level.
High	Mandatory Label\High Mandatory Level	S-1-16-12288	3000	HI	Administrators run here.
System	Mandatory Label\System Mandatory Level	S-1-16-16384	4000	SI	Most system services run here.

How Objects Get and Store Integrity Levels: Mandatory Labels

Vista stores integrity level differently for processes, users, and objects. Vista stores an object's integrity level inside a special System Access Control Entry (SACE, pronounced to rhyme with "ace"), which is on that object's System Access Control List (SACL, pronounced to rhyme with "ACL").

The SACL: It's Not Just for Audits Anymore

"SACL" and "SACE" don't ring any bells or, perhaps, the bells tinkle but a mite faintly? Given how little they've done for us since NT 3.1's appearance, that'd be no surprise. If you've ever audited object access, however, then you've used them. In addition to space for a discretionary ACL, every securable object has space for a *system* ACL. Don't go looking in the Orange Book, Common Criteria, or the like for SACLs—they're not there. But back when they were working on NT 3.1, Microsoft said "hey, as long as we're creating places for the DACLs we need for that C2 certification, why not leave one for our own purposes?" and so they added a SACL.

Microsoft envisioned using the SACL and its component SACEs for many things, but the only thing that SACLs have ever held have been instructions about what to audit. Most of the nine things that Microsoft lets you audit, like logons, use of privileges, system events, and the like consist of nothing more than just on/off switches in group policies that enable or disable some class of audits. But if you flip "Audit object access" on, you won't get any information in the Security event log because you must first go to every object for which you'd like Windows to track access and describe how specific you'd like Windows to be in reporting that access. For example, suppose you want Windows to watch activity on a particular file. You can't just tell Windows, "watch all access attempts on the file `test.txt`"—that's not enough information by half. Windows wants to know, "who should I report on, and what kind of activity should I report on—when she tries to read? Write? Change an attribute? And should I report the successes, failures, or both?" As anyone who's ever done object access auditing knows, you've either got to be very specific about what you'd like to see, or face mountains of audit logs. Anyway, when you specified exactly who you wanted watched, what activities you wanted watched, and whether you wanted successes, failures, or both tracked, then that information went into the SACL as one or more SACEs and, from 1993 to now, that's about the only use the SACEs and SACLs have had.

You can see the SACEs on any object by right-clicking it, then choosing Properties. In the property page that appears, click the Security tab and then the Advanced button. In the dialog box *that* raises, click the Auditing tab—in Vista, you'll have to first click a Continue button to make User Account Control happy—and you will, on the resulting page, see any SACEs on that object. In most cases, however, it'll be empty, as most folks don't do much object auditing.

WIC's Mandatory Labels: Lost in SACE

"Danger, danger, Will Robinson!" (Sorry, couldn't resist.) If you just read that tip, then you may be wondering something. After all, I've already said that (1) everything's got an integrity level in Vista, (2) it's stored as a new kind of access control entry called a "mandatory label," (3) that mandatory label ACE is actually a special SACE, and...(4) you just read that the chances are good that any given file's SACL—the list of its SACEs—is empty. Okay, Robot, *now* you can talk. Go ahead....

"That does not compute, Will Robinson! If all objects have mandatory labels that are actually SACES then how can their SACLs be empty urrgh..."<slight sound of thump as the Robot's head slumps forward and his lights go out when some miscreant flips his normally obscure power switch>.

I've always wanted to turn off that robot. Anyway, our metal friend is right, or at least his inference engine is, because I left off two factoids.

- First, Microsoft decided for some reason *not* to show the mandatory label SACE in the GUI in the Auditing tab. As far as I can see, there are no GUI tools that will show you an object's mandatory label SACEs. There *is* a command-line tool that we'll discuss later, but it's limited in capabilities. Meanwhile, *I've* written a command-line tool that does things that the built-into-Vista tool does, and more—but we'll meet that in a minute.

- Second, in actual fact the vast majority of objects in Windows *have* an integrity level, but it's only an *implicit* one. Most things do not have an actual mandatory label SACE because of the WIC Second Directive.

 The Second Directive of Windows Integrity Control is "if an object doesn't have an *explicit* mandatory label, then treat the object as if it had a mandatory label identifying that object as being of medium integrity."

It was probably a good move on Microsoft's part to store integrity levels as something in an object's SACL, because so many kinds of objects already *have* SACLs. Thus, without having to replace *too* much of Windows' plumbing, we get a mandatory control infrastructure in addition to our already existing discretionary one.

Viewing Object Integrity Levels: Meet *chml* and *icacls*

So how *do* we view an object's mandatory level? Well, actually, Windows doesn't have a tool that does that. (Or at least it didn't until just a few weeks before Vista's release.) But *I* do.

The Tools: *icacls* and *chml*

You see, back when I was first working on this Windows Integrity Control stuff, I asked everyone at Microsoft who'd listen, "what tool shows me an object's integrity level? What lets me *change* an object's integrity level?" To both questions, I got a blank stare and the answer that "there is no tool that can do that." They were partly right, because there *is* a tool in Vista that lets you *set* integrity levels and, yes, it does let you view integrity levels sometimes, but not all of the time.

It seems, however, that almost no one in the Microsoft world knew of this tool, a command-line program named icacls that Microsoft intends to use to replace cacls, a command-line application that's been around since NT 3.1, if I recall right. I say that virtually no one knew about icacls because *I* found it when I started playing with RC1, only to find that it just plain didn't do what its Help claimed that it could do. Finally I found a helpful soul at Redmond who confirmed that yes, icacls would work by the final release, but didn't work in RC1.

It *did* get fixed, but only in Build 5744, which Microsoft released in mid-October. I couldn't wait that long, so I wrote my own program that did what icacls did, and (he said, modestly) a bit more. I called it "chml," for "change mandatory label." Get it like this:

1. Open up Internet Explorer.
2. In the address bar, type **www.minasi.com/vista/chml.htm**.
3. Click on the hyperlink to download **chml.exe**.
4. When prompted, click the Save button.
5. Save it to a folder that you can write to; the **c:\mystuff** folder we've been using works fine.
6. Open an elevated command prompt.

> I took you through all of that rather than just saying "go to such and such URL and save this to c:\windows" because Internet Explorer runs in low integrity and Explorer runs in medium integrity and cannot write files to the Windows directory; in contrast, from an elevated command prompt, *you* can. It's just part of getting used to Vista. Another perfectly good approach is to save chml.exe to some folder and modify your system's path to include that folder.

7. Change directory to **c:\mystuff** with **cd \mystuff**.

Viewing Integrity Levels with *chml*

1. From the elevated command prompt, type **copy chml.exe c:\windows** so that it'll be somewhere that we can get to from any directory.
2. Then query **notepad.exe** by typing **chml c:\windows\notepad.exe**, like this:

    ```
    C:\mystuff>chml c:\windows\notepad.exe -b
    c:\windows\notepad's mandatory integrity level=unlabeled (medium)
    ```

    Notice that **chml** tells you that **notepad.exe** has a medium integrity level, but that it comes by that integrity level by default.

3. To see one with an explicit integrity level, type **chml c:\users*yourusername*\appdata\locallow -b**, and press Enter, where you should substitute your username for "*yourusername*". For example, I'm logged in as "mark," so running **chml** would look like this:

    ```
    C:\mystuff>chml c:\users\mark\appdata\locallow -b
    c:\users\mark\appdata\locallow's mandatory integrity level=low
    ```

    Notice two things:

- First, as promised, there *are* things on your computer that are low integrity right out of the box. (And when I say "low integrity," I'm not talking about the salespeople who sold you the computer. Or, God forbid, Vista Home Basic.)
- Second, notice that in this case you don't see the "unlabeled."

Viewing Integrity Levels with *icacls*

Let's next try those jobs out with the built-in tool, icacls. To see icacls in action, just

1. Open a command prompt, either elevated or not.

2. Type **icacls c:\windows\notepad.exe** and press Enter.

3. Type **icacls c:\users*yourusername*\appdata\locallow**—and substitute your username for "*yourusername*" and press Enter.

You'll see something like Figure 4.1, which I'm presenting as a screen shot rather than text because the format of icacls' output tends to make it wrap on the page and become basically unreadable.

FIGURE 4.1   Reading mandatory labels with *icacls*

Hang on, I know it's ugly, but please don't run away! Learning to interpret icacls output is important because, again, *this* is the only tool, GUI or otherwise, that comes with Vista and lets you examine or modify an integrity level. icacls's output is something of a mixed bag of permission information because it

- Only shows you the contents of the discretionary ACL and any mandatory labels; anything that's in the system ACL that *isn't* a mandatory label doesn't show up. That means that if either Notepad or LocalLow had auditing SACEs on them, then icacls would not report them.

- Because icacls only shows you the ACEs that are actually there, it cannot tell you that, for example, Notepad has an *assumed* medium integrity level. But just remember, if you do not see anything with "Mandatory Label" at the beginning of it, then there's no explicit label for integrity levels, and it's treated as medium.

- The stuff that looks like (OI)(CI)(NW) is a shorthand way of describing the permissions that the ACE confers. In this case, it means

  - "Give any files in this folder an integrity level of low like the parent folder." (OI)

  - "Give any subfolders in this folder an integrity level of low like the parent folder." (CI)

  - "Do not allow any process of a lower integrity level to modify this folder." (NW)

  That shorthand is part of the Security Descriptor Definition Language that I mentioned earlier, and I will present a short guide to it a bit later.

Decoding Mandatory Labels

icacls presented LocalLow's integrity label as it did because that's the official Microsoft format for displaying labels. It looked like "Mandatory Label\Low Mandatory Level," a label that I introduced earlier but did not explain in detail. It means that

- The "domain" part of the object name is "Mandatory Label." This name derives, recall, from Orange Book talk.

- The "object name" part will be one of the following values:

  - System Mandatory Level

  - High Mandatory Level

  - Medium Mandatory Level

  - Low Mandatory Level

  - Untrusted Mandatory Level

NOTE You may recall that there is another level, the "Installer" or "Trusted Installer" level, but I didn't name it in the above list. Honestly I've never seen an object that runs at that level—it's an integrity level given only to processes as far as I can see—so I can't report what, if anything, icacls would report for such an object. I have seen the other labels, however.

In case this "Mandatory Label\Low Mandatory Level" doesn't make sense, yet compare it to another ACE as presented by icacls, the first one on "LocalLow." icacls presents it as

Vista64\Mark:(F)

In comparison, icacls shows the mandatory label like so:

Mandatory Label\Low Mandatory Level:(OI)(CI)(NW)

In general, ACEs confer permissions, and, simplified, there are two parts to every permission: who's getting the permission (the "trustee" in Microsoft terms), and what level of permission he's getting, like "full control" or "Read" or the like. In icacls output, the trustee is on the left side of the colon, like "Vista64\Mark," and the permission amount is on the right of the colon, as in "(F)," which means "full control."

Now, mandatory labels, the SACEs where Microsoft stores information on integrity levels, don't really fit into that model because the trustee, the thing that's getting the label, is obvious: it's whatever object the SACE is on. In "Vista64\Mark," the "Vista64" part is essential, as it identifies where to find the computer that holds the Mark user account. But mandatory labels are domain and computer-independent. Given that, all that a mandatory label need convey is the integrity level that the object has. But the fact is that because Microsoft was trying to use an existing storage mechanism for the mandatory labels—a SACE—then they had to make the data fit into that container's rules, and, again, the rules are that the absolute minimum amount of information that any ACE needs is "who gets this?" and "what do they get?" Normally that first part is expressed as a combination of an account name and the domain or local system that the account lives in, but that really didn't make sense here, so Microsoft just arbitrarily gave it a "domain name" of "Mandatory Label."

Technically, the thing on the left-hand-side of the backward slash, whether it's a local system name, a domain, or "Mandatory Label," is called the "authority" that issued the name.

Changing Object Integrity Levels

From the beginning I've been kind of twitchy about this whole idea of stuff that I can't change, so I was very, very interested in discovering what, if anything, I could do to change an object's integrity level. Here's the short version:

- Users *can* change an object's integrity level if they have a new-to-Vista user privilege known in Microsoft privilege as `SeRelabelPrivilege` that lets them modify an object's mandatory label.

- Any user with that privilege will get a split token when logging on, as that privilege is one of the Notorious Nine, as you read in Chapter 2.

- Anyone wanting to read an object's mandatory label only needs "read permissions" on the object. To change an integrity level by modifying a mandatory label, that user would also need "change permissions" *and* "take ownership" on that object.

- Users with `SeRelabelPrivilege` can raise or lower an object's integrity level, but they cannot raise that object's integrity level above their own.

Let's take these in turn so that we can start messing with integrity levels.

The New "Modify an object label Properties" Privilege

Recall that mandatory controls, as laid out in the Orange Book and similar standards, can be "mandatory" in varying degrees. In their weakest form, they might be nothing more than rules created by administrators to restrict the discretionary powers of standard users; in the extreme they could be iron rules built right into the operating system that no one can change. Windows' implementation of Windows Integrity Controls is somewhere in the middle, and permits administrators to loosen or tighten things a bit.

Right out of the box, Vista's Windows Integrity Controls are unbending—if something is of medium integrity, it's staying that way. But that changes if you grant the right to change mandatory integrity levels to someone—and heck, why not yourself? The new privilege's English name is "Modify an object label," short name SeRelabelPrivilege. Here's how to get it.

> **WARNING**   You'll need local administrative powers to modify your user rights to make this work, as has been the case since Windows 2000. If your test machine is a member of an Active Directory domain and your domain admin has locked down your user rights, then you'll either have to go talk to her, just follow along with the screen shots, or set up a stand-alone test system that's not a member of the domain to do this stuff. I am a huge fan of virtual machines for this kind of stuff, and both Microsoft and VMWare offer very nice and free virtual machine managers. Personally, I like VMWare Workstation, even though it runs just under $200. It has repaid its cost over and over and over....

1. Open up your system's local Group Policy Object Editor. Either type **gpedit.msc** from a command line, or click Start ➤ All Programs ➤ Accessories ➤ Run... and fill in **gpedit.msc** and click OK.

2. Click Confirm at the Consent UI unless you've disabled UAC or you've started gpedit.msc from an elevated command prompt.

3. Navigate to Computer Configuration ➤ Windows Settings ➤ Security Settings ➤ Local Policies ➤ User Rights Assignment.

4. Scroll down to find "Modify an object label." Double-click it.

5. In the resulting "Modify an object label Properties" dialog box, click the Add User or Group button.

6. In the resulting field labeled "Enter the object names to select," type in your username, or perhaps just punch in **Administrators** to give all local administrators this privilege. (If you *do* enter Administrators, though, be sure to click the Object Types button on the right-hand side of the dialog box so that you can check the check box next to Groups. For some reason by default the User Rights Assignment area of group policies only wants you to enter usernames rather than groups. By checking this box, it'll accept a group name.) Click OK until you get back to the Group Policy Object Editor.

7. Close the Group Policy Object Editor.

At this point, you've got the privilege on your account, but not your token. So don't forget Windows Security 101: log off and log back on to give Windows a chance to include that new privilege in your token.

Permissions Needed to Change an Integrity Level

Before you can change an integrity level, you'll need some permissions—but how much? Recall that integrity levels are implemented as system access control entries, and "access control entry" is just another word for "permission." You may also know that files have 12 low-level permission types and folders have 13, and in both cases there are specific permissions named "read permissions" and "change permissions"—permissions about permissions, you might say. Therefore, it's no surprise to hear that reading an object's integrity level requires only the "read permission" permission.

Changing an integrity level, however, is a bit of a surprise. You need the "change permission" permission, of course, but you *also* need the "take ownership" permission. Why? Because one of the other 12 or 13 low-level permissions is "take ownership." Therefore, anyone who can change an object's permissions can give herself ownership of a file, and ownership is of course a pretty big thing. Therefore Vista requires not only "change permission" permission to modify an integrity level, but the "take ownership" permission as well.

Changing an Object's Integrity with *chml*

Once you've gotten `SeRelabelPrivilege` and have sufficient permissions (you already did, so there's nothing to do in this case), and have `chml.exe` in `c:\windows` so that it's on your path, you can take `chml` out for a spin, but this time, we won't just *look* at integrity levels…we'll change them. For this exercise, let's continue working in `c:\mystuff`, so open up an *elevated* command prompt and a nonelevated command prompt, and navigate to `c:\mystuff` on both of them with `cd \mystuff`. Then dig out the `createfile` program from `vistafiles.zip`, which recall you downloaded from `http://www.minasi.com/vista` in Chapter 2 and do this:

1. From the unelevated command prompt, type **createfile hltest.txt** and, of course, press Enter. You've now got a simple text file named `hltest.txt`.

2. Verify that you can modify this file by opening it with Notepad. Change a character or two, save the file, and close Notepad.

3. Examine its mandatory integrity level by typing **chml hltest.txt -b** and pressing Enter. You'll see that it has a medium integrity level because we haven't given it a mandatory label yet.

4. Now switch over to the elevated command prompt.

5. Raise `hltest.txt`'s integrity level to high by typing **chml hltest.txt -i:h -b** and pressing Enter. You should get a response like

   ```
   Integrity level of hltest.txt successfully set to high.
   ```

 chml's syntax for changing integrity levels is "chml *filename* -i:*level*," where *level* can be u, l, m, h, or s for untrusted, low, medium, high, and system, respectively. "s" won't work, though, because you're only running at a "high" integrity level. (It's in there because I'm hoping to figure out how to make it work one day.)

6. Use `icacls` to verify that you've raised `hltest.txt`'s integrity level by typing **icacls hltest.txt** and notice the line saying "Mandatory Label\High Mandatory Level" label. You can see a similar result by running `chml hltest.txt -b`.

Changing an Object's Integrity with *icacls*

icacls finally started working with Build 5744 as I was finishing the book, so I can show you how to change a file or folder's integrity level with this syntax:

```
icacls filename /setintegritylevel H|M|L
```

To which icacls will respond

```
processed file: filename
Successfully processed 1 files; Failed processing 0 files.
```

So, for example, to change hltest.txt's integrity level to low, you'd type

```
icacls hltest.txt /setintegritylevel L
```

As with chml, changing a file's integrity level requires having SeRelabelPrivilege, an elevated command prompt, and both "change permissions" and "take ownership" permissions on hltest.txt.

Testing Out WIC's Prime Directive

Back when we started discussing this topic, I said that the big payoff about WIC was that lower-integrity processes could not modify higher-integrity objects. Now that we've got a file that's got a high integrity level, let's see what might happen if we try to mess with that file.

1. Start Notepad from the Start menu, not your elevated command prompt, and read c:\mystuff\hltest.txt. Now, because you started Notepad from the Start menu in the usual way, then it will get your standard user token, assuming that you haven't disabled UAC. (If you did, then most of what you'll see here won't work.) Forgive me for jumping ahead a bit, but please just trust me when I say that Notepad is running at medium integrity level right now.

2. Change the text a bit.

3. Click File ➢ Save to save the file.

   Notepad will complain that it "Cannot create the C:\mystuff\hltest.txt file; Make sure that the path and file name are correct." That's Notepad's less-than-clear way of saying, "I got an Access Denied message from the operating system when I tried to write out a new hltest.txt file." Now let's demonstrate that Notepad *can* modify hltest.txt, when Notepad's got the right integrity level.

4. Click OK to clear the error dialog, Esc to clear the File Save dialog, and close Notepad, choosing "Don't save" when it asks you what to do with the changed file.

5. *Now* start up Notepad by clicking Start ➢ All Programs ➢ Accessories and then right-click Notepad and choose "Run as administrator."

6. Click Continue at the UAC prompt. Again, we'll cover this in more detail soon, but for the moment let me note that Notepad now runs in high integrity.

7. Open c:\mystuff\hltest.txt.

8. Modify the text again.

9. Click File ➢ Save. Notice: this time, no errors, as the process (Notepad) had an integrity level equal to or greater than the object (`h1test.txt`).

10. Exit Notepad.

Summarizing, here's what we've seen in this section and with these exercises:

-   You can raise or lower an object's integrity level so long as you've got `SeRelabelPrivilege` and are running as an administrator. You've *got* to be running elevated with "Run as administrator" because you may recall that `SeRelabelPrivilege` is one of the Notorious Nine privileges that get removed from your standard user token.

-   You must have the "read permissions," "change permissions," and "take ownership" permissions on an object to view and modify its integrity level.

-   You can use `chml` or `icacls` to make the change.

-   You can raise or lower any object's integrity level as high as your integrity level, and no higher.

By the way, if you've sat through or read some of the early material from Microsoft about Windows Integrity Controls, then you may have heard that users with the "modify an object's label" privilege could only *lower* an object's integrity level. That may have been true for early betas of Vista, but it's not true now. As you'll learn later, the highest integrity level that a user can get is High, so that's as high as you'll ever raise an object's integrity.

I know what you ~~hacker~~ security expert types are thinking. "No problem, I'll just schedule an integrity-changing command via the at.exe program and, as at.exe runs under LocalSystem—which runs at the system, not the high, level—then it can raise an integrity level all the way to system. Or perhaps I'll have that run in a Startup script, as that runs at LocalSystem." As the folks say where I grew up in New York, fuhggedaboutit. Microsoft's apparently read a couple of those "how to hack Windows" books and plugged those holes, dagnabbit. I think there *might* be a way to build a service—services run as system integrity—but I'm not a good enough programmer to write one of those. Also, I suspect that Microsoft has thought of that as well.

Default Low Integrity Folders

Before moving along to examine how users and processes get integrity levels, let me mention a few cases where Vista's designers have made use of the ability to set integrity levels on folders. They're there in support of Protected Mode Internet Explorer:

-   \Users*username*\AppData\LocalLow,

-   \Users*username*\AppData\Local\Temp\Low, and

-   Several objects in \Users*username*\AppData\Local\Microsoft\Temporary Internet Files\Low (which is a System file, so you won't see it by default)

User Integrity Levels

We've just seen how objects get and store integrity levels. Next, let's take on user accounts to see where they get their integrity levels.

User Integrity Levels Depend Solely on Privileges

As far as I can see, users in the Vista world can only get either a high integrity level or a medium one, although I imagine that there might be cases where someone might log onto a Vista box anonymously, which would get them an "untrusted" integrity level. But which do you get, high or medium? Basically, anyone running with a standard user token will have a medium integrity level, and anyone running with an administrator token gets a high integrity level. But why does *that* happen?

Well, recall from Chapter 2 that User Account Control gives you a split token when you log on if you're either a member of the Fearsome Four local groups or have one of the Notorious Nine user privileges. I therefore expected that if I turned off UAC altogether, created a user, and added it to, say, Network Configuration Operators—one of the Fearsome Four—then when I logged it on, it'd have a high integrity level. (I'll show you how to determine your integrity level in a moment.) I was surprised to find that the user account ran at medium. I got the same result for adding the user account to Power Users, another member of the Nine—a user that's a member of Power Users and Network Configuration Operators runs just as a medium integrity user.

But add that user to either the Backup Operators or Administrators group, and its integrity shoots up to high. The rules for assigning a user an integrity level, then, seem to be quite simple:

- In determining your user account's mandatory integrity level, your group memberships don't count. The Fearsome Four are irrelevant save in a backhanded way, because...

- What *does* matter is the set of user privileges that you enjoy. If your user account includes any members of the Notorious Nine, then your logon gets a high integrity designation for this session and any others where it has one of the Nine as a privilege. If it lacks all of the Nine, then it gets a medium integrity level.

Where Users Store Integrity Levels

Although user accounts are securable objects, there doesn't seem to be any way to apply mandatory labels to them, and apparently nothing good would come of doing so. So where does a user account carry its integrity level? Vista assigns an integrity level to a user's token at logon. Recall from Chapter 2 that upon logon you get a token that contains

- Your SID

- The SIDs of any global and universal groups to which you belong

- Your privileges

As I briefly mentioned in Chapter 2, Vista also marks your token as medium or high (or, theoretically, anything else) by adding a kind of fake group SID along with your group SIDs to your token. But where many SIDs are long strings of numbers, an "integrity SID" looks like a simple

`S-1-16-value`

Where *value* is some arbitrary number. Look back to Table 4.1 and you'll see that *value* is 0 for the untrusted integrity level, 4096 for low integrity, 8192 for medium integrity, 12288 for high integrity, and 16384 for system integrity. But *where* did they get *those* numbers? Well, for those of us in the audience who've have had to do a lot of decimal-to-hex and back conversions, those numbers might ring a bell, because while 0, 4096, 8192, 12288, and 16384 may not look like they make much of a pattern, let's recast them in hex, where they become 0, 1000, 2000, 3000, and 4000—now, *that* makes some sense! And that all means that we're ready to actually see our integrity level.

Viewing User Integrity Levels

The Vista tool for seeing your current integrity level is the command-line utility `whoami` (which we met in Chapter 2, recall) either with the `/groups` or `/all` options. For example, if I'm logged onto a Vista computer and I start up an unelevated command prompt and then type

`whoami /groups /fo list`

Then among the output I'll get is this:

```
Group Name: Mandatory Label\Medium Mandatory Level
Type:       Unknown SID type
SID:        S-1-16-8192
Attributes: Mandatory group, Enabled by default, Enabled group
```

Notice that `whoami` calls this a "group" and refers to its name by a now-familiar one: "Mandatory Label\Medium Mandatory Level" which, we now know, is Vista's wordy way of saying "medium integrity level." Notice also the SID, 8192, which Table 4.1 told us is the one associated with a medium integrity level.

Give it a try yourself on a Vista box. Once you've seen the S-1-16-8192 SID, create an elevated command prompt and try it again to see the S-1-16-12288 prompt.

Process Integrity Levels

Given that Windows Integrity Control's Prime Directive is that no process can modify an object of higher integrity level, it's really the integrity levels of *processes* more than users that feature heavily in WIC, so let's take a look at process integrity levels.

How Processes Get Their Integrity Levels

Processes get their tokens by mixing two things that we've already learned in this book. First, recall from Chapter 2 that processes basically get their tokens from whomever started them; if Joe starts Word while he's logged in as a standard user with a medium integrity level, then

Word will usually have a token with a medium integrity level. But remember that a process is nothing more than a copy of an EXE file running in memory, and that you've learned in this chapter that any file can have an integrity level embedded in it. When Vista starts a process, it uses this algorithm to decide what integrity level it gets.

- Rule 1: if someone with a high integrity level starts a process, the process runs with high integrity.

- Rule 2: if you start a process with "Run as administrator," the process runs with high integrity.

    If you're running as a standard user when you start a process, though, the rules change a bit.

- Rule 3: if you start a process while running as a standard user, then the process either gets an integrity level equal to the one on your token (medium), or on its EXE file, whichever is lower.

- Rule 4: it's always possible for one process to start another process at a lower integrity level, but for a process to start a process at a higher integrity level requires user approval through UAC.

    Let's take a few examples to clarify this:

Example 1: Run as administrator   Suppose I right-click the Notepad icon and choose "Run as administrator." The Consent UI appears and I choose Continue. Notepad is now running in high integrity mode.

Example 2: Started by an administrator   Suppose I'm logged onto Vista as a member of the local Administrators group. I double-click the Notepad icon. What happens? Well, assuming that UAC is enabled, then I've got a split token, and unless I request elevation, then Notepad gets my standard user token. The actual `notepad.exe` file is unlabeled and therefore gets medium integrity level. As both the user token and the EXE file are of medium integrity, the process—Notepad—runs at medium integrity level.

Example 3: Started from an elevated command prompt   I've started an elevated command prompt by right-clicking the Command Prompt icon and choosing "Run as administrator" and then Continue at the Consent UI. From that prompt, I type `notepad` and press Enter. What happens? Because I've started Notepad from the elevated command prompt, it inherits my S-1-16-12288 "high integrity" token. Rule 1 kicks in, so Notepad runs as high integrity.

Example 4: Starting a low integrity EXE file   Suppose I've used `icacls` or `chml` to label an EXE file as low integrity. I'm running with a standard user token and I just double-click its icon—and do *not* start the EXE by right-clicking it and choosing "Run as administrator." Now Vista has a process to start that inherits a token at medium integrity, but whose EXE file is marked "low integrity." What happens? The program runs as low integrity.

    We'll do some exercises that underscore this soon, but first let's get some more techie details out of the way.

Viewing Process Integrity Levels

Where does a process store its integrity level, and how can we see it? Well, a process clearly has an integrity level stored in its EXE file, but, as we saw earlier, that's only one factor in determining the integrity level that it ultimately gets, and, besides, a process can get quite different integrity levels at different times depending on who started it and how she started it, so clearly looking at the integrity label on the EXE is not the way to go.

Instead, a process stores its integrity level in its token, which can vary from run to run. To see a process's current integrity level, then, we need to peek into its token, which lives only in the computer's RAM.

> That's unless, of course, the application is designed to read its own token and report to you on command. The only application that I know of that does that is whoami.exe.

You might think that integrity levels would be a perfect thing for Task Manager to show, but it doesn't, so we're on our own. Sucking up an application's token "on the wing" might make for some fancy programming, but thankfully we needn't, as Mark Russinovich has created Process Explorer, and you can find that at http://www.sysinternals.com. (Or at least you can now. By the time you read this, it'll probably be on Microsoft's site, as they bought Sysinternals. Too bad they didn't do it earlier—maybe they would have tossed Task Manager in Vista and replaced it with Process Explorer.) Start it with "Run as administrator" or it won't have the privileges that it needs to peek into other processes, and you'll see something like Figure 4.2.

FIGURE 4.2   Running Process Explorer on Vista

Process	PID	C...	Description	Company Name	Integrity Level	Virtualized
System Idle Pro...	0	96...			n/a	
iexplore.exe	22...		Internet Explorer	Microsoft Corporation	Low	Virtualized
cmd.exe	25...		Windows Command P...	Microsoft Corporation	Medium	
cmd.exe	22...		Windows Command P...	Microsoft Corporation	Medium	
dwm.exe	21...		Desktop Window Man...	Microsoft Corporation	Medium	
dwm.exe	21...		Desktop Window Man...	Microsoft Corporation	Medium	
explorer.exe	22...		Windows Explorer	Microsoft Corporation	Medium	
explorer.exe	32...	1.52	Windows Explorer	Microsoft Corporation	Medium	
ieuser.exe	31...		Internet Explorer	Microsoft Corporation	Medium	Virtualized
MSASCui.exe	23...		Windows Defender Us...	Microsoft Corporation	Medium	
MSASCui.exe	33...		Windows Defender Us...	Microsoft Corporation	Medium	
taskeng.exe	21...		Task Scheduler Engine	Microsoft Corporation	Medium	
taskeng.exe	31...		Task Scheduler Engine	Microsoft Corporation	Medium	
VMwareTray.exe	24...		VMwareTray	VMware, Inc.	Medium	Virtualized
VMwareTray.exe	32...		VMwareTray	VMware, Inc.	Medium	Virtualized
VMwareUser.exe	24...		VMwareUser	VMware, Inc.	Medium	Virtualized
VMwareUser.exe	26...		VMwareUser	VMware, Inc.	Medium	Virtualized
cmd.exe	35...		Windows Command P...	Microsoft Corporation	High	
procexp.exe	30...		Sysinternals Process ...	Sysinternals	High	
procexp64.exe	36...		Sysinternals Process ...	Sysinternals	High	
csrss.exe	448		Client Server Runtime ...	Microsoft Corporation	System	
csrss.exe	500		Client Server Runtime ...	Microsoft Corporation	System	
csrss.exe	28...		Client Server Runtime ...	Microsoft Corporation	System	

Process Explorer - Sysinternals: www.sysinternals.com [Vista64\Mark]

File Options View Process Find Users Help

CPU Usage: 3.03%   Commit Charge: 38.41%   Processes: 52

Well, actually, your copy of Process Explorer will look like that screen shot if you click View ➤ Select Columns, where you'll get the option to choose what you want Process Explorer to show you. I added two checks: "Integrity Level" and "Virtualized." (We're not going to use Virtualized in this chapter, but you may find it interesting if you read the last chapter. It tells whether or not a particular application will get the benefit of file and Registry virtualization.) Notice that this particular computer has processes running in low (Internet Explorer), medium, high, and system-level integrity levels.

Seeing Processes in Action

Now that we're conversant with the ways that objects, users, and processes get their integrity levels, let's try them out to see for ourselves how they work. Here are a few step-by-step demonstrations of integrity levels in processes.

Setting Up

We'll do these examples pretty much as before. In addition to Vista, you'll need chml.exe and Process Explorer. Once you've got those, get set up like so:

1. Open up two command prompts: one elevated, one not.

2. Change their default directories to c:\mystuff.

3. Start up Process Explorer with a high integrity token by right-clicking it and choosing "Run as administrator."

4. Now view the setup with Process Explorer. You should see two instances of cmd.exe, which is the Command Prompt. One will be running at medium integrity level, and the other at high.

Example: Starting a Low Integrity Application

Next, let's see how to create a low integrity process, and see how an EXE file's integrity isn't always the sole determinant in its process integrity. There isn't a nice command-line tool to launch any given application as a low integrity process, which is kind of odd, as I'd have guessed that cmd.exe or the start command would have contained that ability. But we've got our own tool to accomplish this: chml.

1. From the elevated command prompt, copy cmd.exe to mystuff by typing **copy c:\windows\system32\cmd.exe** and press Enter.

2. Then create a couple more copies by typing

```
copy cmd.exe lcmd.exe
copy cmd.exe hcmd.exe
```

3. Next, let's set their mandatory labels to "low" and "high," respectively, by typing

```
chml lcmd.exe -i:l -b
chml hcmd.exe -i:h -b
```

In case that font isn't clear, the first chml's -i: option is followed by a lowercase "L." Both commands should succeed, as long as you ran them from the elevated command prompt. Now we've got a high-integrity cmd.exe and a low-integrity one. In the *nonelevated* command prompt, type **hcmd** and press Enter. The only output you'll get will be a line or two of copyright and Windows version information, like

```
Microsoft Windows [Version 6.0.9421]
Copyright © 2006 Microsoft Corporation.  All rights reserved.
C:\mystuff>
```

So we started up a copy of Command Prompt whose file had a high integrity level and ran it from a medium integrity command prompt… what integrity level does this new process have? Well, we *expect* that anything started from a medium integrity level process won't be able to run any higher than medium integrity, as UAC hasn't popped up the Consent UI, but let's check it out: type **whoami /groups /fo list** and press Enter.

What happened? The last group reported was probably the Mandatory Label section, with "Mandatory Label\Medium Mandatory Label" reported, so things worked as expected, and hcmd.exe ran as medium integrity despite its file integrity.

4. Now try lcmd; in the unelevated command prompt window that you just did the whoami in, type **lcmd** and press Enter. Again, you should see the copyright and version notice, and a prompt. Again, type **whoami /groups /fo list**.

What did you get this time? If all went well, that last group was "Mandatory Label\Low Mandatory Label," with a SID of S-1-16-4096. Mission accomplished, we've got a low-integrity command prompt running!

> By the way, if you don't want to pick through all of the groups when doing a whoami /groups /fo list to find the one with the "Mandatory Label" line in it, just type **whoami /groups /fo list | find "Label"** and press Enter. The "find" filter is case sensitive, so be sure to type "Label" rather than "label."

Internet Explorer Protected Mode and WIC

You've already read that the version of Internet Explorer 7 that comes with Vista has something called "Protected Mode" that is, as far as I can see, one of the main reasons why Windows Integrity Control exists in the first place.

Vista's Internet Explorer 7—and the "Vista" part is important, as the version of IE 7 that runs atop XP SP2, 2003 SP1, and 2003 R2 does *not* behave in the same way—splits itself into two processes, `iexplore.exe` and `ieuser.exe`. (A close look back at Figure 4.2 will verify that.) `iexplore.exe` runs in low integrity, and `ieuser.exe` runs in medium integrity. Most of the surfing happens with `iexplore.exe`, which cannot write to anywhere except the Temporary Internet Files folder and the other low-integrity folders that I listed earlier. That's also true for IE 7 add-ons, so even if you load some malware, then it will only run in low integrity and so will be limited in what it can damage, although it can still read any file that discretionary ACLs don't block it from reading. (We'll see how you can change that later, to tighten up security a bit.) Further, IE 7 by default will not load an ActiveX control unless it's signed, so at least if you get some malware you'll know who wrote it!

But while touting the benefits of Internet Explorer 7, Microsoft doesn't always make clear that all of these benefits from low integrity only come when running Internet Explorer in Protected Mode, so it's important to be aware of when you are aren't using it. Take a look at Figure 4.3 to see what I mean.

The important point is on the status bar at the bottom of the window frame, where you see "Protected Mode: On." It's on by default, although you can turn it off by clicking Tools ➢ Internet Options and then clicking the Security tab to show something like Figure 4.4.

FIGURE 4.3 Internet Explorer 7 in Protected Mode

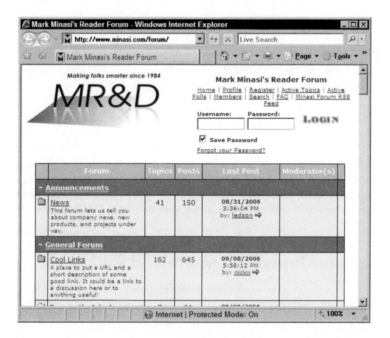

FIGURE 4.4 Enabling/disabling IE 7's Protected Mode

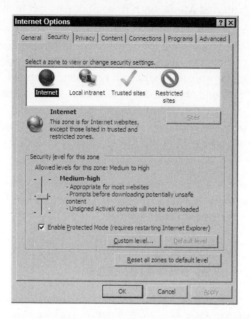

Now, that *looks* like the old IE security tab we've seen many times, but look below the slider on the left of the figure, and notice "Enable Protected Mode (requires restarting Internet Explorer)." Shutting it off is as easy as that, and you *don't* want users doing that. I don't think it'll be that long before we see websites trying to get people to shut off Protected Mode with enticements like "oh, sorry you can't see the pictures of the naked people because Protected Mode is blocking IE from showing them. Follow these directions to disable Protected Mode...." You can keep them from doing that by enabling the group policy setting in Computer Configuration ➢ Administrative Templates ➢ Windows Components ➢ Internet Explorer ➢ Security Page ➢ Internet Zone named "Turn on Protected Mode." If you turn this on, then the users can no longer disable Protected Mode.

Using the setup that we've already got running, you can verify the main effect of disabling Protected Mode—losing `iexplore.exe` as a low integrity process:

1. Start up Internet Explorer.

2. Look in Process Explorer if you've still got it running, and if not, then start it elevated, and note that `iexplore.exe` runs in low integrity.

3. Then in Internet Explorer, click Tools ➢ Internet Options and then the Security tab.

4. Uncheck "Enable Protected Mode (requires restarting Internet Explorer."

5. Click OK and then click OK on the resulting message box that says, "The current security settings will put your computer at risk."

6. Close and then restart IE.

7. Refresh Process Explorer by pressing F5.

8. Now you can verify that without Protected Mode, both IE components run in medium integrity level.

The point here was to underscore that if you disable Protected Mode in Internet Explorer, then you basically strip away the biggest part of the anti-spyware, anti-malware improvements that Vista offers. If you need to visit specific websites that cannot work in Protected Mode, then just put them in your "Trusted sites" zone because if you turn back to the Security tab of Internet Options on IE, notice that if you click between the Internet, Local intranet, Trusted sites, and Restricted sites zones, then you'll see that you can choose to enable or disable Protected Mode just for those zones and, in fact, by default the Trusted sites zone does not enable Protected Mode.

Another way to disable Protected Mode is to start Internet Explorer from the command line on an elevated command prompt.

A Prime Directive Puzzle: WIC and Deletes

Remember what I call "Windows Integrity Control's Prime Directive?" It says that "no process can modify an object with a higher integrity level." We saw that in action much earlier in this chapter when we created a file named h1test.txt and set its integrity level to high, and then opened it in Notepad. Recall that when we tried to save the file, Notepad couldn't, because Notepad was running as a medium integrity level process and was trying to modify a high integrity level process. That was a nice demonstration of the Prime Directive.

But now try *this* one.

If you've still got h1test.txt around, great; if not, just redo the steps in the earlier exercise. Then, from the unelevated command prompt,

1. Type **whoami /groups /fo | find "Label"** and press Enter to verify that you are indeed running with medium integrity level.

2. As you created this folder, you can give yourself full control of it, so let's do that by typing **icacls c:\mystuff /grant yourusername:(f)** and press Enter.

3. Finally, type **erase h1test.txt** and press Enter.

Note the distinct lack of an "access denied." Look in the folder, h1test.txt is gone, gone, gone! Now, I know that some of you folks who are just sitting and reading this without trying it out are skeptical, so consult Figure 4.5 if you are in doubt.

Testing File Delete Permissions with *icacls*

How the heck did *that* happen? The answer lies not in some new feature or bug in Vista, but in an old fact of life for permissions: the permissions for deleting files are looser than for almost anything else in NTFS. Where it's possible to, say, keep someone from reading a file once and for all by applying a single ACE to that file that says, "deny the 'read' permission to such-and-such person," you can't do that with file deletion.

FIGURE 4.5   A medium integrity process deletes a high integrity object!

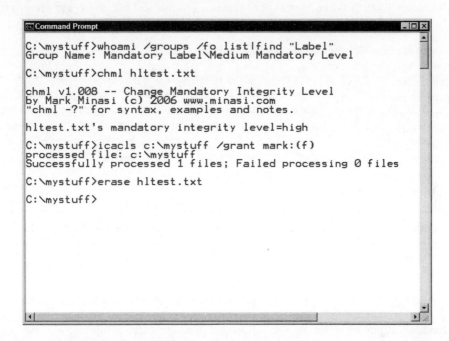

```
Command Prompt                                                    _ □ ×
C:\mystuff>whoami /groups /fo list|find "Label"
Group Name: Mandatory Label\Medium Mandatory Level

C:\mystuff>chml hltest.txt

chml v1.008 -- Change Mandatory Integrity Level
by Mark Minasi (c) 2006 www.minasi.com
"chml -?" for syntax, examples and notes.

hltest.txt's mandatory integrity level=high

C:\mystuff>icacls c:\mystuff /grant mark:(f)
processed file: c:\mystuff
Successfully processed 1 files; Failed processing 0 files

C:\mystuff>erase hltest.txt

C:\mystuff>
```

Here's an outline of a more specific example that you can try out to prove it to yourself on *any* system, from NT 3.1 up to Vista:

1. Create a folder.

2. As you are the owner of the folder, you can give yourself full control of the folder; do that.

3. Inside the folder, create a file.

4. As you are the creator of the file, you can *deny* yourself the right to delete the file; do that.

5. Try to delete the file; it will succeed.

All of that's easy enough to do from the GUI, but describing how to do it's a whole lotta clicking and dragging and, besides, I love preaching the Gospel of the Command Line, so if you'd like to try it, then start up an unelevated command prompt and type these commands. Where I've typed "mark," the account that I'm logged in as, just substitute your username. Start from c:\mystuff so you've got createfile close to hand.

```
md c:\test
icacls c:\test /grant mark:F
createfile c:\test\killtest.txt
icacls c:\test\killtest.txt /deny mark:(D)
erase c:\test\killtest.txt
```

Most of those commands should be clear—md makes directories or, as we've come to say since Windows 2000, "folders," createfile creates a simple text file, and erase erases a file. icacls lets me modify permissions of all types and its syntax looks like

```
icacls objectname /grant|/deny username:permission
```

That looks a little ugly but let's pick it apart to see how it works. *objectname* is just the name of the file or folder that we want icacls to work on. Use /grant to create a new "allow" ACE, or /deny to create a new "deny" ACE. *username* is whomever you want to give this new ACE to, and—here's the only troublesome part—*permission* is a set of one or more one- or two- character "codes" that refer to one of the 12 low-level file permissions or 13 low-level folder permissions. You can find them in the following Table 4.2.

TABLE 4.2 Permission Codes

If this refers to a file, then it means...	If this refers to a folder, then it means...	Code
If this file is an executable, allow the user to execute it	Bypass traverse checking	X
Read the data in this file	List the files and folder in this folder	RD
Read the basic attributes of this file (system, hidden, read-only, archive)	Read the basic attributes of this folder (system, hidden, read-only, archive)	RA
Change the basic attributes of this file (system, hidden, read-only, archive)	Change the basic attributes of this folder (system, hidden, read-only, archive)	WA
Read the extended attributes of this file (author, copyright, description, rating—basically any of the Vista "tags" or "metadata")	Read the extended attributes of this folder (author, copyright, description, rating—basically any of the Vista "tags" or "metadata")	REA
Change the extended attributes of this file (author, copyright, description, rating—basically any of the Vista "tags" or "metadata")	Change the extended attributes of this file (author, copyright, description, rating—basically any of the Vista "tags" or "metadata")	WEA
Change permissions on this file	Change permissions on this folder	WDAC
Read permissions on this file	Read permissions on this folder	RC
Delete this file	Delete this folder	D
Write or change the data in this file	Create a new file in this folder	WD
Append data to an existing file	Create a new subfolder in this folder	AD

TABLE 4.2   Permission Codes *(continued)*

If this refers to a file, then it means...	If this refers to a folder, then it means...	Code
Change this file's owner	Change this folder's owner	WO
	Delete files and folders in this folder (short for "delete child," as objects inside folders are called "child objects")	DC

You can include more than one permission; just separate them with a comma. For example, to give the account "jane" the ability to read permissions, write permissions and take owner-ship—recall that's the set of permissions that an account would need in order to modify a mandatory label—then I'd type

```
icacls c:\test /grant jane:(WO,RC,WDAC)
```

Anyway, returning to the example above, it worked like a charm. And, for the unbelievers, I offer a screen shot of a run of this in Figure 4.6. I included a `whoami /groups` to prove that, again, I was running there as a standard user, not an administrator.

FIGURE 4.6   Mark amazingly deletes the file even though he is denied the "delete file" permission!

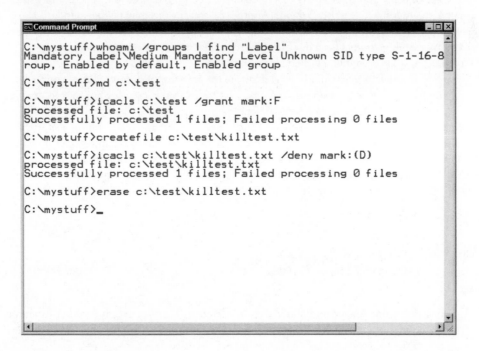

Denying File Deletes Is Different from Denying Most Things

What's going on here is not a Windows bug, but a design decision that Microsoft made. Consider that when you delete a file, in actuality *two* things happen. First, of course, you delete the actual object that is the file. But at the same time, you *modify* the object that is the folder.

 If that's not clear, think about what a folder is. It's really nothing more than a list of the files and subfolders inside of it. Adding a file adds something to the list, deleting one subtracts one. But in both cases, you have modified the list, and the list is a securable object…so you need the proper permissions.

So if deleting a file does two things—deletes the file and modifies the information in the folder that used to contain the file—then that seems to imply that I would need *two* permissions to delete a file:

- The "delete" permission on the file object
- The "delete subfolders and files" permission on the folder that contains the file

Now, I'd think that you would need *both* of those permissions to delete a file. But not everyone agrees; for example, I've seen Unix implementations that allow someone with administrator-level control of a folder to delete a file, even if that person has no permissions to the file itself. Were I in charge of maintaining a folder full of home directories and eliminating unlawful material but I couldn't have or, for legal reasons, might not want to have access to the particular files, I could see the logic of being able to delete "`stolen commercial music.mp3`" or "`nakedbabe.jpg`" without actually being able to open them. (Another reason for this may be that standard Unix/ Linux file permissions are a bit less flexible than NTFS file permissions; see Chapter 6 in my *Linux for Windows Administrators* for a discussion of this. That may have motivated the original Unix ability to delete a file even if you lacked access to the file.)

Whatever the reason, ever since NT 3.1 it's been the case that Windows allows you to delete a file if you have either of the two permissions. Try, for example, creating another folder with another file in it, and then give yourself "delete" permission on the file, but deny yourself the "delete subfolders and files" permission on the `c:\test` folder, and tell Explorer to apply that permission to "this folder only." Or you could do it from the command line as before except now I'm denying myself the "DC" permission, which is the "delete subfolders and files" permission—the "DC" stands for "delete children," a geekspeak way of saying "delete subfolders or files." Delete `c:\test` to start fresh and type

```
md c:\test
icacls c:\test /grant mark:F
createfile c:\test\a.txt
icacls c:\test\a.txt /deny mark:(DC)
erase c:\test\a.txt
```

Again, that ran fine for me and allowed me to delete `killtest.txt`. It is *only* by denying the Mark account both the "delete" permission on the file and the "delete subfolders and files" permission on the folder that `killtest.txt` doesn't get deleted.

How Blocking Deletes via WIC Can Fail

Okay, so now we know that keeping someone from deleting a file under NTFS has, since time immemorial (well, since July 1993), required blocking their ability to delete the actual file, *and* blocking their ability to delete subfolders and files in the folder that contains that file. But the original question wasn't really an NTFS permission question, was it? The original question was "if `hltext.txt` is a file with a high integrity mandatory label, then why can a medium integrity process delete it?" Here's why:

- As before, blocking deletion requires the file "deny" and the folder "deny." Put another way, Windows lets you delete a file if you have *either* a file "allow" or a folder "allow." There's nothing like in Windows permissions that I know of, as normally the first time Windows sees a "deny," the whole operation's terminated.

- There was no file "deny delete" in the `hltest.txt` example. Instead, there was the difference in mandatory integrity levels, which act as a "deny" and trump any discretionary ACLs. You couldn't see what was going on under the hood, but this part worked as expected, and the medium integrity process was blocked from deleting `hltest.txt`...

- ... *but* Vista knew, as all versions of NT have known, that just because the file "deny" has kicked in doesn't mean that the fat lady has sung yet. So Vista said to the folder that `hltest.txt` was in, "do you have any problem with this medium integrity process deleting one of your files or subfolders?" Now, the *folder was labeled as medium integrity* (as it was not labeled), and a medium integrity folder has no problem with being modified by a medium integrity process. Result: `hltest.txt` is history.

In short, Windows Integrity Controls *do* trump DACLs, but there was only a Windows Integrity Control to trump the file part, and none to trump the folder part.

The Solution: Ensuring That WIC Protects Objects

Now we're ready for the solution to the problem of "how can I use Windows Integrity Controls to keep lower-integrity processes from deleting higher-integrity objects." The best solution is to put items of a given integrity into folders of that integrity. Then the "delete file" attempt will fail against the higher-integrity file, and the "delete subfolders and files" attempt will fail against the higher-integrity folder.

To see this, try these commands out. As before, start with both an elevated and unelevated command prompt, both set with `c:\mystuff` as their default directories.

From the elevated command prompt, we'll create a subfolder of `c:\mystuff` called `c:\mystuff\high`. We'll then grant our user account full control of `c:\mystuff\high` and all of its contents. After that, we'll raise `c:\mystuff\high`'s integrity level to high. Then we'll create a file called `test.txt` inside that file, and it will inherit the file's high integrity level. Finally, from the unelevated—medium integrity—command prompt, we'll try to delete `test.txt`, and verify that it fails.

First, move to the elevated command prompt and type these commands:

```
md c:\mystuff\high
icacls c:\mystuff\high /grant yourusername:(OI)(CI)F
```

```
chml c:\mystuff\high -i:h -b
createfile c:\mystuff\high\test.txt
```

Then, move to the unelevated command prompt and type **erase c:\mystuff\high\ test.txt**. The file is erased, and you can see a sample run on Figure 4.7.

FIGURE 4.7   Mandatory integrity wins at last!

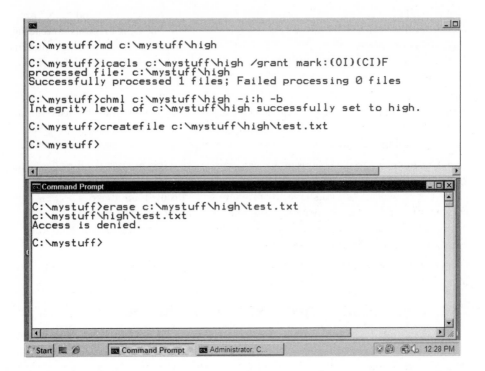

The moral of this story is simple: things are best secured with integrity levels if they are in a folder with similar integrity levels.

Using WIC ACEs to Restrict Access

We've already seen a couple of examples of how Windows Integrity Controls can restrict a program from modifying or deleting a file. That's WIC's default behavior, but that's not all that Windows Integrity Controls can restrict. They can also stop a lower-integrity process from reading a higher-integrity object, or, if the object is an EXE or related file, WIC can stop a lower-integrity process from executing the program in that file.

I've already told you that to protect a file or a folder from lower-integrity processes reading that file or folder, you just have to add a special kind of ACE that is recognized by the operating system as a mandatory label to the file or folder that says, "this is an object of such-and-such integrity level," and that that's how WIC protects objects from being written. But I've not told you the entire story because in actual fact there *is* no kind of ACE that merely declares an object's integrity level; instead, the ACE says "this object has integrity level such-and-such," yes, but the ACEs that we've applied so far *also* say something like "and it does not wish to be written by lower-integrity items." There is room on that ACE for you to add that the object should not be read from, or executed.

chml lets you do this with the -nr, -nx, and -nw options. "NR," "NW" and "NX" are, as you've probably guessed, Microsoft's shorthand designation for the restrictions on reading, writing, and executing, respectively. For example, to give a file named test.txt a high integrity level and to tell the operating system not to let lower-integrity processes *read* the file, just type

```
chml test.txt -i:h -nr -b
```

icacls does not have the ability to create NX or NR WIC policies; it can only create NW entries.

Thus far you've not had to worry about including -nr, -nw, or -nx because I wrote chml to assume an NW option whenever none of the three were specified. The internal structure of the mandatory integrity ACE leaves room for all three of the options, so you could even lock test.txt right up with

```
chml test.txt -i:h -nr -nx -nw -b
```

(It doesn't matter what order you specify the -nr, -nx, or -nw options; just be sure that the first option is the file or folder's name.) You can see this in action with just a few commands. As before, start up two command prompts, one elevated and one not, and navigate to c:\mystuff in both. Then, from the elevated command prompt, type these lines:

```
createfile a.txt
chml a.txt -i:h -nr -nx -nw -b
```

Then, from the nonelevated command prompt, type **type a.txt**. You'll get an access is denied message.

Where could you use this? Well, if you really wanted to tighten up the protection from the Internet that Windows Integrity Control seems to have been designed for, then you could set an NR ACE on your entire C: drive and make exceptions for the few built-in low integrity folders.

That, by the way, is just a thought; I've not had time to test it, so *please* don't do it without testing it thoroughly first!

Along those lines, this is one area of WIC that honestly disturbs me a bit. What if a bad guy were to install some malware on your system and then figured out how to set all of the files, folders, and Registry keys relevant to the malware to system integrity? My *guess*—I'm not a good enough programmer to get this to work yet—is that because I notice that system services run in system integrity level, then there may be a way to write a service that can manipulate integrity levels all of the way up to system. Time will tell.

Things WIC ACEs *Can't* Do

When I learned of Windows Integrity Controls, I was fascinated by this new dimension to Windows security...but I imagined more. So I spent some time searching down some blind alleys. In this section, let me save *you* the trouble of visiting those alleys.

You Cannot Apply Mandatory Labels with Group Policy

The whole idea of applying "no read up" mandatory labels wholesale across an operating system appealed to me, as I really liked the notion that I could point to, say, my personal finance files and do something like

```
chml c:\personalfinance -i:m -nr
```

With the idea that I could be nearly certain that malware from the Web would be unable to read my personal finance files, no matter how clueless I was in visiting the wrong websites. That led me to thinking that it'd be neat to construct a whole structure of NRs, NXs, and NWs for my computer's folder structure. That led to the notion that after I'd figured all of that out that I might want to apply those NRs, NXs, and NWs to many systems on my network. But how to do that? Well, one of the best ways to roll out a set of new NTFS permissions wholesale across a network is through group policies. So I wondered if I could use group policies to roll out mandatory labels.

Unfortunately that does not work; I tried such an application with a security template and nothing happened save for a few choice errors. As it turns out, I was just being a bit clueless. When asked about the possibility of rolling out integrity labels with group policies, the Microsoft folks said that they really didn't have any plans for supporting anything like that. I guess I was just a bit overeager to play with my new tools. But I still think that many people will want a capability like this; perhaps in Windows Vienna?

You Cannot Create Standard Permissions That Name Mandatory Labels

I was told in an early WIC briefing that you could use the integrity levels in regular old access control entries —you know, a regular old allow or deny permission. That led me to think that perhaps I could create a file that you could access solely on the basis of your integrity level, rather than being a member of Users, Administrators, or the like. To create such a thing, I first removed all existing permissions from the file, wiping it clean of all discretionary ACEs.

Next, I wrote a program that allowed me to add just about any kind of ACE to a file that I wanted to. That gave me the flexibility to set the file up so that it had just five discretionary ACEs that looked like this:

- Mandatory Label\System Mandatory Level: Full Control

- Mandatory Label\High Mandatory Level: Full Control

- Mandatory Label\Medium Mandatory Level: Full Control

- Mandatory Label\Low Mandatory Level: No Access

- Mandatory Label\Untrusted Mandatory Level: No Access

Looking at its permissions in the Vista Security tab on the file's Properties page looked like Figure 4.8.

FIGURE 4.8   A file with only label-related ACEs

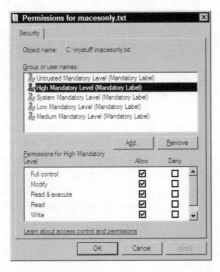

Again, that doesn't work, but it may bring a chuckle, as it's sort of the "security research" version of some of those amusing pictures of would-be heavier-than-aircraft that people built in the late 19th and early 20th centuries but that never went anywhere. The exercise *did*, however, teach me something quite useful about icacls. I'd spent a few days writing a program that would let me paste an arbitrary SID into a permissions ACE so that I could produce that chimera that you saw in Figure 4.8, only to learn later that icacls could do the job for me. You've already seen that icacls will create permissions with its /grant and /deny options, but you haven't seen yet a neat feature of those commands. Instead of specifying a user or group name in an ACE, you can specify a SID by prefixing it with an asterisk. Thus, to create a permission that grants the Everyone permissions of Full Control on a file named a.txt, you could type

```
icacls a.txt /grant *S-1-1-0:F
```

(Recall from earlier that S-1-1-0 is the SID of the Everyone group.)

Thus, I could have saved myself the trouble of creating the program to add ACEs, as icacls could have done the job with references to *S-1-16-0 (the untrusted integrity level), *S-1-16-4096 (the low integrity level), and so on, like so:

```
icacls macesonly.txt /grant *S-1-16-0
icacls macesonly.txt /grant *S-1-16-4096
icacls macesonly.txt /grant *S-1-16-8192
icacls macesonly.txt /grant *S-1-16-12288
```

In any case, it was a fool's errand because Microsoft chose not to extend WIC to (in my opinion) its fullest potential, but at least now you're saved the time of carrying out similar errands, and I got a chance to show some of icacls' syntax.

A Note on Modifying System Files

During some of the early betas of Vista, I am told—I wasn't yet investigating Windows Integrity Controls so I can't personally verify it—that Microsoft labeled all of the Windows system files with, not surprisingly, the "system" integrity level. This apparently caused no end of heartache to beta testers because whenever a new version of the Vista beta appeared, those testers—who were logged on as administrators and therefore running mere high integrity processes—could not delete the old operating system. A person inside Microsoft told me that someone there had created an application called obliterate.exe that was the only thing that could wipe old Vistas off a hard disk.

Needless to say, having to run an unsupported in-house application to remove a copy of Windows from a hard disk was not popular. Particularly inasmuch as the millions of beta testers did not receive a copy of that apocryphal tool, Microsoft tried another tack in protecting operating system files, a quite significant if quietly done one: they completely rebuilt the default NTFS file permissions on things in the \Windows directory.

In Window Server 2003 and XP, the default permissions for the `\Windows` directory for the Administrators group was a simple "Full Control." The owner of the `\Windows` directory was the aforementioned Administrators group as well. In Vista, things are a lot different, as you can see in Figure 4.9.

FIGURE 4.9   New default permissions on the `\Windows` directory

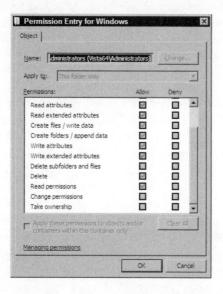

First of all, Vista's `\Windows` folder does not inherit any permissions from the root directory. Microsoft (probably wisely) set up your operating system's hard disk so that any loosening of the permissions on C: (or whatever drive you put your OS on) will not loosen the Windows permissions a whit. In the `\Windows` folder, the local Administrators group has almost full control, but lacks permissions to

- Delete subfolders and files
- Change permissions
- Take ownership

This is a very subtle but powerful change in a few ways. First, these permissions do *not* inherit to subfolders as is normally the case; they only apply to the `\Windows` folder. Microsoft did that because they've been very closely fine-tuning the NTFS permissions on the Windows folder. And notice the other two: "change permissions" and "take ownership." Where have we seen this before? Yeah, you've got it—those are the permissions needed to change a file's integrity level. I guess Microsoft's aim here was to set things up so that an administrator running in elevated mode who inadvertently ran something that tried to lower the integrity level or in fact loosen the permissions of any of the operating system files in `\Windows` would trip a few alarms. (Of course, it also caused me some heartburn the first time I tried to change `notepad.exe`'s integrity level to high when trying to construct a useful example!)

But it doesn't stop there. Ready for the really big change? We Administrators are no longer the owners of the \Windows directory for the first time in, well, *ever*, from the Windows point of view. (Ah, *that's* what's been giving me the creeps about Vista. I *knew* this thing didn't treat me like The Boss as the old operating systems did. And no, I wasn't referring to Bruce Springsteen.)

Those changes continue as we move down to System32. Again, Microsoft has removed any inherited permissions on System32 and hand-tuned them. This happens also in a number of other folders, including Drivers. Apparently Microsoft is thinking, as with the \Windows folder, that disconnecting inheritance will greatly slow down any malware that seeks to borrow an administrator's powers to open up the entire \Windows directory in one fell swoop. Once again, each directory does not give Administrators the ability to delete files and subfolders, change permissions or take ownership.

Was this a good change? Some will argue yes, some no, but I know one thing: this will cause more than a few heated discussions around the water cooler or, more likely, the beer pitcher. Let me try to summarize what the two points of view will probably be.

Those who say that it's a bad idea will name, or at least be thinking, a few things:

- First of all, pre-built permissions that don't make admins the owners of a system are a pain in the neck for administrators who are used to being able to do anything that they want on their systems. (Imagine loud emphasis on the word "their," accompanied by a pound or two on the table. There might even be a one-word pleading to their favorite deity thrown somewhere.) This is the "dang, this is going to make my work harder" reason. And, speaking as an admin of several decades, they're right.

- Second, they will argue, also correctly, that any computer criminal worth his salt will just take ownership of \Windows, give himself full control, and then move on to \Windows\system32 and do the same, and then \windows\system32\drivers, and so on. There is, they will argue, no structural barrier to an administrator taking control of a Windows system, just the irritation factor of having to do dozens of things to take that control, rather than having it immediately handed to him. True hackers, they will argue, would be *attracted* to the challenge of cracking a Vista box. I'm not so sure about this argument, but I've heard it.

On the other hand, those who like the changes will argue that

- These barriers are not insurmountable, but they *do* exist. They're sort of like tripwires: they don't stop you, but they do sound the klaxons that there's someone trying to do a Bad Thing to the system. Better yet, they're a simple barrier that remind us that we're treading in dangerous waters, a simple reminder to the well-intentioned but perhaps inattentive administrator that "oops, that wasn't what I meant to do." In fact, speaking of tripwires, this might be just the sort of thing that the new Event Viewer's event triggers capabilities were built for.

- Obstacles don't have to be perfect to be effective because after all, *no obstacle is perfect*. The vast majority of attacks on a system *aren't* dedicated hackers. They are, instead, just some mindless worm, bot, or just something that some pathetic script kiddie found on the Internet and is trying to hack you with because, well, you and he are on the same cable modem trunk.

Who's right? I don't know. But personally I side with the latter group. There's an old quip that "to err is human, but to really screw things up requires a computer." Simple missteps can mean serious damage, so I'd argue that a few "are you sure's" now and then aren't the worst thing in the world.

And besides, it's not like you can no longer control your system. If you want to restore your Vista system to the Good Old Days of administrators' owning the \Windows directory and having full control of all of its folders, then that's entirely possible—after all, there's nothing stopping you from taking ownership of those folders, as that's a privilege that administrators always have.

Dialing Up Custom Labels

For the last section in this chapter, I want to delve into a more advanced topic—low-level control of mandatory integrity levels. You've seen throughout this chapter that objects signify their integrity level through special access control entries called "mandatory labels." Knowing how to construct and apply a custom label lets you control not just integrity level, but whether folders will propagate their integrity level to their contents, what sort of restrictions they impose, and the like; with a knowledge of labels you can also remove mandatory labels altogether.

Meet SDDL Strings

When I say that we'll be directly manipulating mandatory integrity labels, I mean that we'll be using chml's -wsddl: option to directly compose and write onto an object something called a Security Descriptor Definition Language (SDDL) string. To see what that means, here's a quick example. For example, if you were to type

```
chml testfolder -wsddl:S:P(ML;CIOI;NWNR;;;HI)
```

You would be telling Vista, "there's a folder on the system named 'testfolder.' Please find it and give it a mandatory integrity level of high. Also, tell the folder to ignore any attempts by lower-integrity processes to either write it *or* read it. Please ensure that any objects inside this folder get those instructions as well, but block any integrity labels from this folder's parent." Quite a bit for just "S:P(ML;CIOI;NWNR;;;HI)," eh?

That bunch of capital letters, colons, semicolons, and parentheses is a compact way of describing access control entries and access control lists is the SDDL string I referred to earlier. To crack that code, you've got to learn SDDL, and that's basically what we'll be doing in this section. The -wsddl option gets its name from what it does, as its job is to "write SDDL strings." With the -wsddl option, you can craft and apply SDDL strings to do anything that we've talked about in this chapter, and other things as well. (And icacls won't let you build your own SDDL string even though they finally fixed it!)

Understanding the Secret Language of Bs: SDDL Label Syntax

(That's "Bs" as in Orange Book Bs—mandatory access control systems. After all, without mandatory integrity labels, there's no building a mandatory access control system.)

When NT 3.1 came out, about the only thing that you could put permissions on were printers, files, folders, shares, and Registry keys, if memory serves. As time has gone on, Microsoft has added more and more "securable objects," places that will accommodate an access control list. But writing out all of the details of just a single access control entry can be a lengthy affair, particularly when you take into account the many kinds of permissions that a file or folder might offer, and when you consider all of the options for permission inheritance that popped up in Windows 2000. So Microsoft developed a shorthand method of describing an object's owner, its primary group (something you have probably never needed to worry about, nor will you likely ever worry about it in the future, as it's there for POSIX compatibility), its discretionary access control list, and its system access control list. We'll focus on that system access control list, as that's where the mandatory label lives.

A Windows Integrity Control label SACE, when written in SDDL, looks like

```
S:sacl_flags(ML;ace flags;integrity control policy;;;integrity level or SID)
```

For example, in the SDDL string `S:AI(ML;CIOI;NR;;LW)` the SACL flag is `AI`, the ACE flags are `CIOI`, the Windows Integrity Control policy is `NR`, and the integrity level is `LW`. To see how to decode all of that, we'll consider each piece in detail.

WARNING   Remember, SDDL strings all use *capital letters*. Using lowercase letters in SDDL strings will, in my experience, always fail.

The SACL Designator

The first part of the SDDL string, `S:`, means "the information following is a SACL." More complete SDDL strings can have designators `O:`, which precede the object's owner, or `G:`, which precedes the object's primary group, or `D:`, which precedes the object's DACL. The SACL `S:` designator does not vary, and must always be capitalized. There is only one SACL per object, although Vista's programming interfaces differentiate between SACEs that are just auditing entries and those that are mandatory labels. That's why running `chml filename -sddl` yields only the mandatory label SACE, and no audit SACEs.

The SACL Flags

SACLs and DACLs changed significantly with the advent of Windows 2000 because of inheritance. You can, however, tell any object to ignore any inherited ACEs and to only use explicitly defined ACEs. Take a look at Figure 4.10 and you'll see what I mean.

FIGURE 4.10   A typical DACL

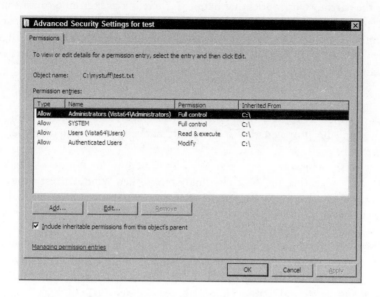

This is a discretionary ACL rather than a system ACL, but I chose it because it's a bit more "complete," which helps illustrate what I'm trying to explain. First, a reminder about ACEs and the ACL: this is one ACL, and it contains four ACEs. It is the ACL on an object, the file `test.txt`. And now the important point: notice the check box in the lower left-hand corner, the one labeled "Include inheritable permissions from this object's parent." Unchecking this would cause all of this object's DACEs to go away, because as you can see by the "Inherited From" column, they are all inherited.

The SDDL way of saying, "uncheck the 'Include the inheritable permissions from the object's parent,'" is to add a SACL flag of P, which is short for "protect this object from inherited SACEs" according to Microsoft documentation. So, for example, if I were to put a SACL like `S:P(ML;;NR;;;LW)` on a file, I'd be saying, "here's a SACL for you, *and* ignore any SACEs from your parent."

Remember that here, "parent" means the folder that the file lives in. Recall that a files or subfolders inside of a folder are said to be "child objects."

There are two other possible SACL flags: AI and AR, although you'll probably never, ever see AR. P is easy to understand because it corresponds exactly to that check box in the user interface, but there's nothing in the user interface that corresponds with AI or AR.

Recall that by default most child objects—files and subfolders—inherit the DACEs and SACEs on their parent object, the folder that they live in. But how do those DACEs and SACEs actually get copied—"propagated" is the term people use in inheritance talk—to the child objects? I mean, it's not like you've got to remember to push a "refresh permissions" button whenever you change a folder's DACL or SACL, and yet the children inherit whatever new thing you did to the parent, so how does that happen? There is a background routine in Windows that watches for changes in permissions on a folder and, when that happens, it springs into action and propagates the new DACEs and SACEs to child objects. That, in turn, may trigger propagating them to "grandchild objects" so long as those grandchild objects aren't blocking inheritance. That can go to "great-grandchild objects" and so on. On a big system with a complex folder structure and a slow CPU and disk, this might take a while. (I've never seen it, but it's possible.)

To keep track of which ACEs have been completely propagated and which are still in the process of being completely propagated, Windows automatically puts a flag on any changed ACLs, an AR flag that basically says, "Windows, I'm a modified ACL, can you come propagate me to my child objects?" AR is a flag put on an ACL *by* Windows, *for* Windows. Once Windows has completed propagating an ACL to its child objects, then Windows resets the AR flag to AI. That's why you will find an AI flag on many objects' SACLs; it just means that the object's SACL includes one or more inherited SACEs, and that Windows has completed propagating those SACEs.

You can see this by opening up an elevated command prompt and navigating to c:\mystuff. Then create a new folder c:\mystuff\testfolder and give it a high integrity level. By default, chml creates folder permissions that propagate to child objects. Then create a file inside testfolder called test.txt, and examine its SDDL; you will see the S:AI flags. You can do that with these commands:

```
md testfolder
chml testfolder -i:h -b
createfile testfolder\test.txt
chml testfolder\test.txt -sddl -b
```

You'll get a response of

```
SDDL string for testfolder\test.txt's integrity label=S:AI(ML;ID;NW;;;HI)
```

Reviewing, then, on any given SACL you may see no flags, or you may see P if you've blocked inheritance on an object. In addition to P you may see AI and in theory AR, but I doubt it.

The SACE Type

With the SACL designator and SACL flags out of the way, it's time to explore the SACL's one and only security access control entry. In SDDL-ese, ACEs—both discretionary and system— are set off by parentheses. The next character in the SDDL string, then, is a left parenthesis.

The SACE has six parts, four of which we will use: the SACE type, its inheritance flags, the integrity level policy, a couple of parts only relevant to Active Directory objects, and the integrity level. We'll take them in turn.

The first item in a SACE is the "SACE type." For years, auditing SACEs mainly came in a few varieties: "audit" SACEs, "object audit" SACEs, "object alarm" SACEs, and "alarm" SACEs. (I can't say that I've ever used one of the alarm SACEs.) Windows Integrity Controls brought a new kind, a "mandatory label" type of SACE. SDDL designates SACE types with one- or two-letter abbreviations, and ML is the one for mandatory labels. Hence, every integrity label has the same SACE type, and thus they all start out (ML.

SACE Flags

Just as a SACL could have flags, so also can each SACE in the SACL. You may see no flags on a mandatory label, or you might see some combination of these five, which I'm identifying by their two-letter SDDL abbreviations:

- CI, or "container inherit"
- OI, or "object inherit"
- NP, or "inherit but do not propagate"
- ID, which indicates that this is an inherited SACE
- IO, or "inherit only"

Whether or not you realize it, you've probably bumped up against these flags before. Take a look at Figure 4.11 to see what I mean.

Figure 4.11 shows you the dialog box that you'll see if you ever want to create a fine-tuned permission on a folder. Clearly it's a discretionary ACL rather than a system ACL, but the dialogs work the same. The drop-down list box labeled "Apply to:" might be better labeled "Inheritance instructions." There are seven of them, and one more important control on that dialog box—the "Apply these permissions to objects and/or containers within this container only" check box. You'll see that each of those eight functions corresponds to different combinations of the five SACE flags.

FIGURE 4.11   Standard "create a new ACE" dialog box with "apply to" options visible

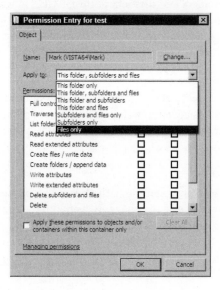

No Flags: "Apply It to Me"

A SACE with no flags applied to a folder cannot be inherited, so no files or subfolders in that folder will get the SACE. The folder itself will get the SACE, however. The "no flags" scenario usually makes more sense on files than it does on folders, as files can't have child objects. (In fact, most of the SACE flags don't make sense on files for that same reason—they can't have child objects.) In short, by default a SACE applies to the object that it was applied to. It's only when you start adding flags that things change from that simple default behavior.

CI: "Copy This to the Subfolders"

A CI, "Container Inherit," flag tells Windows not only apply this SACE to this object, but also to propagate this to any containers *inside* this object. So, for example, suppose you applied a low mandatory label's SACE with the CI flag to a folder named C:\folder1. Any folders inside C:\folder1 would inherit a low mandatory label, as would any folders inside *them*. But any files in C:\folder1 would not inherit a label of any kind. CI wouldn't make sense on a file because it has no child objects to propagate to.

OI: "Copy This to the Files"

OI, "Object Inherit," works like CI, except instead of restricting inheritance to folders, it restricts it to files. When you create a file, the default inheritance in Windows is CIOI, so that both files and subfolders in a folder inherit that folder's permissions. OI wouldn't make sense on a file because it has no child objects to propagate to.

IO: "I Don't Want it, But the Kids Can Have It If They Want"

IO, "Inherit Only," tells Windows, "I've applied this SACE to such-and-such folder, but don't apply its effect to that folder." I know that doesn't sound like it makes sense, and in truth it *doesn't* make sense if it were the only flag on a SACE. But now consider a combination of CI, OI, and IO. CI and OI say, "let my child subfolders and files inherit this SACE," and IO says, "…but don't apply it to me." IO wouldn't make sense on a file because it would basically be saying, "don't apply this SACE to me," and inasmuch as files don't have child objects, then there would be no one *else* to apply it to, which would essentially nullify the SACE.

NP: "Okay, the Kids Get It, but Not the Grandkids"

The NP, "inherit but do not propagate," flag lets the SACE propagate to the subfolders and files inside a folder, but no further: the grandkids get left out. If you check that box in the Permissions dialog that says, "Apply these permissions to objects and/or containers within this container only," then you'll get an NP flag on your SACE.

ID: "I Didn't Start This, I Only Inherited It"

Unlike some other operating systems, Windows propagates inherited ACEs by physically copying them to child objects. Thus, Windows objects may have ACEs that have either been explicitly applied to them, or ACEs that they got when the inheritance process caused Windows to just copy an ACE from a parent. An ID flag in a SACE shows that the object inherited the SACE.

All of that enables us to see how each of the settings in the drop-down list box back in Figure 4.11 work out:

- "This folder only" says to apply the permissions to the folder object, and nothing else. That means no inheritance, which means no flags.

- "This folder, subfolders, and files" means to apply it to the folder object (the default behavior) but then to *also* propagate it to any subfolders or files in the folder. CI propagates to folders, OI to files, so the flags would be CIOI. (Or OICI.)

- "Subfolders and files *only*"—my italics and yes, I know I'm doing this out of order, but I wanted to contrast it with the previous setting—clearly indicates that CIOI is called for, but what's that "only" mean? It means "…but don't apply that SACE to me, the parent folder." To satisfy that need, we add IO, "Inherit Only," for a set of flags equaling CIOIIO.

- "This folder and files" means "this folder" which, we've seen, is the default behavior and calls for no flags, and "files" means OI. The SACE flag for this situation is, then, just OI. Notice that it didn't mention subfolders, so no CI.

- "This folder and subfolders" is the reverse situation: subfolders but no files. Subfolders are containers, so CI is sufficient here.

- "Files only" calls for OI, and "only" calls for IO, so the flags are OIIO.

- "Subfolders only," similarly, is CIIO.

The example output that I offered before, with the SDDL of S:AI(ML;ID;NW;;;HI), has a flag of ID, meaning that it has no inheritance settings, and that test.txt got it through inheritance. Had the SDDL lacked any flags, it would have looked like S:AI(ML;ID;NW;;;HI).

SACE Rights

Thus far, we've seen the type of this SACE—a mandatory integrity label—and its inheritance flags. Next, we see what sort of integrity policy it requires. Recall that Windows Integrity Controls let us opt to block attempts by lower-integrity processes to read, or write, or execute a higher-integrity object. SDDL strings represent that with these flags:

- NR = do not accept read requests from lower-integrity processes.

- NW = do not accept write requests from lower-integrity processes.

- NX = do not accept attempts by lower-integrity processes to execute this object.

A mandatory integrity SACE must have at least one of these, and can have all three. So, for example, all of these SACEs are legal:

- S:(ML;CIOI;NW;;;HI) would just block writes.

- S:(ML;CIOI;NRNW;;;HI) would block reads and writes.

- S:(ML;CIOI;NWNRNX;;;HI) would block reads, writes, and executes.

Once you've installed your integrity policies in your integrity SACE, then add three semicolons, as these kinds of SACEs don't need the next two fields. We're just about done!

SACE Trustee: The Integrity Level

ACEs usually refer to an account that's getting granted or denied some kind of access. The user account or group that's referred to in an ACE is called the "trustee" in Microsoft security-speak. Mandatory integrity labels include a SID, but it's one of a few predefined SIDs that convey an integrity level, the SIDs that we saw back in Table 4.1. Thus, to build a mandatory integrity label SACE that applied to a file and thus didn't need any inheritance rules with a policy that denied executes and marked the file as high integrity, we can look up "high integrity" back in Table 4.1 to get the S-1-16-12288 SID, and build our integrity SDDL string like so:

```
S:(ML;;NX;;;S-1-16-12288)
```

Reviewing, this is a SACE with no SACL flags, is a mandatory integrity label (ML), has no SACE flags because of the `;;` after the ML, enforces a "no execute" policy because of the NX, then we skip two fields and end up with the high integrity SID. That works great, but those SIDs are a pain to type, so Microsoft has predefined abbreviations LW, ME, HI, and SI for low, medium, high, and system integrity levels. With that in mind, we can shorten up the above SDDL string without changing its effect:

```
S:(ML;;NX;;;HI)
```

Using SDDL Strings to Set Integrity Levels

Once you've got an SDDL string, you feed it to chml with the -wsddl: option. To apply the above SDDL string to a folder called c:\noex, you'd type

```
chml c:\noex -wsddl:S:(ML;;NX;;;HI)
```

You can also examine the SDDL string of an existing file or folder by using the -sddl option, as in

```
chml c:\noex -sddl
```

You will find that most files and folders lack an SDDL string altogether, or perhaps they have an empty SACL inherited from somewhere, as when chml reports an SDDL of S: or S:AI. That's SDDL-ese for a SACL without a SACE, or an empty SACL. And that's handy to know because I don't know of any Microsoft tools for *removing* a mandatory integrity label. Do it with chml like so:

```
chml c:\noex -wsddl:S:
```

What else could you do with the ability to handcraft SDDL strings? Well, the options on chml assume that if you want to label a folder, then you want its label to propagate to its child objects. If you don't want the label to propagate at all, then you can add the -noinherit flag. But what if you wanted to give a folder c:\documents a medium mandatory label that protects reads and only have its direct children inherit that label? There's no way from the chml options, but you could build an SDDL string to do it, as in

```
chml c:\documents -wsddl:S:(ML;CIOINP;NR;;;ME)
```

Summary

We covered a lot of new concepts here, so let's summarize the high points:

- Vista includes a notion called "Windows Integrity Control" that is essentially a second set of permissions parallel to but superseding the standard file permissions.
- Under Windows Integrity Controls, every object, user token, and process token are marked with one of six "integrity levels" that are, from least to most trustworthy, "untrusted," "low," "medium," "high," "system," and "trusted installer."
- Files, folders, and other "securable objects" get their integrity levels as access control entries that are, again, sort of like an NTFS file/folder permission, but that are stored on the SACL, not the DACL.
- Users and processes' integrity control labels are stored in their tokens as a group SID looking like S-1-16-*number*.
- By default, the main effect of Windows Integrity Control is to block any process of lower integrity from modifying any object of higher integrity. WIC can also, however, block lower-integrity processes from reading or executing higher-integrity objects.
- Objects without labels are assigned a mandatory integrity level of medium.
- To block lower-integrity processes from *deleting* higher-integrity objects, always keep objects of a given integrity in folders of the same integrity.
- The tools you need to view and manage mandatory controls are `whoami`, `icacls`, Sysinternals' Process Explorer, and my `chml` program.

Windows Integrity Controls are, in some sense, one of the biggest architectural changes in Windows in quite a long time. Their first job, and their main job in Vista, is to protect us from Internet-borne malware. But I'd guess that Windows Integrity Controls will take a larger and larger place in Microsoft's security arsenal.

5

BitLocker: Solving the Laptop Security Problem

BitLocker Drive Encryption is one of the most useful features found in Enterprise and Ultimate editions of Windows Vista. For many enterprises, BitLocker could be the single reason to upgrade from Windows XP. So, what could possibly be so important? Simply put: addressing the laptop security problem.

In a moment we'll examine what this problem is, and, of course, how BitLocker can help you solve it. But first, what is this BitLocker thing anyhow?

BitLocker does two main things:

- It encrypts every sector on the Windows OS volume.

- By using a Trusted Platform Module (TPM) hardware chip, it can check the integrity of early boot components.

This combination protects the operating system and your data from offline attacks—that is, the type of attack that is conducted by bypassing the operating system, or attacks that are attempted when the OS is offline. For example, say a particular laptop is joined to an Active Directory domain. Users must log onto the domain before they can use the laptop, and sensitive files are also protected with NTFS access control list (ACL) entries. But when the laptop is stolen, all the thief has to do is move the hard drive into another computer that is running a different OS. (This other OS could be a completely different OS like Linux, or even just a different installation of Windows.) Suddenly the user password and ACLs don't matter anymore! The thief can read any unencrypted data in an almost trivial exercise.

There are some existing mitigations today, most noticeably the Encrypting File System (EFS) and Rights Management Services (RMS), both of which are also improved in Vista, but both of which need effort and configuration to use and maintain and don't protect *everything* on the disk.

But, first, it is important to understand the scope of the laptop security problem.

The Laptop Security Problem Today

Have you recently received a letter from your bank to let you know that somehow (but surely not because of their fault!) some of your personal information has been accidentally compromised, lost, stolen, or leaked? I have. That makes me (and likely you) the subject of one of the over 93 million records of personal information included in data breaches that have been tracked by the Privacy Rights Clearinghouse since 2005. That's 93,000,000 individuals (less a few unlucky souls who had the misfortune to be in more than one) in less than 2 years (http://www.privacyrights.org/ar/ChronDataBreaches.htm).

While it is definitely not a great feeling to find out that data about you has been breached, would you want to trade places with the IT professionals and CIOs at the companies who have had to write these letters? It has become part of our jobs to safeguard the personally identifiable information (PII), intellectual property (IP), and business intelligence (BI) stored in our systems—and there are growing and dire consequences for failing to do so.

These consequences tend to fall into three main areas: financial consequences, legal or regulatory compliance, and negative image and credibility (and the last two, can in turn, drive the first).

First, losing data costs money. The U.S. Department of Justice estimates that stolen IP cost enterprises $250 billion dollars in 2004. These losses may include a loss of revenue, decreased market capitalization, or being placed in a competitive disadvantage.

Second, regulations abound. The legal framework facing a multinational corporation, for example, includes:

- Health Information Portability and Accountability Act (HIPAA)
- Sarbanes-Oxley Act (SBA)
- Gramm-Leach-Bliley Act (GLBA)
- California Senate Bill 1386
- Securities Exchange Commission (SEC) Rule 17a
- The Organisation for Economic Co-Operation and Development (OECD) Fair Information Practices
- Europe's Directives on Data Protection, and the U.S. Safe Harbor Principles
- Canada's Personal Information Protection and Electronic Documents Act (PIPEDA)
- Australia's Federal Privacy Act

Sorting through this alphabet soup is a task best left to your lawyers. But, we submit that you should realize this: if you are not already legally and morally compelled to protect this data, you soon will be. This brings some ugly fallout. It can cost a lot to become compliant, but it can cost even more to fail to do so: there are civil and criminal penalties waiting.

But, third, something even worse keeps many CEOs up at night: the dread fear of being "above the fold" on the front page of the *Financial Times*, as the subject of a data breach disaster. Image, reputation, and credibility all matter since they, in turn, affect everything from stock price to sales numbers. For example, one survey—way back in 2001—reported that 64 percent of online shoppers chose not to purchase from some vendors because of privacy concerns.

To be fair, there are many causes and potential causes of data breaches, but one particular risk stands head and shoulders above the rest: information workers are increasingly mobile, and hundreds of gigabytes of confidential data goes mobile with them on their company laptops. It's just too easy, in most cases, to get that information off of one of those laptops once it's been stolen or simply lost. The estimate is that every year American companies lose 600,000 laptops—sometimes stolen, but often just left in cabs and airports.

One large multinational company whispers privately that they average losing one laptop a day, just by them being left in taxis—in one city. Disasters can also befall you, such as happened to those companies who had to hire private armed security to guard their offices until the computers or data could be removed in the aftermath of Hurricane Katrina.

But no matter how they're lost, they contain the data that can make or break organizations and careers. For example, you may recall that a government employee in the Veterans' Administration thanked those who defended the country over the past few decades by bringing home a laptop containing a database full of their information…and had his home broken into. And, of course, the data wasn't encrypted. (After all, nothing says "thanks for keeping me safe" like simplifying identify theft.)

Even if you survive all of these calamities, at the end of life of your computer equipment, you still need to decommission it. That is, every computer eventually needs to have the data stored on it securely removed or completely destroyed.

The answer? Encrypt the whole bloody hard disk, and hide the key where it can't be found. That's in Vista in this new feature called BitLocker. In the rest of this chapter, we will examine how BitLocker begins to solve the laptop security problem.

BitLocker Drive Encryption— the Overview

A few years ago, Microsoft began a project called the Next Generation Secure Computing Base, and BitLocker is a direct result of that effort. In designing BitLocker, the System Integrity team in Windows wanted to come up with a solution that included laptop computers (notebooks), desktops, and servers, and provide a way to prevent thieves from using other operating systems or software hacking tools to break or bypass the protection provided by the Windows OS and the file system. That kind of prevention requires encryption.

BitLocker is also designed to provide a transparent user experience. In other words, unlike EFS or RMS, the user doesn't have to do anything complicated to configure and use the protection given by encryption, and the user (and you, the IT guru, and your colleagues in Legal Affairs) can be confident that *everything* is encrypted.

What is in "everything"? In Windows Vista, BitLocker supports the encryption of the entire Windows OS volume (the volume on which Windows has been installed). Later, we describe exactly how sectors are handled, and discuss how to handle the active partition (used for booting). Additional data volumes are not officially supported in Vista, but will be in Windows Server code-named "Longhorn" and Vista Service Pack 1.

When Microsoft first started to talk about BitLocker (then called "secure startup"), it seemed like an interesting but impractical technology because it required a Trusted Platform Module (TPM) chip built-in to the computer. Thankfully, the Vista implementation of Bit-Locker, however, lets you encrypt any system so long as it's got a TPM chip, or else by using a compatible USB flash drive, USB port, and BIOS. (BIOS and USB compatibility is part of the testing done before a manufacturer can put a Vista logo on a computer.)

This allows BitLocker to be used on many existing computers. However, some incompatibilities will still be found. It's a good idea to test system, BIOS, and USB flash drive combinations before committing to a large roll-out.

Clearly, laptop computers are where you need to begin, because they are sometimes stolen and often lost. Desktops, too, are sometimes targeted for theft, or sometimes placed in less-than-secure environments (such as shared lobbies or offices without locked doors). BitLocker will also be included in Windows Server code-named "Longhorn" (and will actually offer additional supported features). Although I hope you don't misplace your server very often, servers are very high-value targets for theft. All of these types of computers contain sensitive data, such as IP and PII.

BitLocker Components

BitLocker contains four main components: a single Microsoft TPM driver, an API called TPM Base Services (TBS), BitLocker Drive Encryption, and a WMI provider.

Like most hardware, a TPM chip needs a driver to expose its functionality to the operating system and, ultimately, to applications. By including the Microsoft TPM driver within Windows Vista, we gain increased stability and can more easily leverage the TPM's security features. To use a TPM with BitLocker, you must allow Vista to use the Microsoft driver. The Microsoft driver works with TPM chips that are at version 1.2 or newer. (For more information, see the section later in this chapter on the TPM.)

TPM Base Services (TBS) is an application programming interface (API) that allows applications to access the services provided by a TPM. In this aspect, even though it is part of the Windows operating system, BitLocker is an "application" that uses TBS. The advantage of this architecture is that *other* applications could also make use of the TPM. After Vista is in the marketplace for a while, I believe we will see other security applications that call on TBS. TBS also allows the TPM to be managed within Windows Vista from the TPM Management Console, instead of forcing users to navigate through endless BIOS screens.

BitLocker Drive Encryption, itself, is the OS component that encrypts and decrypts data on the volume, and uses the TPM to validate the pre-OS boot components. BitLocker has a number of options that can change its default behavior, many of which are exposed through Group Policy settings.

BitLocker is also totally scriptable and manageable. In addition to Group Policy options, BitLocker and TBS both include Windows Management Interface (WMI) providers. WMI is the Windows implementation of Web-Based Enterprise Management (WBEM), so any WBEM console can also be used with BitLocker. More usefully, though, this WMI interface allows BitLocker to be scripted, and Vista includes a scripted utility called `manage-bde.wsf`, which allows you to configure and control BitLocker from the command line or a batch file, either locally or remotely.

It is also worth noting here, even though we talk about it in more detail later in the chapter, BitLocker integrates with Active Directory Domain Services to store TPM and BitLocker information that can be used for recovery.

What Is a TPM?

A Trusted Platform Module (TPM) is a microchip that provides some basic security-related functions, mostly ones that involve encryption keys. To be considered secure, the TPM is installed permanently on the motherboard of a computer. The TPM uses a hardware bus to talk to the rest of the system.

A classic problem with any software-based security solution is that if an attacker can insert malicious code *before* the security software, then the security software can be circumvented. It is also difficult to be confident that any software reporting on its own state can be trusted. Think of rootkits, for example. They make the OS lie. Once you can fake out the OS, what can you trust?

So, a TPM helps address this problem because it can build a chain of trust that starts with hardware. Since this trust begins in hardware, there isn't any practical way to insert malicious code "before" the TPM. The TPM actually validates components of the platform (the computer) and the early boot process very reliably, and BitLocker can rely on this validation.

In many ways, a TPM is similar to a smart card. Although a TPM doesn't store certificates, it can create keys for cryptography and also keep private key permanently within the TPM. If a key created in a TPM is never exposed to any other component, software, process, or person, then, since the private key is never released outside the TPM, it's pretty darn hard to compromise. Because the TPM uses its own internal firmware and logic circuits for processing instructions, it does not rely on the operating system and is not exposed to external software vulnerabilities.

The TPM can also encrypt data provided by the OS, such as symmetric keys used to encrypt large blocks of data. When this type of data is encrypted by the TPM, it can only be decrypted again by the same TPM. This process, often called "wrapping" or "binding" a key, can help protect the key from disclosure. (Sometimes the data being wrapped is called a "blob of data," but "blob" can have a lot of meanings.)

Each TPM has a master "wrapping" key, called the Storage Root Key (SRK), which is stored (and kept) within the TPM itself. A TPM must also have an Endorsement Key (EK), which is permanent once set for that TPM. Other keys are derived from or signed by the EK.

Every time the computer starts, certain measurements are made and stored in the TPM's platform control registers (PCRs). PCRs are discussed in more detail later in this chapter. Accordingly, computers that incorporate a TPM can also create a key that has not only been wrapped, but also tied to specific platform measurements in the PCRS. This type of key can only be unwrapped when those platform measurements have the same values that they had when the key was created. This process is called "sealing" the key to the TPM. Decrypting it is called "unsealing." The TPM can also seal and unseal data generated outside of the TPM. With a sealed key and software like BitLocker, you can lock data until specific hardware or software conditions are met. This process is the basis for the pre-OS boot component validation performed by BitLocker.

There is some bad news, though. To use a TPM, BitLocker requires a TPM that meets the version 1.2 standard, set by the Trusted Computing Group (TCG). If your computer is older than 2006, it is very unlikely to have a version 1.2 TPM (most computers existing today don't have a TPM at all). In addition to having a compatible TPM, your computer must also have compatible BIOS. Most computer manufacturers are releasing Vista-compatible BIOS updates for computers that have version 1.2 TPM chips.

For more information about the TPM specifications, you can visit `https://www .trustedcomputinggroup.org/specs/TPM`. TPM chip manufacturers work with the computer manufacturers, and generally ensure that the TPM meets encryption export requirements, and they may seek certification from various authorities. One example of a TPM chip in common use is the line by Infineon, featured at `www.infineon.com` (`http:// www.infineon.com/cgi-bin/ifx/portal/ep/channelView.do?channelId=-84648& channelPage=%2Fep%2Fchannel%2FproductOverview.jsp&pageTypeId=17099`).

Don't despair: computers that lack a compatible TPM can still use the encryption features of BitLocker, provided their BIOS supports access to a USB flash memory device during the early boot process. There are a lot more of these computers around.

Full Disk Encryption

Since the release of Windows 2000, you have been able to encrypt files stored on your computer's hard disk with EFS. But there are some issues with EFS that prevent it from being the magic bullet to solve the laptop security problem.

EFS requires user interaction to specify which files to encrypt. Although the new group policy settings in Vista allow an administrator to specify that some folders, such as a user's Documents folder, will be encrypted, there are still a great many other places where sensitive data could be stored, such as places like Temporary Internet Files or automatically created backup copies of word processing files. It's very labor intensive to find all of these locations and ensure they are encrypted. BitLocker, conversely, simply encrypts every data sector on the volume. That's why it's called "full disk encryption" or "full volume encryption."

Sometimes, technical terms get thrown around a bit too loosely, so let's agree to use a few of them consistently.

A *partition* is a structure on a physical disk, usually defined in the disk's *partition table* (a specific data structure stored in the first few sectors of a disk). A *volume* is a logical structure in Windows made up of one or more partitions. In Vista, as with other versions of Windows, the volume is what gets a drive letter assigned to it, so what we normally call "drive C:" is a volume.

The *volume manager* is a Windows component that organizes the partitions into volumes, and the rest of the Windows system does not deal with partitions directly. In almost all cases in Vista, a volume and a partition will have a one-to-one relationship, and this is called a *simple volume*. Servers often have other types of volumes. For example, one volume could be stored on several partitions for redundancy or performance, such as in a RAID array. BitLocker works at the volume level, not the partition level. In Vista, BitLocker works with simple volumes.

One partition on the disk is marked as the *active partition*. The active partition is the partition from which the computer boots, or as Microsoft describes it, "The system partition refers to the disk volume that contains the hardware-specific files that are needed to start Windows." Ever since Windows NT was released, this has caused some confusion: the *active partition* is called the *system partition*, and the partition on which Windows is installed is called the *boot partition*, or "the disk volume that contains the Windows operating system files (by default, in the `Windows\` folder) and its support files (by default in the `Windows\System32` folder)." The "easy" way to remember this is that "you boot from the system partition, and the system is installed on the boot partition." In many cases—well, probably *most* cases of client installations before Vista—the boot partition and the system partition are the same. (For more information, see `http://support.microsoft.com/kb/314470/`.)

In most of the Windows Vista documentation you will see the terms *Windows OS Volume*, which means the former *boot partition* and is the volume on which windows has been installed; and *active partition*, the former *system partition*, and it is the partition from which the computer will boot. You can have multiple Windows OS volumes, if you have multiple operating systems installed, but you can only ever have one active partition at a time.

The terms *disk* and *drive* can mean different things depending on context. Drive can refer to a physical unit ("the hard drive failed") or a logical structure ("drive C:"). I try to avoid this the term except to use it when referring to a volume that has a drive letter assigned. End users, however, are probably much more likely to use the word "drive" than the word "volume." And, of course, BitLocker Drive Encryption has the word "drive" in its name.

A *sector* is the smallest addressable block of space on a disk. Almost all sectors today are 512 bytes in size, but as disks keep growing, sector sizes will likely climb. A *cluster* is a group of sectors, and is the smallest block of space that can be assigned to a file. Cluster sizes can vary according to the capacity of your volume, but since nobody I know uses 2 GB (or smaller) hard drives anymore, you can expect most volumes today (2006) to have a cluster size of 4,096 bytes (this is 4 KB, or 8 sectors). This means that if you want to write a 1 byte file, the file will still be assigned an entire cluster, and 4 KB of disk space will be used. (For more information, see `http://support.microsoft.com/kb/314878/`.)

The first sector of a volume is called the *boot sector* and contains code that can be used to start the computer if that volume is also the active partition.

The point of all this defining is to help explain what is not encrypted by BitLocker and how the BitLocker encryption algorithm works.

So what's not encrypted? First of all, to use BitLocker you will need two volumes. The active partition will be a smaller, unencrypted volume that is used to start the computer. Since this is not encrypted, you should avoid storing any confidential information on this volume.

> In fact, administrators should set NTFS permissions so that users cannot write to this volume at all.

The second volume is the Windows OS volumes, with Vista installed. The Windows OS volume will be completely encrypted by BitLocker except for the following:

- The boot sector

- Any bad sectors (sectors marked as unreadable by the file system)

- The volume metadata

The volume metadata is a data structure that BitLocker uses to store encrypted versions of the keys needed to decrypt the data, and some other statistical and reference information about the volume. The BitLocker system writes three redundant copies of the metadata to ensure that if one copy (or even two!) develops a bad sector, you can still get your data from the disk. A BitLocker-encrypted volume, then, would look something like Figure 5.1.

Although the metadata sectors are not encrypted as a whole, any keys stored in the metadata are strongly encrypted with other keys. More about that in a bit.

This architecture means that anything and everything written to the disk is encrypted by BitLocker. In some cases, this means things would even be encrypted twice. For example, if you encrypt a file with EFS, it is encrypted by EFS before being encrypted again by BitLocker.

To achieve this complete encryption, BitLocker uses a filter driver. A filter driver is a kernel-mode software component that communicates with the volume manager and the file system. A simplified view of the BitLocker filter driver architecture looks like Figure 5.2.

FIGURE 5.1   Typical layout of a BitLocker-encrypted volume

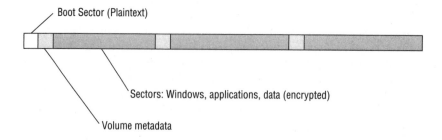

FIGURE 5.2   BitLocker filter driver overview

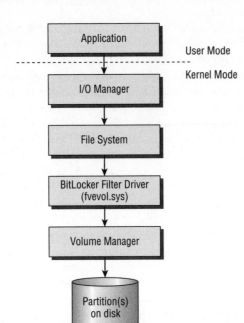

In Windows Vista, you cannot talk to the Windows OS volume without BitLocker knowing about it.

Encryption Algorithm

Up to now, I have simply said that the data is "encrypted" without explaining in much more detail. Let's look a bit more at how the encryption is done.

In 2006, one of the designers of BitLocker, Niels Ferguson, wrote a detailed paper about how the team sought and selected the best encryption algorithm for BitLocker, given the constraints imposed. Microsoft published his paper and you can download the complete PDF here: `http://www.microsoft.com/downloads/details.aspx?FamilyID=131dae03-39ae-48be-a8d6-8b0034c92555&DisplayLang=en`.

The encryption algorithm selected had to meet these goals:

- It encrypts and decrypts sectors that are 512 bytes, but also larger sectors (which will be likely during the lifetime of Vista).

- It must be able to implement different algorithms for different sectors.

- It protects confidentiality of the plaintext.

- It is fast enough to be nearly unnoticeable to users.

- It has been validated by public scrutiny and is generally considered safe.

- An attacker cannot control or predict any of the plaintext by changing the ciphertext.

And, the resulting ciphertext couldn't occupy more space on the disk (since when you encrypt the whole disk, there is no "extra" space).

In the end, Microsoft decided to use the Advanced Encryption Standard (AES), which is well regarded as one of the most secure and robust encryption algorithms. Microsoft, however, added a few additional pieces to the encryption process.

First, a different key is used for every sector on the disk. One part of the key is derived from the sector number. This makes it easy to create, and it doesn't need to be stored or managed, but not easy to discover from the encrypted data. Second, BitLocker adds a two-pass diffuser prior to the AES encryption. It's hard to explain what a diffuser does without delving deep into the cryptography. Basically, the diffuser, in this case, rearranges the bytes before the AES encryption to remove the possibility that changes made to the plaintext could result in changes to the ciphertext that might help an attacker to break the encryption. In other words, it makes the encryption even stronger.

So, after all is said and done, the resulting encryption algorithm looks something like Figure 5.3.

The algorithm is designed to use a 512-bit key, called the full volume encryption key (FVEK). The FVEK is split into two (each part being unique and different from the other). One part is used to derive the sector key, used by the diffuser, and the other part is used for as the AES encryption key. BitLocker is designed to use 256-bit keys for each part, but by default, BitLocker uses 128-bit keys. Longer keys result in higher security but decreased performance. You can configure BitLocker to use the larger key sizes, if desired.

FIGURE 5.3   Overview of the BitLocker encryption algorithm

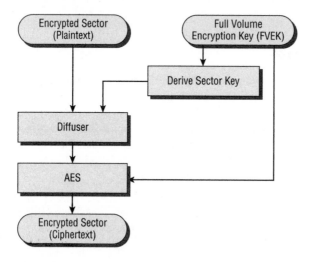

Key Storage

Speaking of keys…where do we get keys and where are they stored? In the preceding section, you learned about two keys, the FVEK and the sector key—but that's just the tip of the iceberg.

We'll start with the easy one: the sector key does not need to be stored. Rather, each time it is needed, it is easily derived, given the FVEK and the sector number of the sector being encrypted or decrypted. There is a good reason to go to all of this trouble. If every sector used the same key, then an attacker could write a large number of identical sectors of known data and try to determine information about the key by seeing what the resulting output looked like. But using the sector keys, this ensures that even identical plaintext data written to different sectors will result in different output ciphertext.

The FVEK is a very, very important key. It's like the master key that can open any door in a large office building. The FVEK is created for each new volume encrypted by BitLocker and is used for every sector that is encrypted. BitLocker stores this key in a handy place: the volume metadata. This means three redundant copies are stored, and that it travels with the encrypted volume. For example, if your motherboard blows up one morning, and you need to remove the disk, the FVEK stays on the disk.

Of course, it won't do to just leave the FVEK lying around in plaintext in the volume metadata. That would defeat the purpose of encrypting the disk. Instead, the FVEK is encrypted with another key, the volume master key (VMK). So, bear with me…in order to use the FVEK to read the data on the disk, you need to have the VMK.

Where's the VMK?

The VMK is actually also stored in the volume metadata. This is what allows BitLocker, in its default configuration, to start up and access an encrypted volume without any user intervention. Again, the VMK is obviously not just stored in plaintext; it too is encrypted, or in the language of BitLocker, it is *protected* by one or more *key protectors*.

In BitLocker, there have to be a number of ways to get the data that is encrypted. An important part of any enterprise-level encryption scheme is planning for the potential of needing to recover data if the normal access to the encryption keys is not available for some reason. For each way to access the data—in normal operation or in recovery after a problem—the VMK is encrypted and stored slightly differently, with a different key protector.

With default settings, BitLocker will create a recovery password and also use the TPM. This will create two key protectors, the "TPM Only" key protector and the "numeric password" key protector. Let's look at the TPM Only key protector.

You may hear someone say that the VMK is "stored in the TPM," but that is not correct. As far as the TPM is concerned, BitLocker is just another application. BitLocker presents a "blob" of data (that contains the VMK) to the TPM, and asks the TPM to "wrap" it (by encrypting it with the TPM's SRK), and seal it (by making decryption available only when values stored in the PCRs match). The TPM then returns an encrypted, sealed, and wrapped version of the data, and that is what BitLocker stores in the volume metadata. In this case, it is both wrapped and sealed by the TPM.

In other words, the VMK is *protected* by the TPM. The TPM is the bouncer at the exclusive club. Nobody gets in without his say-so; but when you show the right VIP guest pass (the integrity check), he simply steps aside.

Whenever talking about recovering encrypted data, you need to talk about how to get it back if something goes wrong. In BitLocker terms, this is called recovery. To facilitate recovery, a second key protector is used. In the graphical user interface, this is called a *recovery password*, although there are two variations used internally: a numerical recovery password or a binary recovery key. Although a "recovery key" and a "recovery password" have slightly different characteristics, the BitLocker user interface only uses "recovery password" to avoid confusing end users. You're not confused, are you?

When you enable BitLocker, you must create a recovery password, which can be stored in Active Directory Domain Services (AD DS), on a USB flash memory device, in a text file, or printed. This recovery password is your emergency "get out of encryption jail" card, and can be used to regain access to the disk no matter what the state of the TPM, or even if a PIN has been set and forgotten. Recovery is discussed in detail a bit later in this chapter.

If you choose to save the recovery password to a folder, or to print it, or if Group Policy is used to store just the recovery password in AD DS, a recovery password that uses only the digits 0 to 9 is created and used as a key protector. If you choose the menu option to save it on a USB drive, or if Group Policy is used to store a full recovery package in AD DS, then the binary version with the full 256 bits is created and used as a key protector. Since the user (by default) must choose at least one method of storing a recovery key, at least one of these key protectors will appear. Depending on the user's choices, you can have both versions.

In any case, another encrypted copy of the VMK is stored in the volume metadata, encrypted ("protected") by the recovery password or recovery key. See later in the chapter for a discussion about using the recovery password. Figure 5.4 shows these relationships.

You may have wondered why Microsoft bothers with the VMK. It would have been possible to just to apply the key protectors to the FVEK and store it, but that would run the risk of needing to perform some computationally expensive operations a little too frequently. Instead, the VMK provides a level of abstraction that is essential to making it efficient to keep data encrypted on the disk. Here's what I mean by "a level of abstraction": one of the basic principles of security and encryption is that if a key is compromised, *everything that was encrypted with it must be re-encrypted.*

Imagine a situation where someone loses a recovery password, and they are worried that it might fall into the wrong hands. If the recovery key unlocked the FVEK, you would want to create a new FVEK and re-encrypt the data. But, think about that for a minute. How big is your hard drive? How long does decrypting it and re-encrypting it take? Re-encrypting the data is an "expensive" operation, so we'd like to avoid it. By using an intermediary key (in this case, the VMK), it reduces the likelihood that the drive would need to be re-encrypted.

In fact, it also opens up some interesting features. Sometimes, you might want to disable BitLocker. It would be a rather time-consuming task to decrypt the drive, do whatever you wanted to do, and then re-encrypt the drive. Instead, you can turn off BitLocker temporarily.

FIGURE 5.4   Default key protectors

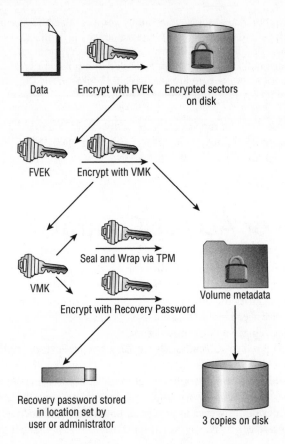

In this case, the VMK is encrypted with a new key, and that new key is simply written to the volume metadata in the clear. (This key, cleverly enough, is called a "clear key.") So, to access the data in this case, the clear key is easily read (no TPM, user input, or validation required), and used to decrypt the FVEK. This is still a type of key protector, although explicitly designed to not "protect" access to the data.

When you reenable BitLocker, a new VMK is generated, the clear key protector is deleted, and the other key protectors (such as the TPM and the recovery password) are reapplied to the new VMK, including resealing with the TPM. This means that the data did not have to be re-encrypted, and the user did not have to replace recovery passwords, or, for example, learn a new PIN. Abstraction can be your friend.

Yes, there is a slight risk that the keys could be compromised if an untrusted person gained access to the computer while a clear key is in effect. Therefore using a clear key—or "disabling" BitLocker without decrypting—and then reenabling the original keys is not recommended in high-security environments. It's also not a very secure idea to leave BitLocker in the Disabled state—with a clear key—for long periods of time.

You might want to disable BitLocker like this if you were deliberately making changes to your computer that would otherwise invalidate the signatures stored in the TPM PCRs, such as upgrading to a new motherboard, or to move a BitLocker-protected drive from one computer to another.

Authentication or Access Control

BitLocker doesn't replace Authentication or Authorization (or Access Control).

In this default configuration, the TPM provides validation of the pre-OS boot process—and that can be very valuable—but the security of your systems absolutely depends on the security of the OS as well. You must configure user accounts, strong passwords, and NTFS permissions as appropriate. BitLocker does not replace any of those items.

For example, if a laptop is configured to automatically log on a particular user, BitLocker does not interfere with that process. When that user then leaves the laptop in a hotel bar, yes, the data is encrypted, but—big deal—as soon as someone turns the computer on, the automatic logon would just happen—with or without the authorized user's presence. What the default BitLocker configuration does do, however, is prevent an attacker from succeeding in bypassing the Windows Vista logon screen by removing the hard drive and attaching it to their own computer.

There is no doubt that the default configuration was the result of some security tradeoffs. Many users were simply unwilling to perform extra steps at startup; you will need to evaluate your environment, and determine if the default configuration meets your needs.

Increasing Security with Additional Key Protectors

In many cases, the protection offered by BitLocker in its default configuration will be a vast improvement, and is probably enough for most day-to-day routine business information. But in those cases where the information stored on a computer has a high value, or you just want to increase the security, then you can configure BitLocker to use key protectors that work with the TPM, but add a second layer or factor.

Because these two types of key protectors work with a TPM—and only with a TPM— sometimes they are called "TPM+" or "TPM plus" protectors. BitLocker gives you the option of using a PIN or USB-based cryptographic key (called a *startup key*) that is then required, in addition to the TPM, before the disk can be unlocked.

To be sure, this adds an extra step at startup and means that the system cannot start without the user providing the correct input or presenting the correct USB device. Some users will resist this and complain about the inconvenience. Others will actually embrace it, and be pleased to see the evidence that their confidential data is more protected.

Without a TPM or startup key, everything needed to decrypt the disk is stored on the disk, albeit protected by the TPM, and even the TPM is guaranteed to be with the computer. When you use a PIN or startup key, you are able to physically remove some of the required information, and make it impossible to start the computer when that information is not present. This is a form of two-factor authentication.

PINs

When configured to use a PIN, the Windows Vista boot manager interrupts the boot process and prompts the user to enter a PIN. The PIN can be from 4 to 20 digits long. This happens long before any Windows shell or graphical user interface is loaded, so the prompt looks something like this:

```
Windows BitLocker Drive Encryption PIN Entry


Enter the PIN for this drive.




Drive Label: BHYNES-VISTABDE OS 10/1/2006
Password ID: 107241EE-A2F1-4553-978C-BC758F240D95

Use the function keys F1 - F9 for the digits 1 - 9. Use the F10 key for 0.
Use the HOME, and BACKSPACE keys to clear incorrect digits.

Press ENTER after the PIN is typed. Press ESC for recovery.







    ENTER=Continue                                              ESC=Recovery
```

The PIN is not a password that can unlock the drive (or decrypt the VMK, and certainly not the FVEK), and it must have the TPM available as well. (This means that the PIN is not a recovery password.)

The TPM has a secured storage area used to hold authorization data (or "auth data," as you may sometimes see it called), and PINs are the primary use of this area. When a PIN is set, a version of the PIN is stored in the TPM's auth data. When the TPM is asked to unseal a key, it can compare the PIN being entered by the user to the information stored in the auth data storage. If they entries do not match, the keys are not unsealed, and the disk remains locked. The PIN is not stored on the disk (neither in the volume metadata, nor in a file under the control of the OS).

Because the PIN system is hardware based, it is well protected. The TPM specification includes an "anti-hammering" feature. If an attacker tries to guess the PIN by entering random or sequential numbers, the TPM will detect this and make it more and more time consuming to enter PINs.

Startup Keys

If you prefer to have a physical "key" required to be present each time the computer is started, you can use a startup key. A startup key is a cryptographic secret stored on a USB flash drive (also called a "USB key" or "USB stick"). It is important to note that the startup key—by itself—is not enough to unlock the disk. The TPM must still unseal keying information. (When BitLocker is configured to operate on a computer without a TPM, a startup key works differently. That kind of startup key is discussed a bit later in this chapter.)

In this configuration, it is not the VMK itself that is sealed and wrapped by the TPM. Instead, BitLocker encrypts the VMK with a new key (usually just called an "intermediate key" or IK) and writes that encrypted version to the volume metadata. The intermediate key is then made into two parts. One part is sealed and wrapped by the TPM. The other part is turned into a 256-bit structure and written in plaintext to the USB flash memory device. When the computer starts, the BitLocker code in the boot manager checks to see if the required startup key is present. If it is, BitLocker combines the key on the USB flash memory device with the key information unsealed by the VMK, and recreates the intermediate key. This intermediate key is then used to decrypt the VMK.

With the first release of Vista, you cannot use both a PIN and startup key, although that has been announced for Vista Service Pack 1. You cannot use a PIN unless your computer has a compatible TPM (see Figure 5.5).

The choices you make about PINs or startup keys will affect what your users need to do when a computer is started. You probably do not want to use either for computers that must restart automatically when a user is not present. While you could use a USB startup key and simply leave it in the USB port, that would rather defeat the purpose of using one, wouldn't it?

There are also a couple of obvious security considerations (well, they seem obvious to me, but somehow escape some end users): If you have a PIN, you should not tell it to other people or write it on a sticker on the laptop cover. If you are using a USB startup key, you should not store the USB key in the laptop bag, because, when you leave the laptop in the taxi, you'll leave the key with it. Maybe you should use that little loop and put your USB startup key on your keychain, and treat it like your other keys.

FIGURE 5.5   BitLocker TPM and TPM+ key protectors

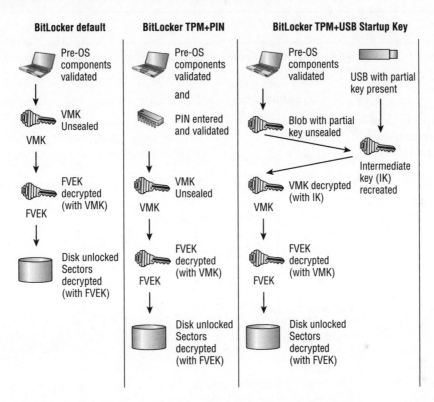

Boot Process Validation (Integrity Check)

Before we end our discussion of BitLocker and TPMs, it's time to delve a bit more into what "pre-OS component validation" is. The concept behind BitLocker is not just about encrypting data; in fact, the encryption was almost a means to an end. What BitLocker strives to deliver is a trusted computing experience, in which you can be assured that your computer is trustworthy, that it has not been compromised. This is a tough goal.

The TPM architecture includes 24 platform control registers (PCRs). Each PCR holds a specific measurement representing the state of a component of the system (or "platform"). Most of the measurements stored in the PCR are calculated with some form of hash. Table 5.1 shows what is measured by each PCR.

TABLE 5.1   PCR Measurements

PCR	Measurement
PCR 0*	Core Root of Trust Measurement (CRTM), which includes the BIOS and any platform extensions
PCR 1	Platform and Motherboard Configuration and Data
PCR 2*	Option ROM Code
PCR 3	Option ROM Configuration and Data
PCR 4*	Master Boot Record (MBR) Code
PCR 5	Master Boot Record (MBR) Partition Table
PCR 6	State Transition and Wake Events
PCR 7	Computer Manufacturer Specific
PCR 8*	NTFS Boot Sector
PCR 9*	NTFS Boot Block
PCR 10*	Boot Manager
PCR 11*	BitLocker Access Control
PCRs 12–23	Reserved for Future Use

The PCRs with * are those that BitLocker uses by default.

As the early startup process begins, the TPM first measures each component and stores the measurement in the appropriate PCR. In each case, the component is measured before control is given to that component. A component cannot change any earlier PCR value, so if an attacker inserted malicious code in the Boot Manager (PCR 10), that change would make the measurement stored in PCR 10 different from what it was before, and the malicious code could not change what was recorded as its measurement, or the earlier measurements, either.

The importance of this is easy to grasp: the OS can now reliably know if the components loaded before the OS have been changed. Changing one of these components could be a legitimate part of computer maintenance, but it could also indicate a concerted attempt to attack the OS, by installing a virus, spyware, or a rootkit, for example.

You can configure BitLocker to be more restrictive or less restrictive by telling it to examine a different set of PCRs; however this might not be what you really want. For example, you could configure BitLocker to include PCR, which would detect the addition of a PCMCIA card. For many laptop users, this would be too cumbersome, but perhaps in your situation, that's exactly what you want: to ensure no PCMCIA cards are added.

Enabling BitLocker for the First Time

So now that you have kept up this far, you are officially blessed with the author's permission to enable BitLocker and encrypt your Windows OS volume. The steps to turn on BitLocker are very simple, provided that your disk is set up beforehand. Here's what to do.

First make sure you have:

- A computer that meets the minimum requirements for Windows Vista.

- A TPM microchip, version 1.2. Some computer manufacturers require you to explicitly activate the TPM in the BIOS; however, most should simply allow Windows to detect it and communicate with TPM Base Services.

- A Trusted Computing Group (TCG)–compliant BIOS.

- Two NTFS drive partitions—one for the active partition (the "system volume" from which the computer will start) and one for the Windows OS volume (on which Vista will be installed). The active partition must be at least 1.5 GB.

- The BIOS set to boot first from the hard drive with the active partition, not the USB or CD drives.

New computers designed to support Windows Vista are expected to ship with the hard disk configured with two partitions, in a way that is compatible with BitLocker. However, if you are upgrading from Windows XP or you have installed Windows Vista on a hard drive partitioned with only one partition (volume) you are going to need to configure your hard drive into two partitions first.

If you are doing a "clean" install, you can set up the disk with the correct partitions during the Windows Vista setup. Note that this will erase anything you might already have on the disk. Here are the steps to follow, as per the "Windows BitLocker Drive Encryption Step-by-Step Guide," published by Microsoft (see `http://www.microsoft.com/technet/windowsvista/library/c61f2a12-8ae6-4957-b031-97b4d762cf31.mspx#BKMK_S1`):

1. Start the computer from the Windows Vista product DVD.

2. In the initial Install Windows screen, choose your "Installation language," "Time and currency format," and "Keyboard layout," and then click Next.

3. In the next Install Windows screen, click System Recovery Options, located in the lower left of the screen.

4. In the System Recovery Options dialog box, choose your keyboard layout and click Next.

5. In the next System Recovery Options dialog box, make sure no operating system is selected. To do this, click in the empty area of the Operating System list, below any listed entries. Then click Next.

6. In the next System Recovery Options dialog box, click Command Prompt.

7. To use the Diskpart tool to create the necessary partitions, at the command prompt, type **diskpart**, and then press Enter.

8. Type **select disk 0**.

9. Type **clean** to erase the existing partition table.

10. Type **create partition primary size=1500** to set the partition you are creating as a primary-type partition.

11. Type **assign letter=S** to give this partition the S: designator.

12. Type **active** to set the new partition as the active partition.

13. Type **create partition primary** to create another primary-type partition. You will install Windows on this larger partition. Because no size is specified, it will default to using all of the remaining space on the drive.

14. Type **assign letter=C** to give this partition the C designator.

15. Type **list volume** to see a display of all the volumes on this disk. You will see a listing of each volume, volume numbers, letters, labels, file systems, types, sizes, status, and information. Check that you have two volumes, that they are NTFS, and that you know the labels.

16. Type **exit** to leave the diskpart application.

17. Type **format c: /y /q /fs:NTFS** to properly format the C: volume.

18. Type **format s: /y /q /fs:NTFS** to properly format the S: volume.

19. Type **exit** to leave the command prompt.

20. In the System Recovery Options window, use the close window icon in the upper right (or press ALT-F4) to close the window to return to the main installation screen. (Do not click Shut Down or Restart.)

21. Click "Install now" and proceed with the Windows Vista installation process.

When installing Vista, choose the larger volume, not the active partition, as the destination for Vista.

If you already have a Vista installation, but only one volume, you have limited options with the RC1 version of Vista. Only repartitioning a new disk (or clean installation) is officially supported. There are a number of repartitioning tools out there, and there is the shrink command in the diskpart tool. However, to repartition a live system to turn it into a compatible state for BitLocker is not for the faint of heart.

At the time Windows Vista releases, there should be some help. The BitLocker team announced on their blog in June 2006 that they were working on a utility to automatically reconfigure the disk to support BitLocker (see `http://blogs.technet.com/bitlocker/archive/2006/06/09/PartitionVistaB2.aspx`).

After Windows Vista has been successfully installed and the system has the correct volumes configured, follow these steps to enable BitLocker on your computer:

1. Click Start ➢ Control Panel ➢ Security ➢ BitLocker Drive Encryption.

2. If the User Account Control dialog box appears, verify that the proposed action is what you requested, and then click Continue.

3. From the BitLocker Drive Encryption screen, click Turn On BitLocker on the Windows OS volume. If your TPM is not initialized, you will see the Initialize TPM Security Hardware Wizard. Follow the directions to switch on the TPM and reboot your computer. Once the TPM is initialized, click Turn On BitLocker on the system volume again.

4. In the Save the recovery password dialog box, you will see the following options:

    - Save the password on a USB drive. Saves the password to a removable drive.

    - Save the password in a folder. Saves the password to a network drive or other location.

    - Print the password. Prints the password.

5. Choose any of these options to preserve the recovery password.

6. From the "Encrypt the selected disk volume" dialog box, confirm the Run BitLocker System check box is checked and click Continue.

7. Confirm you want to reboot the computer by clicking Restart Now. The computer reboots and BitLocker ensures that the computer is BitLocker-compatible and ready for encryption. If it is not, you will see an error message alerting you to the problem before encryption starts.

8. If it is ready for encryption, the Encryption in Progress status bar is displayed. You can monitor the ongoing completion status of the disk volume encryption by dragging your mouse cursor over the BitLocker Drive Encryption icon in the toolbar at the bottom of your screen.

These steps are based on the Microsoft documentation, available at `http://www.microsoft.com/technet/windowsvista/library/c61f2a12-8ae6-4957-b031-97b4d762cf31.mspx`.

The actual encryption process will take some time, but your computer will remain usable during the conversion. The actual time will vary depending on the amount of free space on the volume (since free space can be handled more quickly than space in use), but a good rough estimate is about 1 minute per gigabyte, so a 250 GB drive will likely take between 2 and 3 hours.

Using BitLocker without a TPM

It is a simple fact that, right now, not many computers have TPM version 1.2 chips and BIOS that are compliant with Vista and meet the TCG specifications. As time marches on, most new computers will include these features. As for existing computers…well, hardware companies would normally rather sell you a new computer than spend a lot of money updating the old ones, but most appear to be issuing new BIOS updates for recently manufactured computers. But, if your computer has an older TPM chip (such as version 1.1) they cannot be upgraded. (Remember, they are a hardware security device, after all.)

A computer without a compatible TPM cannot use the pre-OS boot validation features that a TPM and its PCRs offer. However, non-TPM can use the encryption feature with a startup key (a USB flash memory device).

You will notice, however, that if you try to enable BitLocker on a computer without a TPM, you will not be able to do so, by default. The BitLocker user interface was designed to be as simple and clean as possible, for the typical user, and to leverage the security provided by a TPM. In order to enable key protectors (with a TPM) or to use BitLocker at all without a TPM, you must configure BitLocker to use advanced setup options. You configure this mode using Group Policy or the local computer policy settings.

Here are the steps to do so with local policy settings on one computer:

1. Click Start, and type **gpedit.msc** in the Search box. Press Enter.

2. From the Group Policy Object Editor screen, click Local Computer Policy ➤ Administrative Templates ➤ Windows Components and double-click BitLocker Drive Encryption.

3. Choose Control Panel Setup: Enable Advanced Setup Options. You will see the "Setup Wizard Configure startup" option for "TPM computers" dialog box.

4. Change the selection to Enabled and choose "Allow BitLocker without a compatible TPM." Then click OK.

NOTE   Between steps 1 and 2, you will see a UAC prompt, which you're probably becoming familiar with by now. You can also use any method you like to reach the local computer policy settings or a Group Policy object that applies to this computer.

When used without a TPM, a startup key is markedly different than a startup key used with a TPM. When used with a TPM, the startup key and the TPM data are combined as one key protector. On the other hand, a startup key used without a TPM is a key protector all on its own.

When enabling BitLocker on a non-TPM computer, a new recovery key is created and written to the USB drive. Thus, the USB drive holds a binary key that can directly decrypt the VMK. The USB startup key is then the only thing needed to access the BitLocker protected volume. In fact, a USB startup key on a computer without a TPM is exactly the same thing as a "recovery password stored to a USB drive" on a computer with a TPM. In other words, without a TPM, you are using a recovery key on a USB drive every time you start the computer. This is depicted in Figure 5.6.

FIGURE 5.6   BitLocker on a computer without TPM

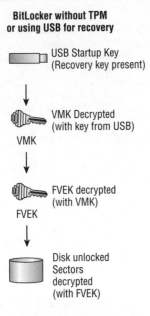

**BitLocker without TPM
or using USB for recovery**

USB Startup Key
(Recovery key present)

VMK Decrypted
(with key from USB)

VMK

FVEK decrypted
(with VMK)

FVEK

Disk unlocked
Sectors
decrypted
(with FVEK)

Summary of Key Protectors

Sometimes, keeping track of the different key protectors can make your head spin. Table 5.2 will help.

TABLE 5.2   Key Protectors

Name	Command line Term	Descrip.	Notes	Computer can auto start?	Requires TPM 1.2	User must present object (USB drive)	User must enter data
TPM Only	-tpm	Uses the TPM to encrypt, seal, and wrap the VMK.	Created by default. TPM will not unseal the VMK unless the integrity check passes.	Yes	Yes	No	No

TABLE 5.2 Key Protectors *(continued)*

Name	Command line Term	Descrip.	Notes	Computer can auto start?	Requires TPM 1.2	User must present object (USB drive)	User must enter data
Recovery Password	-Recovery Password -rp	A 48-digit number that can be typed by a user for recovery.	Either a recovery key or recovery password is created by default. Can be easily stored in AD DS.	No	No	No	Yes (48 digits)
Recovery Key	-Recovery Key -rk	A binary key used to encrypt the VMK.	Called a "recovery password" in the setup wizard for simplicity. Either a recovery key or recovery password is created by default. A recovery key is written in machine-readable form to a USB drive.	No*	No	Yes	No

TABLE 5.2   Key Protectors *(continued)*

Name	Command line Term	Descrip.	Notes	Computer can auto start?	Requires TPM 1.2	User must present object (USB drive)	User must enter data
Startup Key (for non-TPM computers)	-Startup Key -sk	A binary key used to encrypt the VMK.	Stored on a USB drive and behaves identically to a recovery key. Cannot decrypt the VMK if the USB drive is not present.	No*	No	Yes	No
TPM+PIN	-TPMAndPIN -tp	Uses the TPM to encrypt, seal and wrap the VMK, but sets auth data in the TPM	TPM will not unseal the VMK unless the integrity check passes and the correct PIN is entered.	No	Yes	No	Yes (4 to 20 digits)

TABLE 5.2   Key Protectors *(continued)*

Name	Command line Term	Descrip.	Notes	Computer can auto start?	Requires TPM 1.2	User must present object (USB drive)	User must enter data
TPM+USB Startup Key	–TPMAnd Startup Key –tsk	Uses the TPM to encrypt, seal, and wrap part of an intermediate key, and stores the other part on a USB drive. The VMK is encrypted with the intermediate key.	TPM will not unseal the partial key unless the integrity check passes. Cannot create the intermediate key or decrypt the VMK if the USB is not present.	No*	Yes	Yes	No
Clear Key (Bit-Locker "Disabled Mode")	Use the disable command	Encrypts the VMK with a new key, and writes the new key in cleartext to the volume metadata.	Used when temporarily disabling BitLocker when you don't want to decrypt the data itself. Offers no protection, disables BitLocker.	Yes	No	No	No

* Unless the USB drive is left sitting in the USB port. But the readers of this book are so naturally good-looking and innately intelligent that they would never even consider such a foolish thing. And they have great taste in books.

Recovery

Ever misplace your car keys?

With BitLocker protecting the data on your laptop, there are a few situations that might come up, where suddenly, you (or one of your users) is locked out. Situations might be:

- A forgotten PIN (in the TPM+PIN scenario)
- A lost startup key (TPM+USB startup key or non-TPM computer)
- Integrity check failure (TPM only, TPM+PIN or TPM+USB startup key)

In any of these cases, BitLocker will refuse to unlock the Windows OS volume, and you will not be able to start that installation of Windows Vista. Even if you start *another* installation of Windows Vista (or another OS) from a different partition, or swap the disk into a different machine, you still will not be able to access the data.

This is a good thing—if it means an attacker is being thwarted. It would be a bad thing, though, if it means you can't get to your data because you've simply made a mistake or a piece of hardware has failed. (For maintenance, hopefully, if it is a planned situation, you've disabled BitLocker previously with a clear key, but sometimes, unplanned things happen.)

Instead of simply unlocking the disk, BitLocker code (running in the Boot Manager), will display a screen called the "recovery console," which looks like this:

```
            Windows BitLocker Drive Encryption key needed.


                    Insert key storage media.


            Press ESC to reboot after the media is in place.




        Drive Label: BHYNES-VISTABDE OS 10/1/2006
        Key Filename: 4E65A3A7-35F3-4810-92AA-B6B833A78CD6.BEK



    ENTER=Recovery                                        ESC=Reboot
```

If you encounter the recovery console, you have only a few options:

1. Can you fix the situation? In other words, can you undo whatever caused BitLocker to go into recovery? Can you find the missing startup key? Can you connect the drive back to the original computer? If so, restart the computer and proceed as normal. If that is not possible, answer questions 2 and 3.

2. Do you have a recovery key? Recall that a recovery key is the recovery password stored on a USB drive during BitLocker setup, or the USB startup key used with BitLocker on a computer without a TPM. If there is no recovery key, then continue: ask yourself question 3.

3. Do you have the recovery password? These 48 numeric digits have now become important to you. They might be in some of the following places:

    - Stored in Active Directory
    - Stored in a text file in a folder specified during the BitLocker Setup wizard
    - Stored in physical, paper file or binder, as the page printed during the BitLocker Setup wizard
    - Carried in your wallet, purse, or briefcase: if you ensure it is separate from your computer.

Chances are that if you are part of an enterprise deployment, either the recovery key or recovery password will be stored centrally and managed through the company's help desk or similar organization. If you are reading this book, you might well be one of the administrators responsible for setting up that central system.

Let's take a closer look at some possible recovery scenarios that could occur in the real world.

Recovery Example 1: Desktop Hardware Failure (Stand-Alone System without a TPM)

Alice is self-employed and depends every day on her desktop computer. It's an older model, so it doesn't have a Vista-compatible TPM. Alice has upgraded to Windows Vista Ultimate Edition, and because she works with clients that store confidential information, she has encrypted her disk with BitLocker, configured to use a USB startup key.

One afternoon, Alice is shocked to find that her display is acting oddly. By the end of the day, it is no longer showing her any information. It is unusable. Alice eyes the computer belonging to her husband, Bob, and decides he won't mind if she puts her drive into his computer long enough to get this urgent proposal finished. (Since they bought their two computers together, they happen to be identical models—which makes this scenario oh so much easier to write.)

When she starts Bob's computer with her disk, she is prompted with a BitLocker screen, prompting her to insert her key media. Alice inserts her USB startup key, and restarts the computer. At startup, BitLocker finds the correct startup key for the disk, located on Alice's USB flash drive, and unlocks the hard disk. Alice finishes her proposal and lands a lucrative contract.

Recovery Example 2: Laptop Hardware Failure (TPM-based)

Alice's contract is so lucrative, and both computers are so old, that Alice and Bob decide to head out to buy new computers. Bob selects a top-of-the-line laptop, complete with a TPM 1.2 chip and a TCG-compatible BIOS. Bob configures his laptop to use BitLocker in the default TPM-only mode, and relies on a strong Windows password to guard access to his computer.

> **NOTE** Any truly overboard geeks who want to know what things happen to Alice and Bob when they go out together can visit http://rogers.phy.bris.ac.uk/ denzil/denweb4.html.

Bob spends several weeks using his new laptop; then one day, it just totally dies. Bob rushes back to the vendor, and learns that a manufacturing defect has taken out his mainboard. The board is replaced in record time, and Bob leaves happy...except that when he starts his computer, he receives the following BitLocker prompt:

```
                Windows BitLocker Drive Encryption key needed.


                        Insert key storage media.


                Press ESC to reboot after the media is in place.








    Drive Label: BHYNES-VISTABDE OS 10/1/2006
    Key Filename: 4E65A3A7-35F3-4810-92AA-B6B833A78CD6.BEK




 ENTER=Recovery                                        ESC=Reboot
```

Bob realizes that since his TPM was a permanent part of his old mainboard, there is no way to unseal the VMK that was protected by the TPM.

Bob is a bit obsessive, so when he configured BitLocker, he saved a recovery password to a file, he printed a copy, and he also created a USB recovery key. Since the USB recovery key is in his locked filing cabinet, he retrieves it, inserts it into the USB port on his laptop, and restarts the computer. Bob is thrilled to see how easily BitLocker recovery works and returns the USB key to the filing cabinet.

The next morning, however, Bob is surprised to see the save prompt return again. Each time he restarts his computer, he has to perform the same recovery steps. Since Bob is a clever fellow, he surmises that his BitLocker keys have not been sealed by this new TPM.

Since Bob doesn't really want to invest the time to decrypt and re-encrypt his drive, he remembers a clever thing he learned by reading ahead in this chapter to the section on the command-line interface, so he launches an elevated command prompt and types:

```
manage-bde.wsf -protectors -delete -type tpm c:
manage-bde.wsf -protectors -add -tpm c:
```

It only takes an instant to create the new key protector. After that, BitLocker reliably unlocks his encrypted disk, based on the integrity check performed by the new TPM.

Recovery Example 3: Lost USB Key (Computer with a TPM)

Bob's sister Carol works for a multinational corporation that manufactures shoelaces. Carol has a domain-joined laptop computer that—in the face of stiff competition from Velcro, zippers, and the whole sandals-with-socks movement—has been configured to use BitLocker with a TPM and a USB startup key. Upon arriving at her destination, the she turns on her laptop, and is greeted with the request for storage media, similar to this:

```
                    Windows BitLocker Drive Encryption key needed.


                            Insert key storage media.


                 Press ESC to reboot after the media is in place.






        Drive Label: BHYNES-VISTABDE OS 10/1/2006
        Key Filename: 4E65A3A7-35F3-4810-92AA-B6B833A78CD6.BEK



    ENTER=Recovery                                          ESC=Reboot
```

The USB media must be present during the early stage of startup to be used; if you insert the media after the boot manager code has begun, you need to restart the computer. Carol suddenly realizes that the last time she started the computer (with her USB key) was while waiting for her flight in the airport waiting lounge. A sinking feeling hits her as she remembers the USB key sitting on the chair beside her in the lounge. A thorough check of bags and pockets indicates it has been left behind.

Since there is no practical way to recover the missing USB key in any reasonable amount of time, Carol knows that she must use BitLocker recovery, and presses the Enter key.

When this particular drive was encrypted, Carol did not save a recovery key to a USB drive (although she did use a TPM+USB protector), so the USB recovery password entry screen immediately appears, and looks like this:

```
Windows BitLocker Drive Encryption Password Entry


Enter the recovery password for this drive.

    _____   _____   _____   _____

    _____   _____   _____   _____


Drive Label: BHYNES-VISTABDE OS 10/1/2006
Password ID: 107241EE-A2F1-4553-978C-BC758F240D95

Use the function keys F1 - F9 for the digits 1 - 9. Use the F10 key for 0.
Use the TAB, SHIFT-TAB, HOME, END and ARROW keys to move the cursor.

The UP and DOWN ARROW keys may be used to modify already entered digits.






    ENTER=Continue                                        ESC=Exit
```

Carol seems to recall that she printed out a page when she encrypted her disk, but that was a long time ago. Not being sure of what else to do, she calls her company's help desk. A pleasant young engineer makes her verify her identity by confirming the last digit of her zip code and the date of her cat's last tetanus shot, and then reads her a string of 48 digits that he has retrieved from the company's AD DS database. He encourages her to type each block of six numbers as he reads them so that they can be checked for typos.

Ever wanted to know the mathematics behind checking for typographical errors, or why entry screens like this often use short blocks? Surf on over to http://blogs.msdn.com/si_team/archive/2006/08/10/694692.aspx.

After Carol types her recovery password, her computer starts normally. So that she doesn't need to do this again, she has the hotel concierge fetch her a new USB drive, then uses the Manage BitLocker Keys option in the BitLocker section of the control panel (shown below) to create a new USB startup key, and then sends an e-mail to her vet because Fluffy needs a booster shot.

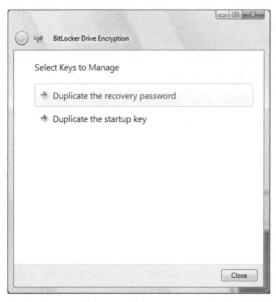

There are some other places where a recovery password can be stored. Notice that the recovery password entry screen shows a GUID for the password, called the Password ID. If you save a recovery password to a disk file, that Password ID is recorded in the file, and also used as the file name.

Recovery Example 4: "Found" Laptop

Alice's arch-rival, Eve, has been sneaking around, following Alice's friend, Dave. Dave is VP of research for a company that competes with Eve. Eve has been stalking Dave, hoping to steal his company's latest ideas. Eve sees Dave pop into a bar after a long day at an industry conference and follows him along. She strikes up a conversation, buys him a few beverages, and he becomes...um...distracted. When Dave is otherwise occupied, Eve slips his laptop into her own briefcase.

Later that night, Eve opens the cover of her long-sought prize, and gets ready to read up on the latest news. But when she powers up the Dave's computer, she is greeted with a prompt for a PIN. She tries Dave's birth date, and then his home phone number...after more random tries, she figures she can just spend all night trying 1111, then 1112, and so on...but she soon notices that the TPM's anti-hammering response makes this approach impossible.

Next she decides to just rip open the laptop and attach Dave's hard drive to another computer. But no matter which computer or which OS she tries, she can see only encrypted data.

Finally, she puts the drive back in the original computer and chooses the recovery option. "Now we're talking" she thinks, and she calls Microsoft Product Support to have them help her "recover" her Vista installation. She is disappointed to learn that it doesn't quite work that way, and that even if she could ever succeed in convincing them to help, there is no way they can get her a key or decrypt the drive.

Recovery Summary

It's impossible to list all of the possible scenarios that might occur. Hopefully, from these examples you can extrapolate to similar situations.

If the disk ends up being unlocked by a recovery key stored on a USB drive, the process is the same as that used by a startup key without a TPM, shown previously in Figure 5.6.

On the other hand, if the user has entered the numerical recovery password (and it's correct) the recovery password is translated into the cryptographic keys required as shown in Figure 5.7. In this case, there are a couple of extra immediate keys, and a dash of salt. (In cryptographic terms, a *salt* is extra information added to increase the complexity of a key, usually to add entropy.)

FIGURE 5.7   Using a recovery password

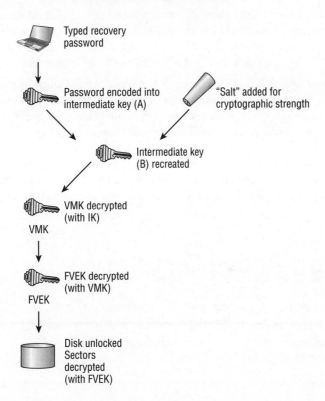

BitLocker using typed recovery password

Typed recovery password

Password encoded into intermediate key (A)

"Salt" added for cryptographic strength

Intermediate key (B) recreated

VMK decrypted (with IK)

VMK

FVEK decrypted (with VMK)

FVEK

Disk unlocked Sectors decrypted (with FVEK)

Recovery is not hard, provided you have a USB recovery key or a numeric recovery password. If you don't, there is no backdoor or secret way to get the information decrypted. So, as the administrators of systems, you need to prepare before disaster strikes. Here are some basic preparation tips:

- If you have an Active Directory domain (Windows Server 2003 SP1 or newer), then store the recovery passwords in Active Directory. There is no reason not to do this. It provides an automatic solution, and this is discussed in the next section of this chapter.

- If you do not have an Active Directory domain, but you are responsible for more than one computer, use WMI or the command-line tool to make backup copies of the recovery password, because you can do this remotely, or even in a startup script.

- If you are responsible for your own computer: make more than one copy of a recovery key (a recovery password moved to a USB drive by the BitLocker setup wizard). You can make as many of these as you want, but keep two contradictory things in mind: you don't want these easily accessible by an attacker, but you do want to be able to get one if you need to. Perhaps keep one in the office safe or a locked desk drawer; or perhaps frequent travelers may leave one in their hotel room while the laptop is out with them in the taxi.

- Use the BitLocker console to create additional recovery keys. Copying the text file with a recovery password to a USB drive is not enough to create the binary file needed to start the computer. Do not leave the recovery key with the computer.

- Also make a copy of the recovery password and store it in an accessible place, but not with the computer. Note that "store" has some interesting possibilities: you could read it to yourself in your own password-protected voicemail. You could keep it in your wallet with your credit cards. The recovery password can be stored in a backup file in a local or on a network drive. Again, though, make sure it is separated from the computer.

You need to spend a bit of time thinking about recovery policies for your organization. We need to be clear: BitLocker does not randomly decide to go into recovery mode just to annoy a user. When BitLocker goes into recovery, it means a security incident has been detected. That may be simple incident as someone forgetting their PIN, or something more complicated, such as an attacker attempting to install a rootkit. Perhaps, though, the "right thing to do" is not to immediately use recovery and to continue as if nothing had happened. Consider policies and practices around determining the cause of BitLocker going into recovery mode, and the proper, safe way to protect that computer, the data it contains, and your network, as you recover that laptop.

BitLocker and Active Directory

In a medium or large business setting, management of computers and keys becomes a huge issue. While you might be able to keep track in your head or in an Excel spreadsheet what the recovery passwords are for 10 or even 20 computers, it becomes harder with 100 or 500, and you are in a totally different universe if you manage tens of thousands.

In a Windows network, most administrators rely on Active Directory (now named Active Directory Domain Services in Windows Server "Longhorn") to manage computers and users. BitLocker leverages Active Directory in two ways: by using Group Policy to manage BitLocker options, and by storing recovery information in Active Directory. (Configuring BitLocker with Group Policy is covered later in this chapter.)

The logical place for an enterprise to store the recovery password for BitLocker-protected computers is Active Directory. For each BitLocker-enabled volume, BitLocker will create an object named `ms-FVE-RecoveryInformation` that stores the BitLocker recovery password and related information. For each computer using BitLocker with a TPM, another object named `ms-TPM-OwnerInformation` is used to store the TPM password (the TPM password is not normally needed to be used by most users). These objects will be subobjects of the computer object.

BitLocker will automatically create these objects and use Active Directory Domain Services to safeguard the recovery information once you have configured AD DS to do so.

In order to store the recovery password in AD DS you need to:

1. Make sure that all domain controllers (DCs) are running Windows Server 2003 SP1 or newer. All DCs that can be used by BitLocker clients must be at this level.

2. Make sure you have the appropriate permissions in the domains and forest to complete the following steps.

3. Extend the Active Directory schema with the BitLocker object and attribute definitions. (Note: if you have installed a DC running Windows Server "Longhorn," Beta 3, or newer, doing so has already extended the schema.)

4. Set permissions on the schema objects allowing computers to back up their own TPM recovery information. The easiest way to do this is with a script file from Microsoft.

5. Configure a Group Policy object to enable the automatic backup of recovery information. (Group Policy options for BitLocker are discussed later in this chapter.) The two specific settings are:

   - Computer Configuration ➢ Administrative Templates ➢ Windows Components ➢ BitLocker Drive Encryption ➢ Turn on BitLocker backup to Active Directory Domain Services

   - Computer Configuration ➢ Administrative Templates ➢ System ➢ Trusted Platform Module Services ➢ Turn on TPM backup to Active Directory Domain Services

By the time Windows Vista is available, Microsoft will also publish a detailed guide on how to configure Active Directory Domain Services. It is expected to include any required scripts or schema extension definition files.

Group Policy Options

As you've read a few times, BitLocker and the TPM Base Services can be configured by using Group Policy. There are two nodes in Group Policy to be aware of:

- BitLocker Group Policy settings are found in `Computer Configuration\ Administrative Templates\Windows Components\BitLocker Drive Encryption\`

- TPM Services Group Policy settings are found in `Computer Configuration\ Administrative Templates\System\Trusted Platform Module Services\`

The following list offers brief explanations of the BitLocker settings. For more details, check out the product help or the "explain text" in the Group Policy object editor.

Turn on BitLocker backup to Active Directory Domain Services   As described above, this setting allows BitLocker to back up recovery information to Active Directory Domain Services.

You can also make two additional selections within this setting. The first, "Require BitLocker backup to AD DS" will configure BitLocker so that if it cannot connect to a DC and successfully back up the recovery information; it will not allow BitLocker to be enabled. This is a useful setting to ensure recoverability, but it also means that the client computer must be connected to the domain to turn on BitLocker (in other words, no enabling BitLocker while flying to your next conference).

The second subsetting, "Select BitLocker Information to store" determines how much information is stored. If you store a full key package, then a copy of the FVEK is encrypted with a key created from the recovery password and then stored in AD DS. This is similar, in essence, to creating another copy of the key information kept in the volume metadata.

There is some increased risk of key exposure when the key package is stored in AD DS, but having it available may make it possible to recover data from a corrupted disk. If the key package is stored in AD DS, you must establish your decommissioning procedures accordingly.

Configure encryption method   This setting allows you to specify the encryption to be used:

AES 128 bit with Diffuser (default)

AES 256 bit with Diffuser

AES 128 bit

AES 256 bit

Configure TPM platform validation profile   Use this setting to choose which PCRs are examined during pre-OS component validation. If you have already enabled BitLocker, you must disable it and reenable it for the change to take effect, so carefully plan before changing this setting.

Control Panel Setup: Enable advanced startup options   This setting controls whether a user setting up BitLocker from the Windows Vista control panel is given choices about creating key protectors.

You have these options:

Allow BitLocker without a compatible TPM

Settings for computers with a TPM:

Configure TPM startup key option:

Allow user to create or skip (default)

Require startup key

Disallow startup key

Configure TPM startup PIN option:

Allow user to create or skip (default)

Require startup PIN

Disallow startup PIN

Remember that you can't have both a PIN and a startup key, so if one is set to "require" the other much be set to "disallow."

Control Panel Setup: Configure recovery options   Use this setting to allow users to have a choice about which recovery options are available in the setup wizard.

Control Panel Setup: Configure recovery folder   This allows you to specify a default folder where the recovery password will be stored, and it would normally be a fully qualified path (\\server\share\path). Note that this is only a default; the user can still choose to store it elsewhere.

Prevent memory overwrite on restart   You can configure your computer so that memory is not wiped when the computer is "warm booted." While this may shorten the restart time, it leaves open a risk that BitLocker secrets could remain in memory. The default is to make sure that memory is overwritten so that BitLocker secrets are removed.

The following offers brief explanations of the Trusted Platform Module Settings.

Turn on TPM backup to Active Directory Domain Services   This setting controls whether the TPM owner password is backed up to AD DS, and, like the equivalent BitLocker setting, allows you to choose whether or not the backup is required. If it is required, you cannot change the owner password (which is usually part of enabling BitLocker for the first time) unless connected to the network and able to back up the new password.

Configure the list of blocked TPM commands *and* **ignore the default list of blocked TPM commands** *and* **ignore the local list of blocked TPM commands**   As part of TPM base services, you can manipulate these three settings to control what functions may be disallowed on the TPM. For BitLocker, you should leave these settings alone.

Managing the TPM and BitLocker in the Enterprise

Group Policy is only one tool that can be used to manage BitLocker. Because BitLocker and TPM Base Services both include WMI providers, there operations are exposed through WMI. If you have a WBEM management console, you can access BitLocker as part of your WBEM strategy. But WMI brings a couple of other interesting features into play.

The first is remote management. Anything that you can do locally through WMI you can do remotely. This makes management of a large number of machines much more palatable. There is one limitation to the remote aspect of managing BitLocker. Part of the TPM specification requires proof of a user's physical presence to take ownership of a new TPM chip, in order to prevent malware from gaining control of the TPM. Xian Ke blogged about the impact of physical presence in a post on the BitLocker team blog, available at `http://blogs.technet.com/bitlocker/archive/2006/05/12/428173.aspx`. In that situation, someone needs to be present at the computer being managed.

The second feature built on WMI is rather helpful for us mere mortals. The BitLocker team has created a command-line tool that does the work of talking to WMI and the BDE and TBS providers for you. The tool is named `manage-bde.wsf` and it ships with Vista. It is expected that there will be a downloadable document detailing the operation of `manage-bde`, but really, the help included with the file is very complete. The following screenshot gives you some idea of the commands available with `manage-bde`.

Notice that the -cn (or -computername) parameter lets you run manage-bde against remote computers.

Here are some examples of using manage-bde to accomplish real tasks. Let's say you have a remote computer on which you'd like to determine whether or not BitLocker is enabled. (Oh, and let's say you've cleverly named your computer bhynes-vistabde.)

```
Manage-bde.wsf -cn bhynes-vistabde  -status c:
```

You'd get results like this:

Since you know that the computer has already had it's TPM activated, perhaps by IT when Vista was installed, and now it is ready to have you turn on the TPM and take ownership, use these commands:

```
Manage-bde.wsf -cn bhynes-vistabde  -tpm -TurnOn
Manage-bde.wsf -cn bhynes-vistabde  -tpm -TakeOwnership NewPassword
```

Your results from these commands will vary depending on the exact state of your TPM. But now, you want to turn on BitLocker, including the enabling of recovery, and verify that encryption has started:

Manage-bde.wsf –cn bhynes-vistabde –on –skiphardwaretest –recoverypassword c:

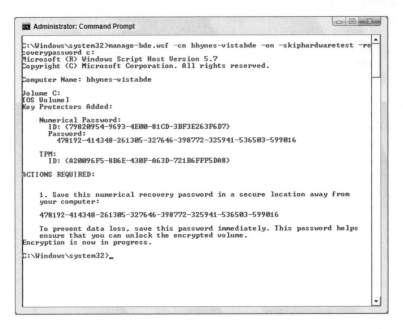

Manage-bde.wsf –cn Bhynes-vistabde –status c:

A few things to note: I happened to give the name of the computer even though I was using that computer's console, so you can use manage-bde locally (with or without the −cn parameter) or remotely (with the −cn parameter). Since I was working locally, this was also evidence that the computer remains fully available when the initial encryption is occurring.

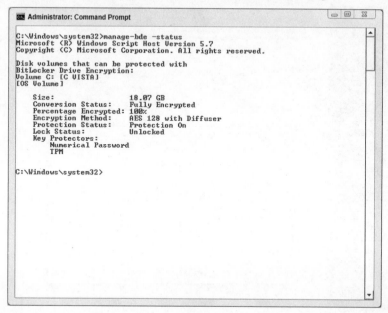

Since I don't consider a picture in a Mark Minasi book to be a "secure location" (although it does qualify as "away from the computer"), I have already changed my recovery password.

Servicing a BitLocker-Protected Computer

A computer is not a static thing. You will need to apply patches, or update applications or even firmware. With BitLocker using a TPM to validate the state of the system, which changes are you allowed to make? What will trigger recovery?

You may recall reading about how the VMK helps BitLocker remain secure on occasions where you may want to disable BitLocker without re-encrypting the disk. This is usually referred to as "disabled mode," but is probably more correct to say that "protection is off." By disabling BitLocker, you can cause the keys to be resealed by the TPM. That is, BitLocker is disabled while you make a change that would otherwise cause recovery, and then when Bit-Locker is reenabled, the new keys are sealed to the new PCR values.

As you can see in this figure, when you use the control panel, you can choose whether or not to decrypt the drive:

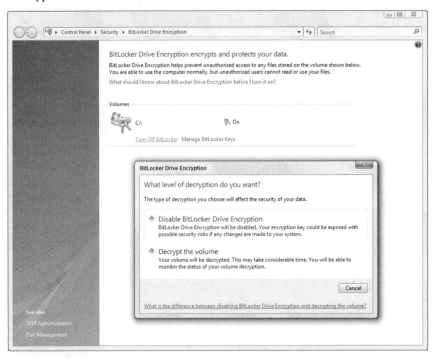

Disabling BitLocker can also be done through the command line, and the status can also be checked. (In fact, for batch files, you can even return the protection status as an ERRORLEVEL value. Pretty clever.)

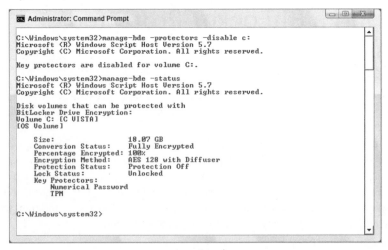

Since the BIOS is hashed by the TPM and monitored by BitLocker, a BIOS upgrade would cause BitLocker to lock the volume and go into recovery mode. Accordingly, you should always disable BitLocker for a BIOS upgrade.

On the other hand, updates to Microsoft Windows Vista sent through the Windows Updates process (including Automatic Updates) are signed and BitLocker aware; therefore, you do not need to disable BitLocker in the course of regular Windows updating.

What's in between is the gray area of other updates. Patches sent by application and software vendors or perhaps upgrades to hardware components or drivers may or may not need BitLocker to be disabled—probably not, if the update is only touching user-mode application software. When dealing with drivers, it certainly won't hurt to be cautious and disable BitLocker, or to be prepared with a recovery password (ideally on a USB flash drive) just in case.

Secure Decommissioning

There comes a time in every computer's life cycle where it needs to be decommissioned. It may be being returned at the end of a lease, or being passed on to a different department, donated to a nonprofit, or just tossed in the recycling system. By now, you should realize that you need to remove any trace of confidential data from the drives in that system.

A number of schemes and tools exist to do this. In software, writing random and fixed values over the disk space hundreds of times is commonly proposed, but to do so is time consuming and expensive. From a hardware standpoint, crushing a disk, drilling through it, melting it, or shredding it are all options. In addition to being time consuming and expensive, these also guarantee that the hardware is wasted and cannot be passed on.

With BitLocker, a new option exists: don't worry about destroying the disk or even clearing the data, just render it permanently inaccessible.

There are two ways to do this: the "I think I want to" way, and the "Yes, Regis, that's my final answer" way. In the first case, by deleting all of the key protectors except the recovery keys from the disk (deleting them all from the volume metadata) you ensure that the system will enter recovery mode every time it starts up. There is no other source of information left that will allow BitLocker to unlock the volume. This lets you be sure that someone buying the computer at a garage sale won't be able to fire it up and read their wife's prescription drug history (no, I am not making that up), but that an authorized user—with a recovery password or USB recovery key—could still get the data back.

If you are sure, and you are sure you're sure, you can take this a step further by deleting all recovery information from Active Directory, and deleting all of the key protectors from the volume metadata. Even if someone still has a USB startup key in their pocket, it won't matter—it would be unusable. Now, BitLocker won't actually let you have *no* keys in the volume metadata, so instead, you replace the recovery key with a random key and don't write it down or save it. Then, remove all of the others.

Now, your disk is a brick.

Another very handy option is the Vista *format* utility. In Vista, format has been written so that it deletes all BitLocker key structures, overwrites that space to ensure their removal, and then formats the drive, so using format with the /Q (for quick) option allows a quick but secure decommissioning.

Is BitLocker secure decommissioning "secure enough"? Well, it's not as secure as wiping the disk with random strings 1,000 times, then drilling holes through the disk, then pulverizing it, sweeping up the shards, melting them down, and shaping them into a metal plaque sent on a spaceship to greet other civilizations—but on the other hand, it costs a lot less.

Each situation is different. If you trust AES 256-bit encryption with an added diffusion algorithm—and you should—then you can be reasonably confident that your computer has been adequately decommissioned.

Planning for BitLocker Deployment

We not sure that our editor will let us talk about what you need to do first as the last section in the chapter, but now that you know how BitLocker works, you're equipped to start planning how to use it. And, indeed, there should be some planning done as you roll out Vista to your business.

While you don't want to be getting the call at 2 a.m. from your boss's boss wanting to know why your company's data is now for sale on the black market; you probably also don't want him calling because he fat-fingered his PIN when he created it and can never get back into his MP3 collection, either.

So, here are things to consider in your planning:

- Hardware requirements. Some business are finding BitLocker to be valuable enough to warrant accelerated purchases of TPM-equipped computers, while others are phasing them in over a longer time. Even without a TPM, though, a computer must have a compatible BIOS to use BitLocker with a startup key.

- Review existing infrastructure and processes. How do you configure new machines as they are received now? Do you want to script BitLocker disk conversion as part of a scripted Windows Vista install?

- Key TPM logistics. Has the EK been set by the computer manufacturer? Who will take ownership of the TPM? How will you address physical presence requirements? Is the TPM enabled and activated, or is it "hidden" by some strange BIOS setting.

- Talk with your hardware supplier or manufacturer. Find out how they propose to address these TPM logistics. Do they build computers with custom images for your company? Will the computers be Vista-logo-compliant? Are the disks being partitioned at the factory in a BitLocker-supported way? What is their plan for all those computers you bought just last year?

- Define BitLocker configuration and key protectors. What protectors will you use? Where will recovery information be stored, how will it be managed? Which computers, users, or types of data require PINs or startup keys?

- Define security and recovery policies. What will you do when a computer enters recovery mode...at headquarters? on the road? What is the response time for getting recovery information out of Active Directory Domain Services? Who will have access to the AD DS information? How will you determine root cause? Don't forget to plan to re-create new keys and recovery material if you've had to recover a computer in the field or give them to a third party.

- Define a computer retirement/decommissioning policy. What level of sanitizing is required? Are internal transfers of equipment subject to the same rules as ultimate disposal?

- Plan and then configure Active Directory Domain Services. You should be using a change management process with your production Active Directory Domain Services installation. Who needs permissions to read recovery data to help users? Do you have multiple forests? (Then you have multiple schemas.) Determine what needs to be changed, and acquire and test any required scripts before implementation.

- Configure Group Policy. Again, change management is your friend. Avoid any surprises by selecting and testing the Group Policy settings. Remember that changes to the encryption setting must be made before you start encrypting disks.

Summary

BitLocker is cool. And it might just save your ass.

6

Post-Boot Protection: Code Integrity, New Code Signing Rules, and PatchGuard

By now you've seen that Vista does indeed incorporate built-in paranoia, and for good reason, as nowadays there is a legion of bad guys. In a change from all previous versions of Windows, Windows Vista randomly reassigns the locations of basic Windows services, making the job of worm writers all the more difficult. One more set of anti-malware provisions includes code integrity, a boot-time check of digital signatures on files, and a new set of rules for 64-bit Windows only. Under these rules, all drivers must be signed. This chapter explains both of those protections in detail. But that's not all for 64-bit systems: the 64-bit kernel contains a feature called "PatchGuard" that attempts to intelligently detect and stop malware.

Address Space Layout Randomization

The first of the post-boot protection tools is simple and yet elegant, as it deals a powerful blow to worm writers. Called Address Space Layout Randomization (ASLR), it does just what its name suggests: it randomizes Vista. Now, that may not sound good, but it is good. You see, if you could peek into your XP system's RAM, you'd find that while there's something different about your computer from everyone else's, there is much that is the same. In particular, the hundreds and perhaps thousands of pieces of Windows in your system load in the same order into your computer's RAM as everyone else's computer. In particular, any Windows DLLs that your system uses are always loaded in the same order.

ASLR changes that by shuffling the actual load order of DLLs at every boot. Its process of doing this allows for 256 different ways to reorder DLLs. This is important because someone writing a program to exploit a buffer overflow has a hard job ahead of him. Sure, the buffer overflow constitutes a way to sneak into Windows code, but once you're in the code, *where are you*? Furthermore, once you're inside, where is the code that you want to modify in order to take control of Windows? Buffer overflow worm writers can really only get to the "fun" code to attack—a web server, the passwords, or the like—by figuring out a relative distance in RAM between where the buffer overflow occurred and where their target code is.

Randomizing the location of system components would, then, really ruin a worm writer's day. I suppose in theory it'd be possible to build a smarter worm, but it'd be a lot of work, if it's possible at all. Address randomization has been a feature of BSD Unix for quite a while. It's a welcome addition to Windows' arsenal.

Giving 64-bit More Armor

Microsoft made its first foray into the 64-bit computing world in Windows XP and Windows Server 2003. Although the 64-bit market has not yet fully expanded, more computer manufacturers are pushing 64-bit processors. While 64-bit processors have been used in servers during the last two years, the fact that they have dramatically come down in price is also making many people move into the 64-bit world for their general computing.

What's so great about 64-bit, though? Is it just another shiny whiz-bang addition that doesn't really matter? Actually, 64-bit processors make working with databases, digital video, and large datasets much faster and easier. In addition, 64-bit clusters have higher reliability than 32-bit clusters.

Vista includes two major updates for the 64-bit architecture (actually, only one is new, but we'll talk about that in a minute): new driver signing rules and a kernel patching protection feature, commonly called "PatchGuard." We'll consider that first.

PatchGuard

Kernel Patch Protection, often referred to as "PatchGuard," is not new to Windows Vista; it was included in the 64-bit editions of Windows XP Professional and Windows Server 2003 SP1. However, it didn't receive too much attention at that time. This lack of fanfare may have been the result of a lack of 64-bit presence in the market. Regardless, PatchGuard is back in the 64-bit edition of Windows Vista, and there's been a lot more people talking about it, including third-party security vendors and antivirus providers.

Before we can talk about why Kernel Patch Protection is contentious or helpful, we must discuss first discuss what it is. Kernel Patch Protection protects the system kernel—the lowest, most central part of the operating system—from tampering. The kernel must be protected since all applications and the Windows graphical interface run on top of it. The kernel is also the first piece of operating system code that runs when you boot your computer. Clearly, if the kernel is damaged, you're in trouble. Microsoft Knowledge Base articles 146419, 155892, and 327101 detail how to recover from a missing or damaged kernel file, but, in all honesty, we shouldn't have to do this. The kernel must be protected. Most kernel problems result from a hardware failure, a malware intrusion, or from a patching error. While Windows can't prevent hardware failures, it can help prevent kernel patching. Vista's User Account Control will help alert you when malware attempts to install. However, if you click Continue or provide admin credentials for a rootkit, you're toast. Or are you?

Let's delve into how Vista Kernel Patch Protection mitigates rootkit and other malware attacks. Again, Kernel Patch Protection only applies to the 64-bit edition of Windows Vista. Microsoft wants to make the Blue Screen of Death (BSoD) history in Vista. The BSoD occurs when an error in the kernel presents itself or when a driver running in the kernel experiences an error. When you see the BSoD in Windows, you know it's time to reboot and hope that it doesn't recur.

Microsoft has always considered kernel patching (also called "kernel hooking") to be a no-no. Kernel patching involves using unsupported methods to replace part of the kernel code or to update ("patch") the kernel. When the kernel is patched, it can become unstable and unpredictable. In fact, you often see the BSoD following a kernel patch being applied. The fact is, most people who patch the kernel are in fact attacking it—malware and virus writers.

There is one major caveat here (which will make it very clear why Kernel Patch Protection is receiving a lot of buzz): antivirus and anti-malware vendors often use kernel patching to intercept system calls from code they have identified as malware. However, by running these programs in the kernel, the vendors can cause problems with the computer's reliability and performance.

When a rootkit is applied to a computer, often, all of its processes are invisible to the user. In fact, if you check the running processes by using Task Manager (Ctrl-Alt-Del in Vista and click Start Task Manager), you won't see the rootkit's processes running there at all. This means that the rootkit is invisible even to the computer's infrastructure itself. By placing itself into the system's kernel, the rootkit can penetrate into the bowels of the operating system to install other malware, such as a keylogger that traps your banking and computer passwords.

How does 64-bit computing on Windows Vista get us out of this nightmare?

 Kernel Patch Protection is currently not supported on 32-bit or ia64 architectures.

Kernel Patch Protection actively monitors the kernel to determine whether any unauthorized kernel patching is being attempted. If Vista does detect that something is attempting to modify the kernel, it shuts down the computer.

While it would be nice if Kernel Patch Protection were a panacea or shield for all malware and viruses, it's unrealistic to believe that. Kernel Patch Protection will not prevent all malware from installing on the computer, but it will prevent malware from attacking the system by using kernel patching. As the most fundamental layer of the operating system, the integrity of the kernel must be preserved.

Great, PatchGuard Breaks My App: What Do I Do Now?

This is where we get into talking about the contentious points of Kernel Patch Protection— where it breaks existing 64-bit applications. If you're running an antivirus or anti-malware application, chances are that the application uses kernel patching to monitor malicious activity. Therefore, 64-bit applications must not modify the kernel or its resources. You can just imagine the horrible user experience caused by a buggy 64-bit application that continually attempts to modify the Vista kernel...shutdown after shutdown.

Where does that leave the antivirus and anti-malware makers in the 64-bit world? There are some alternatives to kernel patching.

- If an application uses kernel patching to inspect network packets, such as a firewall, it can instead use the Windows Filtering Platform (WFP). The WFP allows for an in-depth analysis of TCP/IP packets and the TCP/IP processing path. WFP also enables applications like antivirus and firewalls to both examine and change packets before they are further processed. WFP is a set of services and application programming interfaces (APIs) and cannot be implemented itself as a service. Windows Firewall is based on the WFP technologies.

- Antivirus and anti-malware software can use the "mini filter model" in Vista's file system.

- Applications that need to access the Registry can use registry notification hooks. Microsoft first introduced registry notification hooks in Windows XP.

Applications and drivers that attempt to patch the kernel must be modified to use only supported, public interfaces. If you can't redesign your application or driver to use one of these supported interfaces, then there is no way to perform the action on 64-bit Vista and still be secure.

The truth is that there have been a lot of changes in Vista that impact third-party application developers. Nearly all of these changes were made to improve security in the operating system. However, developers will have to be steadfast about researching application development requirements for Vista. In fact, Microsoft has asked developers that are uncertain or confused by development recommendations and requirements contact them at msra@microsoft.com.

Even Microsoft's applications have to follow the Vista application rules and receive no special treatment. All Vista 64-bit code cannot modify the kernel. Vista is requiring that all developers, whether third-party or Microsoft-based, use secure development methods through supported interfaces.

Applications that perform the following actions violate Vista's kernel patching rules:

- Patch the kernel.
- Modify the interrupt descriptor table.
- Modify the global descriptor table.
- Modify system service tables.
- Use kernel stacks not allocated by the kernel.

Microsoft has also made it clear that it will further enhance Kernel Patch Protection in the future by extending it to protect other kernel resources, but the specific kernel resources have not yet been cited.

So, You Want to Disable PatchGuard

Sorry, you can't disable Kernel Patch Protection on 64-bit systems. There is no exposed user interface for modifying this behavior. In all honesty, disabling this feature would make it easier to run some legacy applications, but it would also place you back into the uncertain realm of random drivers and applications modifying the kernel. Unfortunately, the term "kernel patching" does not immediately communicate its negative impact.

Kernel Patch Protection is disabled in one instance: when a kernel debugger—a separate computer running programs that allow it to peer into the memory and registers of the first computer, used to do low-level software debugging—is attached to the computer.

Code Integrity

A new technology is debuted in Windows Vista as a way to protect Windows files and programs from tampering. This technology is called code integrity or CI for short. What are the threats that make CI necessary? If a vital system file is modified or overwritten by a Trojan or a rogue administrator, suddenly the computer system is compromised. While we have to be realistic and acknowledge that any person who has physical access to your computer can "own" it, there are components in Vista that help limit, and, in some cases, prevent such attacks.

One such technology is Vista's new BitLocker Drive Encryption tool, available in the Ultimate and Enterprise versions of Vista, which you read about in the previous chapter. The fact that your OS's volume is encrypted with up to 512-bit encryption with a key stored away in either a TPM chip or a USB key stored a safe distance away means that even if the bad guys *do* have your laptop, they don't have your data. Ensuring the validity of the thousands of executable files in the \Windows directory is an essential part of maintaining code integrity, and you read in Chapter 4 that Microsoft employed what might be called "Windows Integrity Control Lite" by adjusting the NTFS permissions of the \Windows folder and its subfolders. (Recall that Microsoft calls it Windows Resource Protection or WRP.) Of course, WRP turns out not to be that effective, as takeown command makes taking ownership of Windows folders simple and from there files can be deleted. Oddly enough, WRP does *less* than WFP did because if you delete a file, like notepad.exe, then it doesn't get restored automatically—you've got to run sfc /scannow to make WRP notice the removed file!

Code integrity works by validating the integrity of files by checking the hash value for each file as Windows loads it. A file's hash value is a numeric value derived from a text string. The hash value is used to ensure that the file hasn't been modified, overwritten, or corrupted.

Code integrity also checks files that load in a protected process. The file hashes are stored either in a X.509 certificate embedded with the file or in the Vista system catalog. Vista also checks the integrity of the kernel, the hardware abstraction layer (HAL), and the boot-start drivers during boot. If any file or image fails the integrity verification process, Vista won't load it.

Vista code integrity does not verify the integrity of third-party files and images.

You can ask Vista to check the digital signatures on your files at any time by running the `sigverif` command.

Code integrity also works as a suite of technologies, including technologies discussed later in this chapter, such as the new driver signing rules on 64-bit systems and PatchGuard.

What Can Go Wrong?

There are some potential problems that you could encounter due to code integrity failures, but they're uncommon. Some issues might include:

- A boot-time driver or some code in the kernel fails the code integrity check and Windows won't start up.

- A non-boot-time driver fails the code integrity check and the corresponding hardware device won't function properly after Windows starts up.

- A service fails the code integrity check and Windows behaves in an irregular manner.

- A Windows component fails the code integrity check and you cannot perform a specific task.

Clearly, some of these problems will require you to delve a bit to discover the underlying issue. Here are some code integrity troubleshooting tips.

Troubleshooting Services

To troubleshoot a service failure, check two places. First, check the Services Microsoft Management Console (MMC) snap-in by running `services.msc`. Ensure that the services that are set to run at startup are actually running. Note any services that failed. Second, check the audit log by running Event Viewer (`eventvwr.msc`). Look at the System log underneath the Windows logs and view the Applications and Services logs. Vista also includes a CodeIntegrity audit log, which is located in the Event Viewer at `Applications and Services/Microsoft/ CodeIntegrity`. If you find a problem with a service, there are a few things you can do. If the service is a Windows service, use Microsoft Update to update the service. If no update is available, Google the Web for Knowledge Base or similar articles.

In some instances, the service itself will simply need to be replaced by a copy of the service that has not been tampered with or corrupted. Reinstalling the service and relevant components through a legitimate support channel (Microsoft Update, for example, for Windows services) will resolve this problem.

Troubleshooting Drivers

A boot-time driver failure or kernel code failure is the most clear code integrity failure. If either fails the code integrity check, Windows won't start up at all. You will have to use the Vista Recovery Console by booting into your Vista installation DVD. Then, at the Install Now screen, choose the Repair Your Computer option to access the System Recovery Options dialog, including the new and quite useful Startup Repair option.

Repairing a non-boot-time driver will not require the Startup Repair. Instead, review your audit logs by using the Event Viewer to determine which driver failed to load properly. Vista also includes a CodeIntegrity audit log, which is located in the Event Viewer at `Applications and Services/Microsoft/CodeIntegrity`. You can also check the Device Manager to view devices that are not operating properly. To get to Device Manager in Vista, click the Start button, right-click Computer, and select Properties. In System, click the Device Manager link on the left. In Device Manager, look for any devices that have a question mark (?) next to their description. These devices are malfunctioning, either due to a hardware problem or a missing or failing driver. To repair a failing driver, check with the hardware's manufacturer for an update or to get a pristine copy of the original driver that hasn't been tampered with or modified.

Troubleshooting Windows Components

The best way to troubleshoot a Windows component that is failing code integrity checks is to view the audit log in Event Viewer. Vista also includes a CodeIntegrity audit log, which is located in the Event Viewer at `Applications and Services/Microsoft/CodeIntegrity`. To resolve a Windows component issue, you will have to run Microsoft Update or use the System Recovery Options to repair the installation.

New Code Signing Rules

Vista includes new stricter code signing rules that will most likely impact you. Before we move on to the specifics of the Vista code signing requirements, let's look at why code signing is even required in the first place.

What Is Code Signing and Why Does It Matter?

So, why is it so bad to run an unsigned driver or application? The concept of code signing is based on authenticating the software's publisher. If a publisher signs an application, we can know that the application really came from that specified publisher. We also know that the software has not been tampered with since it was code-signed.

However, a code-signed application is not necessarily a "good" application. For example, `GoodApp.exe` could be signed by EvilCorp and be designed to bundle a seemingly innocuous media player with a keylogger. It's really up to you as the admin to determine what a "good" or "bad" application is, and to then control which applications can be installed by implementing an installation policy or by using installation services. While Vista includes some built-in tools to prevent some bad things from happening to your system, there's no guarantee that your system will be impenetrable if you choose to install a bad application. Once you grant an unknown or malicious application the right to use your administrator access token, all bets are off. The following sections detail which types of drivers and applications must be signed on Windows Vista.

ActiveX Controls

If you download an ActiveX control in Internet Explorer, Vista won't run the control if it is not Authenticode signed. To change this behavior, you can edit the options in Internet Explorer. Figure 6.1 shows the location of the setting.

FIGURE 6.1   Internet Explorer ActiveX controls options

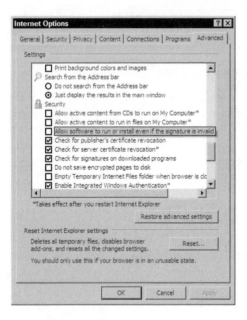

Enabling the "Allow software to run or install even if the signature is invalid" setting will enable both signed and unsigned software to run and install in Internet Explorer. This setting is also controlled by modifying the Security Zone in the Internet Explorer options. The default Internet security setting in Vista is Medium-High, which blocks unsigned ActiveX control installations. Figure 6.2 is a screen shot of the security level.

If you have a managed infrastructure with Active Directory, you can use the ActiveX Installer Service to delegate which ActiveX controls that standard users (nonadministrators) can install and update on Vista. The ActiveX Installer Service uses Host URLs to define permitted ActiveX controls and is an optional component and must be installed on a client computer to be available. A really great feature of this service is that it allows administrators to track ActiveX controls not explicitly allowed in Group Policy that users are attempting to install. When a user attempts to install such a control, like the Flash player, Vista throws event ID 4097. This event lists the ActiveX control, and an administrator can choose to either enable the installation in Group Policy or to not adjust the Group Policy setting.

FIGURE 6.2   Internet Explorer default security level

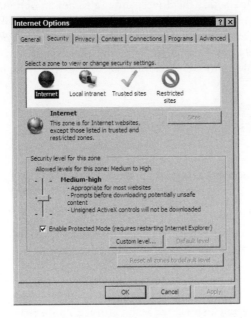

Protected Media Path Requirements

In addition, all software that runs in Vista's Protected Media Path (PMP) must be signed. PMP is Vista's enhanced support for digital rights management (DRM) for next-generation media formats, such as HD-DVDs. In short, this signing requirement means that the content on HD-DVDs will be successfully run and rendered on Vista if content is code-signed. This PMP requirement also impacts display drivers, which will have to include an embedded certificate in order to run on Vista.

x64 Requirements

All kernel-mode drivers and applications and boot-start drivers must be signed in order to run. Kernel-mode drivers and applications run in kernel mode, close to the operating system. Because they run in a protected area, it makes sense that they're required to be signed. A boot-start driver is a driver that the Vista system loader loads at boot-up. Boot-start drivers either have an INF that specifies the start type as "Start=0" or the driver is marked as a "kernel driver" or "file system driver" with a StartMode of "boot."

The kernel-mode software signing requirement is mandatory for 64-bit kernel-mode applications, and you cannot configure Vista to allow unsigned kernel-mode applications to run. Let's say that again: you can't make 64-bit Vista accept an unsigned driver. There's no way around it, short of setting up a certificate server of your own and signing whatever currently unsigned third-party drivers you want to use. We'll talk a bit about that soon. A boot-start driver must have the signature embedded within the driver, and is also not an optional component. If your boot-start driver does not have embedded signature, it won't run. Nor need you stop at drivers and operating system components for ensuring code integrity. You may also recall from Chapter 2 that User Account Control lets you crank up the requirement for signed executables with its User Account Control: Only elevate executables that are signed and validated setting.

Getting Down to Business: Code Signing an Application or Driver

So, now you know that you'll have to code-sign many (or all) of the applications that you will run on your Vista computers. There are really two ways to code-sign an application or driver:

1. Software publishers can code-sign the application or driver with the company's certificate.

2. System administrators can code-sign a released application that was not previously signed by the software publisher.

 Kernel-mode drivers and applications *must* be signed by the software publisher. The publisher must also embed a signature in boot-start drivers before their release. There are no available methods for systems administrators to sign released kernel-mode software or to embed certificates with boot-start drivers.

If you're looking at option 2, chances are the software publisher never signed the original application. Make sure to check with the vendor directly to get updated drivers and applications. If the vendor has not yet provided a signed version, choose between the following two code signing options:

1. Use an internal certification authority (CA).

2. Use a commercial CA.

Make sure that you only sign applications for trusted vendors. This is really a judgment call on you and your company's part. You can also use third-party reputation services to gather information about the vendor, as well.

Using an Internal CA

One reason why you might use an internal CA instead of a commercial CA is to code-sign line-of-business, internally developed applications. If you do use an internal CA, the CA must be trusted. This is a given. To trust a CA in your network, use Group Policy or auto-enrollment to add the root certificate of the internal CA to the Trusted Root Certification Authorities store. You might also want to use an internal CA to have more control over the applications that are trusted in your network. For example, if you choose to allow a developer's certificate, all applications signed with that certificate will automatically be trusted in your network. This situation might not be ideal for some environments. If you want to have more control over what installs, consider using an internal CA to sign a specified subset of the developer's applications. Be careful here, though—re-signing an application developed by a third party and then redistributing that application outside of your network can violate some license agreements and have some litigious results.

Using a Commercial CA

You can also use a third-party certificate from a commercial CA to sign your applications for internal distribution. A big bonus to using this method is that you don't have to spend the time and resources to deploy and maintain an internal CA. Applications signed with this type of certificate will also be able to be trusted outside of your organization or network. You might want to use this method of signing if you need to share your internally developed applications with people outside of your company.

However, there are some downsides to using a commercial CA. You're pretty much dependent on the commercial CA to provide new certificates and certificate updates. Obtaining a certificate from a commercial CA can also be difficult, expensive, and time consuming. You will have to provide information to the third party so that it can verify your organization's identity.

The signing method that you eventually choose will depend on what you want your end result to be. If you need to share your applications externally, use a commercial CA. However, if you already have an internal CA, it can save you time and money to use the internal CA instead of applying to a third-party certificate vendor.

For more information on the actual nuts and bolts of setting up digital signing, you can download a fairly extensive Microsoft white paper on it at http://download.microsoft.com/download/9/c/5/9c5b2167-8017-4bae-9fde-d599bac8184a/64bitDriverSigning.doc. If that link doesn't work, then just Google "64bitdriversigning.doc" to find the white paper.

Getting Down to Business: Deploying an Application or Driver Signed by a Publisher

In order for Vista to know that a publisher is truly trusted in your network:

- The third-party publisher's code signing certificate was issued by a commercial CA.
- The third-party publisher's code signing certificate is trusted in the Trusted Root Certification Authorities certificate store.
- The third-party publisher's certificates are configured in either the user or computer Trusted Publishers certificate stores of your managed computers.

Keep in mind that your network's security will depend on the security of the third-party publisher's private keys if you choose to add a third party's certificate to your trusted store.

Summary

In this chapter, we've taken a peek at how Vista preserves and verifies the integrity of the software that runs on the computer, as well as the integrity of core operating system files. While some of the enhancements are regulated to the 64-bit edition of Vista, these changes tend to be more restrictive for application developers. However, these changes are necessary, even if they will initially be a tax for developers. In the long-run, third-party vendors will see a return on investment through the enhancement of security in both their software and services and in the Windows operating system as a whole.

How Vista Secures Services

7

Every modern operating system I've ever encountered includes the ability to create and run programs that run unobtrusively in the background performing maintenance functions. Unix and Mac OS (which is really just Unix with a neat UI) call them daemons; in the Windows world we call them services.

Over the years, however, the nature of services has made them the target of computer criminals, and that has made security analysts scrutinize services closely. Unfortunately, although we now know how to harden Windows services against attacks, Windows hasn't made doing that toughening very easy...until now. I think you'll be pleasantly surprised at four changes that Microsoft made to Windows services in Vista—three changes we'll cover in this chapter in detail (and briefly in the last chapter).

Services in Brief

Let's start off with a look at what services are and how they work from a security point of view. Services are basically just regular old Windows programs, but with four differences from regular applications.

First, they can run all of the time. As soon as your computer boots, some services start up and run. (Others can start later — you can control that through Vista's service configuration tools.) They tend to do background sorts of activities, like spooling print jobs to the printer as the Print Spooler service does, or constantly watching your Web surfing so as to warn you of potential spyware, as Windows Defender does, to offer just two examples.

Second, they don't need you logged on to run. If you were running a website on your Vista computer—there was a nice, if limited web server shipped with the Vista betas unless they pulled it when Vista goes gold —then your Vista box could merrily respond to Web requests without your having first to log on and start up its copy of Internet Information Services (IIS). That implies that unlike the programs that I discussed in Chapters 2, 3, and 4, services do not get a copy of your security token and don't run as you; instead, they typically run under one of three accounts known as "service accounts":

LocalSystem An account that used to be called "System" in older Windows and that has nearly all-encompassing local powers and the ability to communicate with other systems over a network.

LocalService   An account with very little powers and no ability to network.

NetworkService   An account that is basically LocalService with a limited ability to network added.

Third, while services are, again, nothing more than Windows programs, they don't typically start up the way that most Windows programs do. Most programs are invoked by the name of their EXE file—double-click on the Notepad icon and you're really telling Explorer, "load and execute the file `notepad.exe`." In contrast, services tend not to be directly run but instead run inside a program called a "service host," a program named `svchost.exe`. Another word for this kind of program is a "wrapper" (although without the gold chains and the tendency to spit into the microphone) and its job is to simplify the process of securing services. Not all of your services, however, live inside the same `svchost.exe`. You can view your instances of `svchost.exe` by starting up Task Manager, click the "Show processes from all users" button, then click on the Processes tab, and then the Image Name column to sort the processes by name. You'll see something like Figure 7.1.

As you can see, the Vista system that I'm working on has 13 instances of `svchost.exe` running. To see the services *inside* a svchost, use Sysinternals' Process Explorer, which we met back in Chapter 4, to view your processes. Start it up—don't forget to start it elevated by right-clicking its icon and choose Run as administrator—and find a `svchost.exe`. As you hover your mouse cursor over the `svchost.exe`, you'll get a tooltip that shows you the services living inside that svchost. Or you can just right-click the svchost, choose Properties and then the Services tab, to see something like Figure 7.2.

FIGURE 7.1   Svchosts running on a Vista system

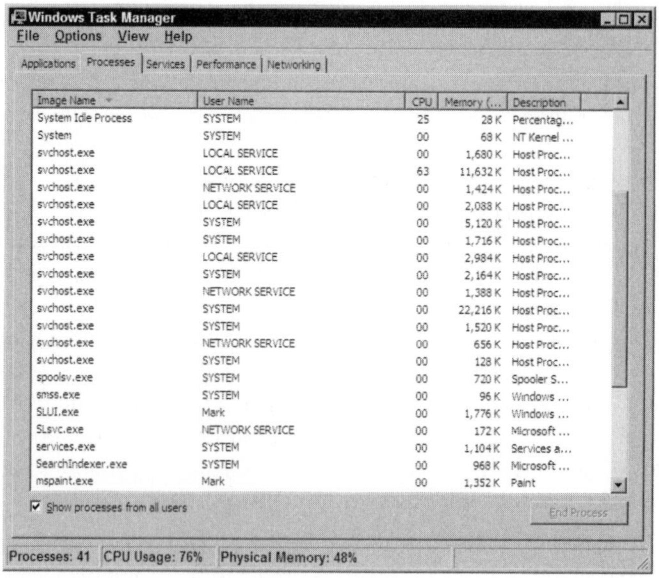

Windows Task Manager

File Options View Help

Applications | Processes | Services | Performance | Networking

Image Name ▲	User Name	CPU	Memory (...	Description
System Idle Process	SYSTEM	25	28 K	Percentag...
System	SYSTEM	00	68 K	NT Kernel ...
svchost.exe	LOCAL SERVICE	00	1,680 K	Host Proc...
svchost.exe	LOCAL SERVICE	63	11,632 K	Host Proc...
svchost.exe	NETWORK SERVICE	00	1,424 K	Host Proc...
svchost.exe	LOCAL SERVICE	00	2,088 K	Host Proc...
svchost.exe	SYSTEM	00	5,120 K	Host Proc...
svchost.exe	SYSTEM	00	1,716 K	Host Proc...
svchost.exe	LOCAL SERVICE	00	2,984 K	Host Proc...
svchost.exe	SYSTEM	00	2,164 K	Host Proc...
svchost.exe	NETWORK SERVICE	00	1,388 K	Host Proc...
svchost.exe	SYSTEM	00	22,216 K	Host Proc...
svchost.exe	SYSTEM	00	1,520 K	Host Proc...
svchost.exe	NETWORK SERVICE	00	656 K	Host Proc...
svchost.exe	SYSTEM	00	128 K	Host Proc...
spoolsv.exe	SYSTEM	00	720 K	Spooler S...
smss.exe	SYSTEM	00	96 K	Windows ...
SLUI.exe	Mark	00	1,776 K	Windows ...
SLsvc.exe	NETWORK SERVICE	00	172 K	Microsoft ...
services.exe	SYSTEM	00	1,104 K	Services a...
SearchIndexer.exe	SYSTEM	00	968 K	Microsoft ...
mspaint.exe	Mark	00	1,352 K	Paint

☑ Show processes from all users   End Process

Processes: 41   CPU Usage: 76%   Physical Memory: 48%

I'm taking the time to underscore out how svchosts work to make an important point: *services don't get tokens—instances of* svchost.exe *do*. Thus, in Figure 7.2, the five services that you see do not each get their own token filled with SIDs and privileges; instead, that particular instance of svchost.exe gets a token that contains privileges and one or more SIDs, and the five services in svchost.exe that share that token. To see that token, click the Security tab, which shows something like Figure 7.3.

FIGURE 7.2   Services running in a given svchost

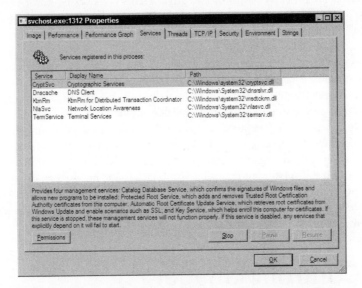

FIGURE 7.3   The svchost's token displayed in Process Explorer

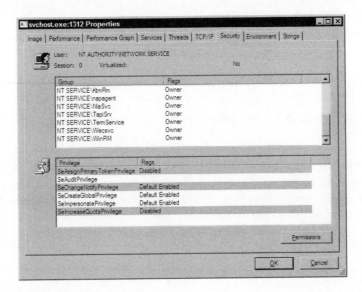

In that dialog, you can see that this particular `svchost.exe` runs under NetworkService rather than LocalSystem or LocalService. In the top half of the dialog, Process Explorer lists the SIDs in the token and there are apparently a lot of them, as I'd have to scroll to see them all. The bottom part shows the privileges that this svchost enjoys. Again, the SIDs and privileges on this svchost's token are the only ones that those five services get, and there's no way to give different SIDs and privileges to any one of those services without sharing them with the other four.

The fourth and final aspect of services is that they are programs that everyone loves to worry about. Listen to anyone talk about Windows security (including me), and eventually you'll hear that services are an entry point for bad guys. That's not because services are any more prone to bugs than any other kind of software. Instead, we worry about services because, again, they run all of the time, because many of them communicate over the network, and because many of them run as LocalSystem.

For example, if, say, Calculator possessed some horrible bug that would allow for a buffer overflow exploit that would enable an attacker to take control of your computer, then we wouldn't panic all that much about it because in order to launch that attack, then the attacker would have to be sitting at the computer (because Calc doesn't network) and Calc would have to be running (because you can only exploit a program's bugs when the program's running). In contrast, if, say, the Background Intelligent Transfer Service (BITS) on every Vista box had that horrible bug, *then* we'd have something to worry about, as BITS runs almost from the moment that you start up a Vista computer, and it *has* to talk to the network to get your software updates. Furthermore, BITS runs as LocalSystem, which means that if an attacker got control of BITS then he'd be able to do anything to your system that the LocalSystem account can—in other words, anything that he wanted to.

Service Control Manager

With the basics of services out of the way, let's next meet the program that manages them, the aptly named Service Control Manager (SCM), and its very useful configuration tool `sc.exe`. SCM has been the Windows component that manages services since Windows 95. SCM mainly:

- Takes care of starting services, whether they start automatically or manually
- Keeps track of which services are currently installed
- Manages communications with currently running services, such as requests to shut down

The SCM built into Windows Vista includes several very important changes that let us harden services more easily.

The Services MMC that you've probably seen before, `services.msc`, is part of the SCM, as is a very useful command-line tool `sc.exe` that existed in previous versions of Windows, but only as a Resource Kit or Support Tools application. Its inclusion in Vista is a welcome one. SCM itself is a program called `services.exe`; a look at Process Explorer will show that all of your svchosts were started by `services.exe`.

`sc.exe` is an extremely powerful command, but it's got a quirk or two. Here's the basic syntax for `sc.exe`:

```
sc [servername] command servicename [options...]
```

You can use sc.exe to control remote systems, as the *servername* parameter suggests. *command* is any one of dozens of commands, only a few of which we will be able to cover in this chapter. *servicename* is something called the "key name" for whatever service you want to control. For example, the Group Policy Client service has key name of "gpsvc." (That human-friendly name "Group Policy Client' is called the "display name.") It's called a key name because gpsvc is the name of the Registry key that contains the configuration information for the Group Policy Client, which is in HKEY_LOCAL_MACHINE\SYSTEM\CurrentControlSet\Services\gpsvc. Just on the off chance that you don't speak Registry fluently, though, you can get sc.exe to cough up the key name from the display name by typing sc getkeyname "*display name*", as in

```
C:\>sc getkeyname "group policy client"
[SC] GetServiceKeyName SUCCESS
Name = gpsvc
```

While we haven't got space to cover all of the sc.exe commands here, let's cover a few basic and useful ones. stop, start, pause, and continue will stop, start, pause, or continue a service, as in sc stop dnscache, which will stop the DNS Client service. getdisplayname will, if fed a key name, produce the service's display name, reversing the display-name-to-key-name lookup we saw earlier. config will, in combination with some options, let you configure a service as you can from the Services GUI snap-in. For example, to make the DNS client service, which again has the key name of dnscache, a manual-start service (not a good idea), you'd type

```
sc config dnscache start= demand
```

Notice a quirk in sc.exe's syntax there: you've got to put a space between "start=" and "demand." All of the options for sc.exe work that way.

How Vista Toughens Services: Overview

You've already read why security analysts worry about services: they're programs that are on all of the time, are often network connected, and often run as LocalSystem. That typically leads security analysts to recommend several things:

- Shut off any unnecessary services. Vista's done this to an extent, and as time goes on we'll probably see more and more advice about what we can turn off safely as we all become more familiar with Vista.

- Replace the LocalSystem account with a lower-power account. That way, if a service is compromised then the attacker only has the power of the lower-power account, and may not be able to do as much damage. XP started this by introducing and exploiting the vastly reduced-power accounts NetworkService and LocalService. But where XP used them for a relatively small percentage of services, leaving most to LocalSystem, Microsoft has reengineered many services under Vista so that they run by default under LocalService or NetworkService.

- Use permissions to deny LocalSystem, LocalService, and NetworkService access to particularly valuable files, folders, or the like. For example, when Code Red hit unpatched IIS servers across the world back in 2000, I must sheepishly admit that my IIS server was hit because I'd not patched it, but I was largely unaffected because I had previously denied the LocalSystem account access to my Web content. When Code Red tried to delete my home page, then Code Red spoke with the authority of LocalSystem…but was rebuffed by its lack of NTFS permissions to even read it. Taking the time to deny service account access to some objects (Registry keys, files, other services, AD objects, and so on) can be a good belt-and-suspenders exercise, but a time-consuming one.

Those last two approaches together comprise a notion called "running with least privilege." The idea is that in the perfect world, every service would run under an account specially built for it that had exactly as much power as it needed…and no more. And, in an even better world (I know, what's better than perfect?), we'd take things a step further and actually explicitly deny those least privilege accounts access to anything that they didn't need.

It's a great idea, but hasn't been practical as it was time consuming and not always fruitful. But Vista incorporates a few changes that offer simpler paths toward running with least privilege and service hardening. Those changes are:

Session separation   Vista largely blocks services from directly interacting with users. As you'll see later, Microsoft created something like a completely separate Terminal Services session and stuck the services in there. You needn't do anything to get this benefit, it's automatic.

Reducing service privileges   Under Vista, you (or the service's developer) can tell the SCM to continue to run a service as LocalSystem, but to strip the svchost's token of any of LocalSystem's unnecessary privileges. The result is that SCM can essentially convert the frighteningly powerful LocalSystem into a tailor-made service account of least privilege! Again, this requires a bit of setup work on either the developer's part or the admin's, but many Vista services appear to have already had that work done for us. (I'll show you how you can view a service's privilege limitations with the `sc qprivs` command and add new ones with the `sc privs` command a bit later.)

Service isolation   You just read that in the perfect world, a given service could access *just* the files that it needed, and no others. With Vista, you (or a service's developer) can accomplish that very thing with just a few simple adjustments. (Again, I'll show you how to control that with the `sc sidtype` command a bit later.)

Network restrictions   A developer can design a service to tell Windows Firewall, "only let me communicate on port X."

We'll consider each in turn.

Session Separation

Ever since Microsoft incorporated Citrix's MetaFrame technology in Windows with Windows NT 4.0 Terminal Server Edition, Windows, or at least Windows in the NT family, has had the notion of *sessions*. A session is basically a set of applications and, usually, a desktop connected to a user. Examples of where you've seen probably seen sessions before include:

Terminal services sessions   Many people can run sessions on a single Windows Server box via Terminal Services. These sessions don't "leak" from one to another, as the underlying session mechanism keeps them apart. Different users can have different desktops and applications even though they run on the same machine, and are totally unaware of each other.

Remote Desktop and Remote Assistance   These are implementations of Terminal Services on XP and Vista and create different sessions, although they're much more limited than the functions offered by Terminal Services on a Server system.

Fast User Switching   XP and Vista can keep track of multiple logged-on users via Fast User Switching. Each logged-on user gets a session in Fast User Switching.

Sessions are numbered from 0 onward, and in Windows before Vista session 0 was known as the "console session." With Vista Fast User Switching, the first person to log on gets session 1, the next session 2, and so on. (That of course assumes that no one logs off; if one person logs on and then off, and then another logs on and off, then they both get a session numbered 1, but of course they won't share desktops.)

In Vista, Microsoft moved all of the services into session 0, and added a few new rules about life in session 0. First, session 0 does not have a user interface of any kind. It can't communicate with the video hardware. It can't pop up messages to users in the other sessions. The only way that it can communicate with other sessions is via the Remote Procedure Call (RPC) protocol, which is a secured method for applications to talk to one another.

Putting services into session 0 and keeping users out of that session has another effect: it makes a common approach to privilege escalation impossible. Over the years, bad guys have created a number of tools whose purpose was to let someone with limited powers—a standard user or even a guest—to "amp up" their power to that of System by taking control of some badly written service. For example, one of the most common approaches was to simply use the `at.exe` scheduler to start up a command prompt, which would then be running as LocalSystem. Well, that won't work anymore.

And as is so often the case with increased security, compatibility suffers. Some kinds of drivers—print drivers in particular—are loaded by a service (the Print Spooler service, in this case) and so live in session 0. That means that if a printer driver were to try to raise a dialog box, perhaps to announce an error or seek some user input while installing, then that attempt to contact the user would fail. There *is*, however, a temporary—Vista-only, it won't appear in subsequent versions of Windows—workaround called the "Interactive Services Detection Service." You can start it on your system by opening an elevated command prompt and typing `net start ui0detect`, and that's a zero in that key name, not the letter "O." Or you can tell Vista to make the Interactive Services Detection Service always start automatically by typing

```
sc config ui0detect start= auto
```

Remember that there must be a space between "`start=`" and "`auto`;" it's a quirk of `sc.exe`'s syntax.

Reducing Service Privileges

As I've already said, a well-secured service would run under a service account that had exactly the privileges that it needed, and no more. But that would imply that Microsoft would have to create a separate service account for each service. While that's a nice idea, it might be a bit difficult to manage, so Microsoft observed something interesting:

 It's not what privileges the service account has that matters. It's what privileges are in the token attached to the service's svchost.exe while it's running.

Now, in previous versions of Windows, that would be one of those "difference that doesn't make a difference" observations; whatever service account your service's svchost ran under would get all of its privileges, and that was that. But we've already seen in Chapter 2 that Vista has the ability to do some interesting filtering of tokens, so Microsoft employed that with services as well.

Developers Can Reduce Service Privileges

Here's how it works: when building a Vista service, a developer may *optionally* include some instructions to the SCM, telling it, "I only need the following privileges." Then, when the SCM loads the service, it creates the token for that service, as has been true in previous versions of Windows. But in Vista, the SCM doesn't just copy the service account's token to the instance of svchost.exe that's running the service; instead, that svchost.exe only gets the privileges that it needs.

In case that's not clear, imagine that you've got a service named CoolSvc that only needs, say, "bypass traverse checking," but runs in a svchost.exe started with the very powerful Local-System service account. When the service starts up, it says to the SCM, "hey, I only need bypass traverse checking," so SCM looks at the SID of the service account that started it—LocalSystem, which you will recall is equipped with about 4,731 privileges—and says "Holy frijoles, that's *way* more privileges than you need to get this job done," and issues the service its token with Local-System's token...but with all of the privileges ripped out except for bypass traverse checking.

Admins Can *Also* Reduce Service Privileges

But what if the developers of your services are lazy and don't bother specifying the limited privileges that CoolSvc can live with? In that case, you can tell the SCM what CoolSvc needs with sc.exe, the all-purpose service control application. The command to do that looks like

```
SC <server> privs servicename privilege1/privilege2...
```

In that command, you specify the list of the privileges with a single slash between them that the service needs, expressed in the shorthand "SEmumble" form. For example, if CoolSvc needed SeShutdownPrivilege and SeChangeNotifyPrivilege, we could inform Vista of that by typing

```
sc privs CoolSvc seshutdownprivilege/sechangenotifyprivilege
```

(That should be one long line; it may have broken on the printed page, but don't press Enter after "CoolSvc.") Once passed to the SCM, that information doesn't disappear; it's stored in a REG_MULTI_SZ entry called RequiredPrivileges in CoolSvc's Registry key, and survives reboots. But how to find out if a service already contains these useful and security-conscious built-in privilege tips? You can then query the SCM to find out what privilege requests, if any, a service makes like so:

```
sc qprivs servicename
```

For example, I can ask the Interactive Services Detection Service what it thinks that it needs like this:

```
C:\>sc qprivs ui0detect
[SC] QueryServiceConfig2 SUCCESS

SERVICE_NAME: ui0detect
        PRIVILEGES          : SeTcbPrivilege
                            : SeAssignPrimaryTokenPrivilege
                            : SeIncreaseQuotaPrivilege
                            : SeDebugPrivilege
```

Aha, I guess I can see why Microsoft turned `ui0detect` off by default. Will ya *look* at the privileges that it needs: "act as a part of the operating system" *and* "debug other processes"—two of the Notorious Nine.

As always with Windows, anything that changes a token doesn't take effect until the account—the service account, that is—logs off and then back on, so to see the effects of your changes, restart the svchost.

Again, let me stress that not every service has this privilege information built in. For example, try querying `sc` for the privileges on lanmanserver, the File Server service: there aren't any. That doesn't mean that the File Server service isn't allowed any privileges—it just means that Microsoft didn't employ their new technology to rein it in.

That's kind of a shame, I think. They're pretty vocal when talking about the security improvements in Vista, but a quick look at a few of the built-in Vista services shows that they've not been configured to reduce their privileges. But given enough time, we admins will probably figure out exactly what privileges we can restrict the Windows services to.

In the event that a service has no `RequiredPrivileges` Registry entry, then SCM treats that service just as services have been treated since NT 3.1: it gets a token with the full powers of its service account.

Special Case: Multiple Services Needing Different Privileges

So no `RequiredPrivileges`, no privilege limitation on its `svchost.exe`'s token; with a `RequiredPrivileges` entry in the Registry, our `svchost.exe` gets reduced privileges, right?

Almost—I left one detail out. Consider: what happens if a svchost.exe contains more than one service, and those services all have a RequiredPrivileges Registry entry?

For example, suppose we've got a svchost.exe running under LocalSystem. That svchost.exe contains Service1, which requires SeDebugPrivilege, and Service2, which requires SeShutdownPrivilege. Remember that even though there is more than one service in the svchost.exe, there is just one token, as it's svchost.exe that gets the token—there is no way to give Service1 and Service2 different tokens if they live in the same svchost.exe. So what's on that token? The union of the RequiredPrivileges values. In other words, SCM builds the svchost.exe a token containing both the SeDebugPrivilege and the SeShutdownPrivilege, and *that* means that Service1 has both privileges, as does Service2. Moral of the story: by default whenever you set up a new privilege, it gets its own svchost.exe. Unless you have a good reason otherwise, keep it that way, or you'll end up having done a lot of work to fine-tune the minimum privilege needs of a bunch of services, only to have them end up with a wide range of privileges anyway.

Reduced Privilege Summary

Vista changes service privileges in that services can enumerate exactly which privileges they need, or allows administrators to modify those lists of required privileges with the sc privs command. The effects of this are that

- In the case where a svchost.exe contains just one service, and that service has no information about its required privileges, then that svchost.exe and thereby that service get a token with the full privileges of the service account.

- In the case where a svchost.exe contains just one service, and that service *has* declared the privileges that it needs, then SCM will give that svchost.exe a token containing only the privileges enumerated by the service. (Although if the service requires a privilege that the svchost.exe's service account lacks, then SCM can't give the token that privilege—the SCM cannot give an account privileges that it lacks.)

- In the case where a svchost.exe contains more than one service that has enumerated its required privileges, the SCM computes the union of all of those privilege needs and gives all of those privileges to the svchost.exe's token.

- In the case where a svchost.exe contains a mixture of services that enumerate their required privileges and services that do not, SCM just copies the service account's token and gives that to the svchost.exe.

WARNING   And in case it's not obvious, configuring a service with a particular set of required permissions that does not include the complete *actual* set of required permissions will inevitably cause the service to fail. For example, NetworkService possesses only a few simple permissions, none of which is SeDebugPrivilege. So running a service in a svchost.exe under NetworkService and specifying that the service requires the SeDebugPrivilege will cause that service to fail, every time.

Service Isolation

Beyond session separation and privilege reduction, Vista takes service lockdown a step further and lets you set up "service isolation." The whole idea of service isolation is to completely remove a service's ability to modify anything on the system except for some small number of objects. That way, if the service stops working for good and starts working for evil, then you have strongly circumscribed the potential damage that it can do. For example, if a given service fell prey to a buffer overflow bug and some miscreant wrote a worm that tried to exploit that bug, then the first thing that the jerk would try to do in the worm would be to install a rootkit on your system. But installing a rootkit involves copying files and fiddling with the Registry, and the whole idea behind service isolation would have already kept the service from being able to modify almost anything on the system. The service would almost certainly not be able to write to the parts of the Registry and file system that would be necessary to get that rootkit installed...and so the worm would fail.

How Service Isolation Works

Microsoft had to make a few structural changes to Vista to make service isolation possible. In brief, they are:

- Every service gets its own SID called, not surprisingly, a "service SID," which can be used to identify that service in a file, Registry, or other type of permission.

- Every service can optionally be restricted such that the service can write to a given object *only* if that object has an access control entry on it that grants write access specifically to that *service's* SID; the service account's SID is of no help to an isolated service when that service wants to write.

- That restriction can be either built into a service by the service's developer, or an administrator can specify that restriction with sc.exe, as we'll see later.

The key to understanding service isolation is, as I've already suggested, that services typically need to write to something—a file, folder, database, Registry key, Active Directory object, or the like—in order to be useful. But of course those are all *securable* objects, as you'll recall from Chapter 4, and so a service needs a write ACE on the securable object that matches an SID on the service's token, or it can't get its job done.

In the pre-Vista days, services got their SIDs from their service accounts and whatever small number of groups those service accounts belonged to. Those were the only SIDs that a service could use to identify itself to an object when hoping to find that the object had a "write allowed" ACE with a matching SID. In Vista, services get not only their service account's SIDs on their svchost.exe's token but they may also optionally get their own SIDs. Using that very specific service SID, Vista's SCM lets you get very, very specific about what objects a given service can modify.

For example, when reengineering the EventSystem service, which manages the event logs, Microsoft looked at how the event logs worked and said "hey, the only files that EventSystem ever needs to write to are the event logs themselves, a bunch of files in \windows\system32\ winevt with the extension .EVT." Vista's service isolation allowed Microsoft to accomplish that. Let's see how....

Restricting a Service's SID

The first piece to understanding service isolation involves understanding restricted SIDs. Under Vista, a developer or administrator can tell the SCM to modify the way that it creates a svchost.exe's token. If instructed, SCM will build the svchost.exe's token so that it gets the service account's SID, as before, but with the addition of a notation that says, "this SID is not good for any 'write' operations."

In other words, a service running in a svchost.exe with this SID can *read* anything that the service account can read, but when it comes to writing anything, then Vista won't let the service use its service account's SID. This is called giving a service a "restricted token."

You can restrict a service's SID with the following command:

```
sc sidtype servicename restricted
```

So let's say for example that we'd like to restrict our friend CoolSvc that we met before in this chapter from writing to anything but a file named c:\mystuff\coollog.txt. (Suppose also that CoolSvc runs in a svchost.exe instance under LocalSystem.) Step 1 in isolating CoolSvc involves restricting its SID; here's a sample run of doing that from an elevated command prompt:

```
C:\>sc sidtype coolsvc restricted
[SC] ChangeServiceConfig2 SUCCESS
```

(Isn't sc.exe's excitement whenever it makes something work downright infectious?)

> Again, we're changing a token's contents, so we've got to stop and start the svchost.exe to make the changes. And yes, I do mean the svchost.exe—if you've got other services sharing that svchost.exe, then you'll have to shut them all down, kill the svchost.exe from Task Manager, and then restart them, or just restart the whole system.

Granting Write Permissions to a Service SID

Clearly now that CoolSvc is a restricted service, it cannot use its LocalSystem SID to write anything, and so it's kind of useless at the moment. If it were to try to write to c:\mystuff\coollog.txt, then NTFS would ask to see its credentials before allowing it to write. CoolSvc would brandish them, only to have NTFS respond "hmm, I see you have a LocalSystem SID, they're *nice*...oh, but I see that it's not usable for write operations. Sorry."

The service will need *some* help in order to write to c:\mystuff\coollog.txt. To accomplish that, recall that Vista's SCM creates a service SID for every service. To see that, look back to Figure 7.3 and you will see that that particular svchost.exe is a member of some groups that we've never heard of before: KtmRm, NlaSvc, TermService, and more. You may recognize those names: they're the names of the services inside that svchost.exe.

These SIDs aren't "complete" SIDs in that they're not separate accounts; they're just labels, sort of like Vista's integrity levels, the SIDs that look like Mandatory Label\Medium Level Label—there's no domain named "Mandatory Label," and no actual group or user account named NlaSvc. But they *can*, believe it or not, be specified on permissions for NTFS, the Registry, and the like.

For example, I can now right-click c:\mystuff\coollog.txt and open its Advanced security dialog, and then click "Add…" to create a new permission. It first asks me to choose a file, group, or whatever, but I want to grant a permission on that file to the CoolSvc Service, coolsvc. To see how I'd do that, look at Figure 7.4.

In that dialog box, you see how I've specified that I'd like to grant a permission on a file (the dialog doesn't show the file's name) to an account with a domain name of "NT Service" and a name of "coolsvc." Once I click OK, it takes Vista a second or two, but it soon realizes that yes, it *does* know of an SID for something called NT Service\coolsvc, and lets me create a permission allowing CoolSvc write access to the file.

FIGURE 7.4   Specifying a service name for a permission

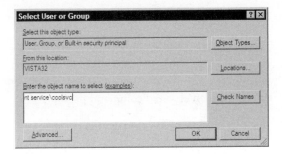

Please remember that this is a cooked-up example. You don't have a CoolSvc on your system, and so won't be able to duplicate exactly what I've done— I've only done that to illustrate the point of how to give a service the permission to modify something.

Instead, by creating SIDs for every service, Vista makes it possible for you to create a permission on an NTFS volume, in the Registry or the like and name a particular service in that permission, enabling you to tell an object that it's okay for a particular Windows service to write to that object, even if nothing else can. At this point, CoolSvc can modify c:\mystuff\coollog.txt, and nothing else.

Understanding the *sc.exe* Restricted SID Commands

Now that I've explained service isolation and how to make it work, let's look a bit further at what sc.exe can do to control service SIDs. As you saw before, you control service SIDs with the new Vista sc.exe "sidtype" command. Its full syntax looks like

```
sc [servername] sidtype servicename none|unrestricted|restricted
```

We've already seen what "restricted" does, or at least part of what it does. The full result of using restricted causes two things. First, your svchost.exe gets to use its service account SID for everything except writing, as you know. But the second effect of "restricted" is to tell SCM to put CoolSvc's SID into its svchost.exe's token. You can't tell Vista not to create a SID for CoolSvc as far as I know, but you *can* tell it whether or not to include the service's SID on the svchhost.exe's token. You can tell SCM not to include the SID on the svchost.exe token with the "none" option, as in

```
sc sidtype coolsvc none
```

This also has the effect of unrestricting CoolSvc's token. Alternatively, you could replace "none" with "unrestricted." In that case, the svchost.exe gets the SID in its token, but that SID is not restricted, and the svchost.exe has full use of its SID from LocalSystem, Network-Service, or LocalService.

To find a service SID's current state of none, restricted, or unrestricted, just type

```
sc qsidtype servicename
```

Or, to view a service's actual SID, type

```
sc showsid servicename
```

And remember to do those commands from an elevated command prompt. Reviewing what we discussed:

- A service always gets to use the SID of its service host.

- A service *also* gets an SID of its own.

- You (or a developer) can potentially take from a service the ability to use its service host's SID for any write operations with the "restricted" setting.

- If you *do* restrict a service, it is absolutely essential to remember to grant the service's service-specific SID write access to whatever it needs in order for the service to get its job done.

- Restart the whole svchost.exe to see the results of your changes.

What about the case where there is more than one service running in a particular service host? Well, if they're all set to either "none" or "unrestricted," then they'll run just fine. *But* if the services in a service host are mixed, with some restricted and some not, then the restricted ones will fail to start. The only way to use restricted services is to ensure that if one service in a service host is restricted, then *all* of the services in that service host are unrestricted.

Restricting a Service's Network Ports

The last bit of service lockdown that you can do in Vista is to instruct Windows Firewall to link particular incoming and outgoing ports to particular services. That way, a compromised system can't start scanning ports. It certainly sounds like a great tool, but unfortunately as I write this in early October 2006, the only documentation about it is a short reference in a Microsoft white paper called "Vista Services." Search Microsoft's site for the paper; the reference is on pages 9 and 10.

Summary

While toughening your system against the risk of services gone wrong was once an arcane art, it's now merely an obscure one. Armed with `sc.exe` and your service names, though, you can restrict service privileges and isolate services through restricted SIDs. As with restricted privileges, a little poking around will reveal that Microsoft did not choose to isolate many services. That means that you may want to experiment with tightening up Vista further yourself...but please do it on a test system!

Well, we've reached the end of the book; thanks for staying with my coauthors and me for so long. I sincerely hope that you've now got a handle on some of Vista security's "big surprises"...so they won't surprise you at a bad time. Thanks again for reading, and drop me a line to let me know what you thought of our deliberately small volume!

Index

Note to the reader: Throughout this index **boldfaced** page numbers indicate primary discussions of a topic. *Italicized* page numbers indicate illustrations.